THE CIVIL WAR DIARY OF EMMA MORDECAI

Diary. May. 1864.
kept by Emma Mordecai at
Rosewood. Near Richmond.

On Thursday, April 18th I left our house on [...]
[s]treet, for the last time. Sister Ellen & Bro[ther]
[Ge]orge had departed early that morning, leavin[g]
[n]ephew George, alone at the house. There we[re]
[re]maining a few articles of furniture to be sent [...]
[a]fter attending to which George & I came away & [...]
[c]ame out to Rosewood in the cars with Augusta [...]
[h]er school was out. I felt strange without a hom[e any]
[m]ore, and very still & quiet, tho' not overcome wit[h de]
[p]ression — the reverse, however, of all excitement. [...]
[h]ad prepared most kindly for my reception, and [my]
[r]oom was the picture of neatness & comfort. She [...]
[m]e very kindly, but we made no demonstration[s or pro]
[f]essions to each other. I only know that my inwa[rd]
[s]olve and humble prayer was & is that I may m[ake]
[m]y residence with her, for as long as it may last, a [...]
[n]ot a torment or inconvenience to her. There was a [...]
[wh]en I should not have doubted this, but the longer we li[ve]
[...] we doubt ourselves, & now I am not certain. I only [...]

The Civil War Diary of
EMMA MORDECAI

Edited and with an Introduction by
DIANNE ASHTON
———— with ————
MELISSA R. KLAPPER

NEW YORK UNIVERSITY PRESS
New York

NEW YORK UNIVERSITY PRESS
New York

www.nyupress.org

© 2024 by New York University
All rights reserved

Please contact the Library of Congress for Cataloging-in-Publication data.
ISBN: 9781479831906 (hardback)
ISBN: 9781479831982 (library ebook)
ISBN: 9781479831944 (consumer ebook)

This book is printed on acid-free paper, and its binding materials are chosen for strength and durability. We strive to use environmentally responsible suppliers and materials to the greatest extent possible in publishing our books.

Manufactured in the United States of America

10 9 8 7 6 5 4 3 2 1

Also available as an ebook

For Rosalyn

Contents

List of Illustrations ix

Foreword xi
RICHARD DRUCKER

Preface xiii
MELISSA R. KLAPPER

Acknowledgments xvii
DIANNE ASHTON

Introduction: Emma Mordecai's Crisis of Home 1

The Civil War Diary of Emma Mordecai,
April 1864–May 1865 85

Notes 223

Index 239

About the Authors 249

Illustrations

Emma Mordecai. 2

Jacob Mordecai 7

Alfred Mordecai. 12

First page of Emma Mordecai's 1864–1865 diary 23

Pass signed by General Weitzel, April 7, 1865 73

Permission to buy brandy for Rosina Young Mordecai,
May 15, 1865 74

Last page of Emma Mordecai's 1864–1865 diary 77

Emma Mordecai's tombstone 82

Foreword

RICHARD DRUCKER

My late wife, Dr. Dianne Ashton, passed away in January 2022 after a long battle with muscular dystrophy. She enjoyed her roles as a scholar of Jewish studies and religion studies, as an esteemed professor and teacher, and as a writer of numerous books on topics including Jewish women's spirituality, the nineteenth-century American Jewish leader Rebecca Gratz, and Hanukkah in America. Due to her illness, she was unable to complete her book project in progress, a scholarly analysis of a diary written by Emma Mordecai, who lived in Richmond, Virginia, during the turbulent days of the Civil War. Dianne was in the process of completing a draft at the time of her passing. Dr. Melissa R. Klapper, Dianne's colleague at Rowan University, generously offered to finish the manuscript.

Dianne wanted to answer a basic question about Mordecai: How would a Jewish woman, living in the Old South, be able to observe Jewish religious practices and yet remain loyal to the values of the Confederacy? Her previous scholarship dealt with similar themes: a dual loyalty to one's nation and religion, a strong resistance to external pressures to convert, and the role of self-expression and creativity in solving these problems. She knew that Mordecai's personal experiences of the Civil War, including her descriptions of relations with family, neighbors, and Union soldiers and her literary expression of these events, would be of great interest to a broad audience.

Because of her disability and the impact of COVID-19, Dianne missed out on opportunities to regularly meet with colleagues to talk about her project and to get feedback. I know from observing her writing her previous books that she found great joy in talking about her work with her colleagues and friends.

Dianne's work was always an important element of our lives together. She was diligent about her scholarship and especially enjoyed working with primary sources like Mordecai's diary. She was also quick to acknowledge the work of other scholars, many of whom she had inspired. She was as committed to me as a life partner as she was to her teaching and scholarship. I always enjoyed and benefited from her knowledge and erudition, as well as her tolerance for others' lack of perspective. She convinced me that Emma Mordecai's diary is an important artifact, and I am sure this book will do the same for all readers.

I am grateful to Dr. Melissa Klapper for offering to complete the book and to Dr. Nawal Ammar, dean of the College of Humanities and Social Sciences at Rowan University, who provided administrative support and general encouragement for the project.

Preface

MELISSA R. KLAPPER

I first met Dianne Ashton when I was a graduate student in the late 1990s. We were introduced at a conference, and she immediately told me how delighted she was to meet another scholar interested in nineteenth-century American Jewish women's history as well as the later period of mass Jewish migration to the United States. I was immensely flattered that someone of her professional stature was referring to me as a "scholar," considering that I was already familiar with her work as a pioneer in the field. When I arrived at Rowan University in 2001 as an assistant professor in the history department, right out of my PhD program, Dianne reached out all the time to make sure I was learning the ropes and to offer her always savvy advice. Eventually I became her colleague, rather than her starstruck admirer, but I never stopped appreciating the mentorship she offered me and so many others. In more recent years, she and I sometimes read and commented on drafts of each other's work, which is how I first became familiar with her interest in the Civil War diary of Emma Mordecai. Since we were in different departments on opposite sides of campus, Dianne and I rarely saw each other at Rowan. It became a running joke that we only were in the same room at conferences. But we were always in the same intellectual room.

When Dianne passed away in January 2022, she had finished most of a draft manuscript for the book she was then calling "Crisis of Home: The Civil War Diary of Emma Mordecai," a project she had been working on for many years. The manuscript consisted of her lengthy scholarly introduction and a full transcript of the diary. She had already identified some illustrations, written a dedication and acknowledgments, and completed a full book proposal. Though Dianne had done all this work, she was a seasoned professional and was well aware that the introduction she had written was not yet in final form and would require substantial further revision in order to secure a book contract.

As a historian of American Jewish women, I had always been greatly interested in this project and had enjoyed several discussions about it with Dianne over the years she had been working on it. After her death, I was very troubled by the prospect that the book would never appear, and I began to discuss the idea of finishing it in her name with her husband, Richard Drucker. He enthusiastically supported the idea, understanding that significant changes would be necessary before publication would be possible. He also graciously supplied me with Dianne's large library of books related to the Civil War era and Southern Jewish history.

As outlined in Dianne's original book proposal, she intended this book for a broad audience of readers interested in the Civil War, Southern history, American Jewish history, American women's history, and American religious history. She chose not to annotate the diary itself but rather to provide all the necessary background information in the introduction, which remains the format here. My aim in extensively revising her draft was to honor these preferences. I have tried to preserve her general style, main topics, and arguments as much as possible while also reorganizing and streamlining the introduction, highlighting additional themes, and expanding the historical and historiographical contexts as necessary. I hope that the end result is a fitting final expression of her scholarly legacy.

I could not have taken on this project without a lot of help, which I am delighted to acknowledge here. First and foremost, I would like to thank Richard Drucker for entrusting me with the revision. He has been a great partner in finding a way to see the book through to publication. Nawal Ammar, dean of the College of Humanities and Social Sciences at Rowan University, offered invaluable support, especially in overcoming a variety of institutional hurdles. As always, I am surrounded by fabulous colleagues in both my own Department of History and Dianne's Department of Philosophy and World Religions at Rowan, all of whom have cheered me on. Nancy Toff of Oxford University Press saved the day at a critical moment. A sabbatical from Rowan University and a Scholar-in-Residence Fellowship at the Hadassah-Brandeis Institute at Brandeis University gave me the time to spend on Dianne's book while also continuing to work on my own book project. Archivists and librarians at the Southern Historical Collection at the University of North Carolina at Chapel Hill, the Jacob Rader Marcus Center of the American Jewish Archives, and the State Archives of North Carolina helped both Dianne and me with illustrations and permissions. Hasia Diner, editor of the Goldstein-Goren Series in American Jewish History at NYU Press, became a staunch ally as soon as I brought the idea of finishing the book to her, and I am so pleased that it is part of the series. I am glad to continue a long-standing relationship with NYU Press by working with Eric Zinner and Furqan Sayeed. Thanks to the anonymous reviewers, who took the time to understand the unusual circumstances and provide extraordinarily helpful feedback and assistance, as did my friends and colleagues Emily Blanck, Bill Carrigan, and Zev Eleff. And I am so grateful to thank, once again, my wonderful family for being loving and supportive in every way: my husband, Noah Gradofsky, who also provided much-needed tech expertise; my parents, Ferne and Mitch Klapper; and my sister Jennie Fine, brother-in-law Josh Fine, nephew Dovie Fine, and niece Sophie Fine.

The Civil War Diary of Emma Mordecai is ultimately a tribute to Dianne Ashton as a fierce advocate of Jewish women's history and feminist religious studies and as a wise and caring mentor. May her memory be a blessing.

Acknowledgments

DIANNE ASHTON

I am very happy to be able to formally thank the institutions and individuals who made it possible for me to undertake and complete this volume. I could not have done it without the generous support of Rowan University, my kind colleagues in the Philosophy and World Religions Department, and Dr. Nawal Ammar, the exceptional dean of the College of Humanities and Social Sciences. My colleagues in the History Department at Rowan University, especially Emily Blanck and Stephen Hague, shared their special expertise. Thanks also to friends and colleagues Melissa Klapper and Harriet Hartman—their enthusiasm for this project meant a great deal to me.

Fellowships funded by the Jacob Rader Marcus Center at the American Jewish Archives brought me to Cincinnati, where I first encountered a transcript of Emma Mordecai's diary amid the rich resources to be found on its campus. The Southern Jewish Historical Society kindly provided me with a valuable grant that paid for the diary's transcription and my further research. Librarians at the Wilson Library at the University of North Carolina, where the original diary is housed in a massive collection of papers belonging to the Mordecai family, graciously provided me access to the digital versions of the diary and other Mordecai papers. It was a pleasure to work with them.

I am grateful to several colleagues for their encouragement and suggestions. Jonathan D. Sarna published the first article that I produced using my research on this diary in the collection on American Jewish women that he edited with Pamela S. Nadell and then reprinted it in the volume he created with Adam D. Mendelsohn that focused on Jews and the Civil War. His support for new work on nineteenth-century American Jews is unparalleled. I am grateful to both Jonathan and Adam for their encouragement and friendly counsel.

My husband, Richard Drucker, made my task easy in too many ways to count, including serving as my first critical reader. I am happy to dedicate this volume to my amazing daughter, Rosalyn.

Introduction

EMMA MORDECAI'S CRISIS OF HOME

Emma Mordecai needed to be alone with her thoughts. On many evenings between April 1864 and May 1865, she sat by candlelight in her new home at her sister-in-law's farmhouse near Richmond, Virginia, to record that day's experiences in a blank book. Other times she wrote as the morning sun streamed through her bedroom window, and she recalled the previous few days' events. Each option gave her the privacy and quiet required for writing. Most likely she sat at a small table with her diary book before her so that she easily could dip her pen into an inkstand for the frequent refills it required. Her pen, if made of wood with a metal nib, improved on the quills that served American writers in the previous century, but, like quills, the incessant need for ink would have confined her to writing indoors. Fifty-one years old and unencumbered by concerns about a husband or children, Emma used those silent moments to think about her new circumstances. She mourned the longtime home in Richmond she had left behind.

It is impossible to know exactly when or where Emma wrote. But the diary she left shows that, as she reflected on her experiences, she coped with displacement and fear. It was the final year of the Civil War, and widespread tumult roiled her world. Her diary reveals how a very private woman weathered the social, political, military, and

economic upheavals around her, survived the dangers in her path, and pondered the fate of individuals close to her. She viewed that year's momentous national events through the private lens of her daily activities. Her diary helped her cope with her personal crisis: her loss of home.[1]

On a broader scale, the Civil War is probably best thought of as a bundle of crises. Most obviously, it tore the country apart both literally and metaphorically. Its death toll is still climbing as historians continue to comb through records.[2] As many as three million men fought in the war, more than two million for the North and between 750,000 and 850,000 for the South, out of a general US population of only thirty-one million. This was a significantly higher percentage of the population than served in any other war in US history. And by one estimate, as many as 35–37 percent of Confederate soldiers and 17.5 percent of Union soldiers were killed or wounded in battle.[3]

Another Civil War crisis was the dislocation of the Southern population. Out of roughly nine million people, including five and a half million whites and three and a half to four million enslaved Blacks, as many as a million people left their homes, either to serve in the military or to escape oncoming armies. A significant number of enslaved people, though difficult to quantify accurately, emancipated themselves by leaving their owners to assist the Union forces in a variety of ways. Considered contraband of war, by war's end, 12–15 percent of the Confederate slave population lived in more than one hundred contraband camps.[4] An untold number of enslaved people took advantage of the widespread disorder simply to escape the South. In an agrarian society in which people stabilized their lives through their economic, familial, and social ties to specific locations and land, dislocation wrought additional emotional chaos for many whites and new challenges and opportunities for African Americans.

There is no doubt that Emma experienced losing her home as a personal crisis. But she was so loyal to the Confederacy that she

Emma Mordecai. (Courtesy of the State Archives of North Carolina)

viewed this loss as a necessary sacrifice. Sacrifice was deeply embedded in the kind of Confederate nationalism that Emma and most of her family members shared.[5] By the time the Civil War broke out, Emma and her few surviving siblings were the elder statespeople of the Mordecais, who over several generations had proven themselves as a thoroughly Southern, white, Jewish family.[6] Their ascendance to middle-class respectability had been fraught and uneven, and at the time Emma started her diary, there were significant class differences among various Mordecai siblings and cousins. But they had achieved whatever status they had by profiting, both literally and figuratively, from their whiteness. As far back as the patriarch Jacob's initial struggling households in Virginia, the Mordecais had first hired and then bought slaves at the earliest opportunity, as was expected of upwardly mobile Southern white families with aspirations to social acceptance. Scholars of the tiny Jewish population of the antebellum South have shown that although Jews like the Mordecais generally were seen as white from the start, they made sure to cement their racial privilege by absorbing—and performing—the racism on which much of Southern society and culture was based.[7] Whether or not they embraced slavery in an instrumental fashion, in order to solidify their whiteness, at least some of them became, like Emma, true believers in white supremacy. Both paths were part of what the historian Eric Goldstein has identified as "the price of whiteness," which required Southern Jews' constant negotiation of racial identification.[8]

It is in this context that Emma's diary should be placed. She was from a family with a remarkable history, she was unusually well educated and articulate, she was devoted to her Jewish faith, and she suffered some privations of war. Her diary is a unique Civil War document written by a unique individual, and as one of the relatively few surviving Confederate diaries kept by a Jewish woman, it is distinctive. Yet Emma was also an entirely typical white, middle-class, slave-owning Southern woman with assumptions and attitudes, particularly about race, that are repugnant to modern readers. She seems to have subscribed fully to a unique Southern domestic ideology that reconciled highly distinct gender roles with racial privilege for white women.⁹ There is no need to rehabilitate her to recognize the importance of her diary as a window into critical Civil War–era themes and topics, including race relations, wartime religion, gendered domestic economies, and Confederate nationalism. While there is an ongoing debate among historians about the many reasons why the Confederacy lost the Civil War, this diary provides support for the interpretation that white Southerners developed a collective national identity and were defeated by military might rather than by domestic disaffection.¹⁰ No one individual's account of the war is sufficient unto itself as evidence for any given historical interpretation, but Emma's fervent patriotism, explicit willingness to sacrifice for her country, consistent interest in the military campaigns of the war, and steadfast belief in the benefits of slavery for whites and Blacks alike exemplify the idea that the Civil War can only be understood by analyzing the dynamic relationship between home front and battlefield.¹¹

EMMA AND THE AMERICAN JEWISH HISTORY OF THE MORDECAI FAMILY

Emma Mordecai's personal Civil War crisis was generated by her own dislocation. Her extended family had settled in Richmond and elsewhere throughout the South over decades of the American Jewish history of the Mordecais, who had lived in North America since before the American Revolution. In 1864, most American Jews had been born abroad. But Emma, her parents, and her siblings were all born in America. Her grandfather Moses Mordecai was probably born in or near what is today Bonn, Germany, but because Jews there lived under many restrictions, he relocated to London. Sometime in the 1750s, he married the much younger Elizabeth Whitlock, who converted to Judaism and changed her name to Esther. For reasons shrouded in the mists of time—and quite possibly by family chroniclers—he was transported to America as a convict, where he finished out a sentence as an indentured servant and became a peddler. By

1756, Moses and Esther lived in Philadelphia. Moses, now a small merchant, served the city in the Independent Troop of Horse, a local defense unit, and joined the city's tiny Jewish community. In the autumn of 1761, Philadelphia's Jews needed to borrow a Torah scroll from New York's Shearith Israel congregation for use in their High Holiday services, and Moses added his name to those who signed the receipt. He also signed the Non-Importation Agreement in which local merchants agreed not to import British goods as a protest against the widely loathed Stamp Act of 1765, which levied extra taxes on British goods sold in Britain's American colonies. Moses firmly supported the revolutionary cause. His eldest son, twelve-year-old Jacob, attended a military school in Philadelphia and joined his fellow students when they escorted the first Continental Congress into the city.[12]

After Moses's death in 1781, events took the family south. His widow, Esther, married Jacob I. Cohen of Charleston, South Carolina, in 1782. Cohen soon established a business partnership in Richmond, Virginia, and moved his new wife and family there. The small city of 3,761 people counted 100 Jews among its residents.[13] Jacob Mordecai's own adventures also brought him to the South. At twenty-two, he fell in love with and married Judith Myers, daughter of the famed New York City Jewish silversmith Myer Myers, in 1784. The young couple settled first in Goochland County, Virginia, where Jacob tried his hand at running a small store. He achieved little there, and two years later, the couple moved briefly to Richmond and then to Petersburg, Virginia, a tobacco market town. Following several failed business ventures, Jacob, Judith, and their children moved on to Warrenton, North Carolina, where they at last found some economic stability, although also family tragedy.

Judith died in Warrenton at age thirty-four, having borne six surviving children. During her final illness, she relied on her younger sister Richea who had accompanied Judith and Jacob to North Carolina.[14] The couple's oldest son, Moses, named for his grandfather, was sent to Judith's parents in New York, where Judith's younger

Jacob Mordecai. (Courtesy of the Jacob Rader Marcus Center of the American Jewish Archives)

sister Rebecca kept an eye on him. Two years later, in 1798, Jacob and Rebecca married, and the couple welcomed seven more children, including Emma in 1812. Meanwhile, Richea married Richmond's Joseph Marx and settled in that city.[15] Judith's half brother, Samuel Myers, had relocated to Petersburg in 1789, but soon he, too, moved to Richmond. Their cousins Slowey and Catherine Hays joined the growing clan there as well. Many of Emma's older siblings also settled in Richmond.

Jacob's love of books and fondness for intelligent conversation became his most respected attributes and also the eventual key to his prosperity. In 1809, he decided to establish a boarding school, and this endeavor became the success for which he and the Mordecai name were most remembered throughout the broader South. One year after the opening of his school, the Warrenton Female Academy, a fine review of it appeared in the *Raleigh Star*.[16] The new school succeeded because it drew on the Mordecai family's greatest strengths: their exceptional education and love of learning, their cohesion as a family unit, and their reputation as a respectable and moral family. The oldest daughter, Rachel, taught school alongside Jacob, while daughter Ellen supervised the residence and the students' daily schedules outside of class. Even fifteen-year-old Solomon served as an instructor.[17] Emma, as the second-youngest child, recalled the school as a family tradition rather than a personal experience. In 1818, when she was only six years old, Jacob sold the school to one of its instructors for $10,000 as part of a plan to move his family to Spring Farm, a four-hundred-acre farm a few miles from their many relatives in Richmond.[18] Jacob's son Augustus and his wife, Rosina Young Mordecai, eventually purchased a neighboring smaller farm, Rosewood. By 1831, Spring Farm, its soil now unproductive and worn out, was for sale, and Jacob joined his many relatives in Richmond.[19] When Emma moved to Rosina's farm in 1864, although she left the home where she had lived with her family since she was nineteen, she remained within the territory that had been familiar to her throughout her life, and she also stayed close to her extensive family network in Richmond.

By the early 1800s, Emma's family was known to many American Jews. Some had heard about the correspondence between her much older sister Rachel and the famed Anglo-Irish author and educator Maria Edgeworth.[20] Rachel admired Edgeworth's educational philosophy and literary talents but deeply objected to the author's insulting depiction of Jews in her 1812 novel *The Absentee*. Rachel corresponded at length with Edgeworth about the matter, and the author took her words seriously. Edgeworth believed her next book, *Harrington*, offered a much improved and even flattering depiction, and she sent Rachel a copy along with a personal note. The Mordecais did not keep this correspondence a secret, and other antebellum American Jewish families praised Rachel for defending the Jews. Philadelphia's Rebecca Gratz was impressed by Rachel's courage and soon followed her example. *Harrington* depicted a marriage between a Jew and a gentile, and Gratz wrote her own letter to Edgeworth expressing her disapproval of that narrative choice.[21]

Emma benefited from the respect shown to her family by Richmond's Jews, who admired her father, Jacob, because of his exceptional knowledge of Judaism. Moses Mordecai had bequeathed a remarkable collection of Hebrew books to Jacob—nineteen in all—and Jacob himself added to their number.[22] Though Jacob had experienced periods of acute religious doubt and toyed with the Christianity that many of his children later adopted, by the time he moved to Richmond, he had recommitted himself to Judaism and taken up more traditional religious practice than had been his habit in earlier periods of his life.[23] Jacob often advised the Richmond community on religious matters, and the community remembered his valuable service. A younger member of Richmond's Jewish community, the sculptor Moses Ezekiel, later recalled that Jacob "was always admired on account of his brilliant intellect, being well versed in Biblical research, the Hebrew language, and its literature; in fact, he was considered an authority on many questions pertaining to Judaism and Biblical interpretations."[24] Late in his life, Jacob served as president of Richmond's Congregation Beth Shalome. Beth Shalome was the sixth oldest Jewish congregation in America and followed the Sephardic rite of Jews descended from those expelled from Spain and Portugal during the Spanish Inquisition, though most of its members were Ashkenazic and had come to America from other parts of Europe.[25] The Mordecai name lent Emma stature in her Jewish community, and the family's high regard strengthened her emotional ties to her Jewish neighbors.

But the Mordecais also were unusual among the South's twenty-five thousand Jews. By the time the Civil War erupted in 1861, more than one-third of Southern Jews resided in Louisiana, especially in and near New Orleans. There were far fewer Jews in the upper South, despite Richmond's sizeable community. The Mordecais' family ties distinguished them from outsiders, both gentile and Jewish, and their tight bonds provided the family with emotional support and a vibrant sense of family pride.[26] They also were proud of being Southerners and enthusiastically adopted the Southern way of life. Any Mordecai family member or relative in the South with means enough, including Emma, owned slaves, just as their economic peers did. Emma's older brother Samuel was a longtime contributor to *The Farmer's Register*, a periodical aimed at an audience of white Southern slave owners that published articles assuming slavery to be the natural social order.[27] During the sectional crisis of the 1850s, Emma and her surviving siblings, always eager to keep up with news and politics, closely followed the debates over disunion and secession, which were particularly acute in both Virginia and North Carolina, where most of them lived, and they came down firmly on the side of secession and Confederate nationalism. As Emma wrote to her brother George just before the war broke out, "If the worst should happen . . . you may be sure that I shall not be found in opposition to my own people."[28]

Only one Mordecai family member of Emma's generation refused to support secession, which was declared in Virginia on April 17, 1861.[29] Emma's older brother Alfred graduated from the United States Military Academy at West Point and had attained the rank of major in the United States Army by the time war broke out. Emma and her siblings nevertheless expected Alfred, raised with them in North Carolina and Virginia, to fight for the South, as his fellow West Pointer Robert E. Lee had decided to do. Lee felt that his primary allegiance was to Virginia and offered his services to the Confederacy soon after war broke out. But Alfred struggled with making a similar choice. He did not want to fight against his old friends and former schoolmates on the Union side, nor against those comrades and relations who fought for the Confederacy. Alfred was fifty-seven years old, a career officer and a well-respected author of two books on ordnance. He had been serving as an ordnance chief in Watervliet, New York, for several years when his siblings urged him to lend his talent and energy to the Southern cause. Alfred refused. In a seventeen-page letter to his family, he explained that he "could not take sides against the South," yet at the same time, he felt that he "should be almost equally reluctant to enter the ranks against those with whom [he had] been so long associated on terms of close intimacy and friendship." Instead, Alfred resigned his commission and gave up "the labor of a whole life." He spent the war in Philadelphia as a civilian. Meanwhile, his son, Alfred Mordecai Jr., also a West Point graduate, fought for the Union in the Army of Northeast Virginia and earned a promotion to brigadier general.[30] Even for as Southern a family as the Mordecais, the war tore at familial bonds, and their experience reflected the rhetoric that envisioned the wartime country as a "house divided against itself," in Abraham Lincoln's words.[31]

Emma began her diary in April 1864, soon after she closed the house on Sixth Street in Richmond, Virginia, where she had lived for years with her widowed mother, Rebecca Myers Mordecai, and her older unmarried half siblings, Samuel (age seventy-eight) and Ellen (age seventy-four). Rebecca had died six months earlier, and the three siblings finally decided they should leave the city for safety. Samuel arranged for the house to be rented by a government official new to Richmond, which had been the capital of the Confederacy since July 1861 and saw its population nearly triple with the arrival of politicians, bureaucrats, displaced Southerners, military personnel,

Alfred Mordecai. (Courtesy of Library of Congress, Prints and Photographs Online Catalog)

and economic opportunists of all kinds.[32] Ellen moved to the large Raleigh, North Carolina, estate owned by her half brother George Washington Mordecai (age sixty-three), where he lived with his wife, Margaret Cameron. George and Ellen left the Richmond house together early in the morning on the same day that Emma locked it up and boarded the local train for the short ride to Rosewood, the farm belonging to her sister-in-law Rosina Young Mordecai. Most likely George had come to Richmond to help the siblings pack their belongings and to accompany Ellen on the long journey. Within a year, Samuel would pass away at the home of the widowed niece in Raleigh whose household he joined after leaving Richmond.[33]

Ellen felt comfortable moving to George's estate because they were siblings who shared a common religious perspective. Although their parents and all their ancestors were Jews, Ellen and George embraced Christianity, as did their siblings Caroline, Rachel, and Solomon at various points in their lives. Ellen repeatedly urged her siblings to seek Jesus but delayed her own actual christening at St. Paul's Church in Petersburg until three months after the death of her father, Jacob, in 1838. Soon thereafter, George became a communicant at Christ Church in Raleigh. Ellen easily settled into George's Christian household.[34] Other siblings, like their brother Augustus, never formally left Judaism but married Christians like Rosina and allowed their children to be raised as Christians. Alfred had remained Jewish and married a Jewish woman, but, perhaps because he chose a military career, he insisted that their son not be circumcised. The Mordecai siblings all negotiated their own religious paths, and although they often strongly disapproved of each other's choices, none of them ever permanently cut each other out of their lives as a result. It is worth noting that even though the American Jewish press tended to cast Southern Jewish women as the ones susceptible to marrying out of the faith, the Mordecai men were more likely than their sisters to do so.[35]

Emma loved Richmond and cherished her close ties to her Jewish relations and her synagogue, Beth Shalome, on Mayo Street. So instead of moving to George's home, where she would always be the younger Jewish sister, she accepted an invitation from her nearby sister-in-law Rosina, who was nearer Emma's own age and, though Christian herself, by temperament much less likely to proselytize than the converted Ellen was. Emma's nephew, also named George, and her niece Augusta came to assist her and accompany her on the short train ride to their home farm of Rosewood, providing affirmation of her welcome there.

Like Samuel and Ellen, Emma had never married. Long before, when she was only twenty-one, her engagement to a man named William Grimes had ended after her brother George withdrew his support for the match, a union that had defied their father's stated wish—doomed to repeated disappointment—that his children, especially his daughters, only marry Jews. George's rationale for approving the match and then changing his mind is unknown, and some years later, after his conversion, he married a non-Jewish woman himself; but the loss led Emma to attempt to take her own life.[36] Perhaps feelings lingering from the painful episode gave her another reason to choose Rosina's household over her brother's home, even many decades later.

The white South's ideas about human nature supported its highly stratified society. Biology was destiny; white women were presumed fit only for wifehood and motherhood. If white women of the middling and upper classes did not marry, they needed to secure a place for themselves under the protection of a family unit because respectable women did not live alone. An unmarried woman from a "good" family was likely to protect her reputation by living with relatives, sharing both their labor and their leisure depending on their class status.[37] Such was Emma's life. By 1864, she was the youngest surviving child of a family that had once included thirteen children, but only George, Alfred, and three half siblings, Samuel, Ellen, and Solomon, were still alive. As per convention, Emma continued to live with family well into middle age.

When the Mordecai siblings dispersed in 1864, they joined a trend that had gathered momentum since war broke out. Many white people who relocated during the war called themselves "refugees." At the start of the war, only the wealthiest classes enjoyed the resources to relocate entire households of both white and enslaved people out of the path of the Union army to safety, eliciting envy from those who were less privileged and remained behind and scorn from those who were already living where the presence of refugees worsened the war-induced food shortages. As many as one thousand such slave owners moved out of the path of the Union forces and headed toward the southern and western parts of the region. In Virginia alone, an estimated two hundred thousand Southerners fled their homes. Meanwhile, those Southerners who sympathized with the Union moved eastward and north, toward areas under the influence of Union forces. Because most white men between adolescence and middle age served in the military, women soon constituted the largest number of free civilians on the move. The pervasive sense of social upheaval and disorder that marked the South's war years stemmed from the widespread instability that exacerbated the disruptions following in the wake of military conquest itself.[38]

Emma never referred to herself as a refugee in her diary. The particular circumstances of her relocation blunted the rough edge of that term. She did not travel far from her own home but only to Rosewood, a mere five miles north of Richmond and adjacent to a farm that her father, Jacob, had previously owned. Perhaps more significantly, Emma probably felt that her move would help her sister-in-law, the widow of Emma's older brother Augustus, who had died seventeen years earlier, leaving Rosina with four young children following the deaths of three others in infancy. In their youth, Augustus had enjoyed Emma's lively and vivacious nature, and the two siblings grew close.[39] Their bond enveloped Rosina in its folds, and Emma was a frequent visitor to the farm. When the war began, Rosina's three sons, all in their twenties, joined the Richmond Howitzers military unit. Only Rosina, seventeen-year-old Augusta (whom Emma fondly called Gusta in the diary), and a number of enslaved people remained on the farm. Emma was a welcome presence.

Emma's nephews were caught up in the huge mobilization of something like 80 percent of draft-age Southern white men; by class, slave-owning status, and inclination, they probably started out as enthusiastic soldiers.[40] White Southerners initially expected the war to last only a few months and cause little disruption. But a year into the fighting, it became clear that long-term mass mobilization would be needed to defeat the Union forces. The Confederacy passed a conscription law in April 1862, the first such in American history, almost a year to the day after the shot on South Carolina's Fort Sumter began the war. The shifting conscription laws revealed the increasingly desperate struggle to fill the military's ranks. When war first broke out, all able-bodied white men between the ages of eighteen and thirty-five were called to serve for one to three years. But service was not compulsory, and most signed up for no more than one year. By 1862, the term of service for men currently serving in the Confederacy's military was extended to three years. Five months later, the Confederacy demanded three years of service from every new draftee. Men who were engaged in work that was deemed too valuable to the home front to be taken from their labor were exempt from service. These groups included railroad workers, civil officials, druggists, and teachers. White men who owned more than twenty slaves were also exempt, prompting resentment, draft evasion, and desertion among some non-slave-owning whites. In the face of a Northern opponent with far greater manpower, the maximum age of conscription was extended to forty-five. In December 1863, the Confederacy stopped allowing men to hire substitutes for the draft. Two months later, the eligible draft age was extended from seventeen to fifty.[41]

The constant expansion of the draft was not without dispute, nor was it adequate to the army's needs. Near war's end, the Confederacy expanded the practice of impressing Black men to serve its military by digging trenches, cooking, and in other ways assisting white men in combat, dragging both enslaved and free Black men into Confederate service.[42] In early June 1864, Emma wrote that her "man" Moses Norrill, still in Richmond, remained indoors for fear he would be "taken up."⁴³ Norrill labored as a hired man for wages that were paid to Emma, who spent some of that money to feed and clothe Norrill and his wife, Sally, whom Emma also owned. This was common practice throughout the South, particularly in urban areas like Richmond, and one that increased in Virginia as agriculture became less central to the state's economy and fewer enslaved people worked on large plantations as a result.⁴⁴

Rosina, six years younger than Emma, may also have wanted her sister-in-law to join her household because she herself was "sickly," as people of her day called it, although Rosina would live for another forty-two years. Emma described chronic headaches and other pains keeping Rosina in bed on most days; whether she had a diagnosable illness is impossible to know. Rosina's fears for her sons' wellbeing surely contributed to her inability to function well. It is easy to see how she might have welcomed Emma, a white woman and a relation, who could help her. As slave owners with close relatives in the Confederate army who lived close to numerous sites of fighting throughout the war, both Emma and Rosina were among those most likely to develop a strong sense of Confederate nationalism, which both seem to have done.⁴⁵

Although Emma had good reason to believe that her coming to live at Rosewood benefited Rosina, she also felt a need to prove herself a useful addition to the household, especially in such uncertain times. The two women had known each other for most of their lives, but their family ties and long-standing relationship did not erase the fact that Emma felt "strange without a home anymore."⁴⁶ For at least a century before Emma wrote those words, "home" had taken on a meaning loaded with emotion and connected to personal identity. Its rise reflected the growing importance of townspeople, a population that included middle-class professionals, small manufacturers and mechanics, and the literary and professional people who influenced politics and culture across western Europe and the United States. The term "home" now connoted privacy, domesticity, and comfort. Appearing first among the Dutch and spreading to England, France, and the German states, this domestic and social ideal was tied to economic shifts that brought people out of farming and into trade and urban life.[47]

The widespread economic and cultural changes that gave rise to the bourgeois home spanned western Europe and the urban centers of North America, but the distinctive features of Southern society modified them significantly. First, the South remained overwhelmingly agrarian. Its cities stayed small and primarily served as hubs for those businesses that supported agriculture rather than becoming competing centers of economic growth. Second, slavery permeated every facet of Southern life. Enslaved people performed the labor done both out of doors and inside residences. The efficient and effective management of household slaves became the most important ability expected of white women. Domestic architecture itself reflected the different ways domiciles functioned in various parts of the country. Homes in the North differed from the farmsteads of the West and the households of the slaveholding South. Southern households of any means included multiple structures, from the main house to the outbuildings to the slave quarters. Kitchens were placed in outbuildings, where heat and smoke would stay apart from the living area of the main house. Thus, historians such as Elizabeth Fox-Genovese have referred to Southern family residences as "households" rather than homes because they remained multistructure units of "production and reproduction ultimately under men's dominance."[48] Yet books, periodicals, visitors from the North and from England, and the abundance of consumer household goods also spread the ideal of the comfortable bourgeois domestic home to the South.[49]

Emma was thankful that Rosina "had prepared most kindly for [her] reception," writing, "my room was the picture of neatness & comfort." The room's neatness, cleanliness, and comfortable furnishings, featuring a table, chair, bed, and linens, included the elements that might make Emma feel at home. But her description of the two women's personal relationship lacks the loving warmth by which many nineteenth-century women described their closest friendships and kin relationships and that had become markers of female domestic relationships. "She received me very kindly," Emma wrote, but the two women "made no demonstration or professions [of affection] to each other."[50]

Emma's diary demonstrates that white Southerners adapted the urban home ideal to their particular circumstances. As someone who had lived in Richmond for a long time, she brought a more urban sense of home with her to Rosina's farm. As she entered life at Rosewood and began writing in her diary, she described herself as "very still & quiet, tho not overcome with depression—the reverse, however, of all excitement." It seems that Emma viewed this move to be something she must do rather than something she eagerly anticipated. Rosina's efforts to make the room attractive and appealing may have comforted Emma, but they did not completely cheer her. She prayed that her time with Rosina, "for as long as it may last," might be "a blessing & not a torment or inconvenience to her."[51] The societal and economic changes that created the bourgeois home and the concept of domesticity meant that homes became extensions of personal identity, especially for women. As men's labor moved out of residences and into commercial, official, or industrial sites, homes increasingly became tied to women's labor, agency, and taste. A woman who left her home moved out of the personal arena that she controlled and that held signs and markers of her own efforts and desires.[52] Emma had run the Richmond family home for years, and her sense of loss was palpable. She was emotionally unsteady. "There was a time when I should not have doubted [my welcome] but the longer we live, the more we doubt ourselves, & now I am not certain—I only hope," she admitted.[53]

Four months after Emma moved in, she wrote that she had "slept badly last night disturbed in mind": "Cannot help feeling sometimes, that I am not living at a home of my own, & think of seeking an independent position."[54] Still feeling like a visitor at Rosewood, dependent on her sister-in-law's hospitality, Emma found that her diary provided a secure location where her own thoughts and emotions could prevail and counter her feelings of displacement. Yet, significantly, this was the only such comment to appear in the diary. "Independent positions" for single women were difficult to find, especially during the economic collapse that the South was enduring. She may have been thinking about a position as a schoolteacher at a women's academy like the one her family had run earlier in North Carolina, but relatively few such institutions thrived during wartime. Moreover, teachers did not enjoy the same respect in the South as they did in the North because Southern white families preferred to hire independent tutors to teach their children at home.[55] In Richmond, Emma had often earned income as a private teacher while continuing to live with her family. Without that home, she would have been forced to become a tutor who lived with a student's family, a type of live-in hired work that was deemed unsuitable for a white Southern lady.[56] The North would have provided far better opportunities for her to teach, as her sister Ellen had done for a while in New York before the war, but that move would require her to live within enemy territory, an utterly abhorrent idea.[57] So she remained with Rosina for the duration of the war and never mentioned moving away from Rosewood again. Instead, she made herself useful, and that usefulness gave her a sense of belonging, focus, and purpose.

Still, Emma was far from cheerful. Her fifty-second birthday on October 6, 1864, might have provided her a reason to celebrate, or at least to lighten her mood, but the reverse occurred. She had paid several visits the previous day, but on the day itself, she wrote, "Nothing to note down." The very brief diary entry noted the weather, a lack of general news, and her complaint, "vertigo & nausea after going to bed—the third Wednesday night that this has been the case with me." Perhaps anxiety caused her symptoms, which were never mentioned again. By contrast, Emma reported, "Rosina uncommonly well," an unusual role reversal.[58]

Rosewood was only a short distance from Richmond, and Emma regularly returned to the city to celebrate events at her synagogue on the Jewish religious calendar, to visit relatives and friends, to shop, and to negotiate with various legal, business, and military authorities to solve problems that arose at the farm due to the war. Usually she traveled by local train, which she called "the cars," available as a result of Virginia's considerable investment in railroads, far more than any other antebellum Southern state.[59] Sometimes she walked or caught a ride in a neighbor's wagon or carriage. The city was never far from her mind and provided a comforting contrast to her life at Rosewood and the lack of a home of her own.

NINETEENTH-CENTURY WOMEN'S DIARIES

If a home is a place where someone feels comfortable, expresses her thoughts freely, places precious objects for safekeeping, and finds emotional sustenance, then Emma's wartime diary functioned as a type of metaphorical home, a site where she could reaffirm her personal self by recording her own version of events and her hopes and fears. However, Emma had some misgivings about this diary, and there is no direct explanation of why she decided to start it other than the significant change in her circumstances. This was not her first foray into keeping a diary. A previous diary, begun in January 1838, opened with buoyant descriptions of parties and visits with family and friends as the new year began. But only a few months later, Emma described the suffering and death of her oldest sister, Rachel, and then, a few months after that, the death of her father, Jacob, along with the anguish and grief that pervaded her family that year. She stopped making entries in August 1838.[60] Perhaps that is why she began her Civil War diary by commenting, "in spite of some experience and all resolutions to the contrary, I have concluded to commence" an account of life on Rosina's farm.[61] She opened this diary by expressing faith that God would protect her and her beloved Confederacy. By the following year, though, Emma was including vivid descriptions of the ways both the war and the Confederacy's collapse challenged her physically, emotionally, and spiritually. Both of her extant diaries, then, describe years that began in hope and optimism but concluded with gloom and despair.

By the last days of the conflict, Emma may have determined to maintain the diary not so much for personal comfort but as a documentary witness to the war and the South's collapse. There is a break in writing at the time that Richmond burned, and Emma returned to the diary later, filling in events from April 1865 and then continuing writing for at least another month. Her reasons for stopping and starting again are unclear, perhaps even to Emma, because by the time she passed the diary along to a new generation of Mordecais decades later, decay and insects had destroyed its final pages, and she made no effort to reconstruct her thoughts or feelings from that period.

Diaries like Emma's were especially common in Protestant, industrializing parts of western Europe and the United States. Protestants, who constituted 90 percent of America's white population by the time of the American Revolution, read the Bible, so Protestant communities required literacy. The secular sectors of commerce and industry also required proficiency in ledgers, instructional manuals, advertising, business correspondence, and meeting notes. As early as the seventeenth century in colonial Massachusetts towns with fifty families or more, parents hired teachers to instruct each child. Writing was equally important.[62] A century later, diaries had been woven into private devotional rituals. In one vivid example, the Newport, Rhode Island, schoolteacher Clara Osborne compiled more than fifty volumes of diaries written "in order to cultivate Christian virtue within" herself.[63] Women, in particular, additionally used the private space of diaries as a means of negotiating their identities.[64]

Although the South counted few public school systems as late as 1860, the region was overwhelmingly Protestant, and white Southerners also shared a widespread literacy and knowledge of the Bible. Biblical references cropped up in political speeches, literature, and private letters by both men and women. Newspapers printed

First page of Emma Mordecai's 1864–1865 diary. (Courtesy of the Southern Historical Collection, The Wilson Library, University of North Carolina at Chapel Hill)

Diary. May. 1864.
kept by Emma Mordecai at Rosewood. Near Richmond.

On Thursday, April 18th I left our house on 6th Street, for the last time. Sister Ellen & Brother George had departed early that morning, leaving my nephew George, alone at the house. There were still remaining a few articles of furniture to be sent away, after attending to which George & I came away & at 3½ came out to Rosewood in the cars with Augusta when her school was out. I felt strange without a home any more, and very still & quiet, tho' not overcome with depression — the reverse, however, of all excitement. Rose had prepared most kindly for my reception, and my room was the picture of neatness & comfort. She received me very kindly, but we made no demonstration or professions to each other. I only know that my inward resolve and humble prayer was & is that I may make my residence with her, for as long as it may last, a blessing & not a torment or inconvenience to her. There was a time when I should not have doubted this, but the longer we live, the more we doubt ourselves, & now I am not certain. I only hope.

The following week I went to town to spend the Passover with my kind cousins, returning at the close of the festival, the time having been spent very satisfactorily, attending the services at the Synagogue, and visiting many of our friends whom circumstances had prevented my seeing before we broke up. By all I was most kindly greeted, & I was gratified at the unvarying regret expressed at our family having left Richmond, & at the kind invitations I received from various friends to pass days or nights with them whenever I could. I returned to Rosewood on Friday 30th. George, meantime had returned to the Army, & Gusta who went out with me, after school, & I found Rose alone, & pretty well, considering she had been exerting herself over much in many ways — I was soon resettled. The weather continues sermons by local ministers. Biblical references wove the scattered households of the South into an imagined community of shared values and imagery that united rich and poor.[65] As the sectional crisis deepened, white Southern politicians, clergymen, and newspapermen alike increasingly referred to their common understanding that biblical support for slavery justified Southern politics. Evangelical ministers often asserted that God approved the South's distinct social order. Religion gave divine sanction to masters of all households, no matter their size or wealth; white men ruled their dependents, both white and Black. That faith in divine support for Southerners' social codes imbued them with confidence in their ultimate military and political success.[66] In addition, letters united white kinfolk and friends living some distance from each other across the South and kept them informed about life-cycle events and social news. Thus, literacy served economic, religious, political, and social purposes for Northerners and white Southerners alike.

Diary writing was a common activity for Southern white women of all ages, including Jewish women like Emma. In New Orleans, seventeen-year-old Clara Solomon maintained a diary of her life during the first year of the war, which included the occupation of her city. Eleanor Cohen of Charleston was also a diligent diarist and for a longer period of time. When she "refugeed" to Columbia, South Carolina (and later to Richmond) with her family in order to avoid Union general William Tecumseh Sherman's "march to the sea," she mourned that "all the labors of years" of journal writing had been destroyed along with most of her family's possessions. She resolved to begin writing again as soon as possible in order to "rebuild from the ashes of despair a new record, and enthrone 'blue eyed hope' as the presiding deity." The widow Phoebe Yates Levy Pember kept a journal of events during her time as head matron of the sprawling Chimborazo Military Hospital in Richmond, which treated seventy-six thousand patients over the course of the war. These and other Civil War–era Jewish women used their diaries and other personal writings as a safe space to express their innermost thoughts at a time when family and region were fraught with political and religious divides.⁶⁷

The Civil War proved to be a diary-making machine. A basic search of the Library of Congress's online catalog turns up thousands of such diaries, written by both men and women in both the North and the South. Generals and ordinary soldiers published memoirs, military units produced collective reminiscences, and women wrote personal reflections and accounts of their experiences. Dozens of Civil War–era Southern women's diaries have been published to date, and many more lie unpublished in historical societies, libraries, and private collections.⁶⁸ An untold number have been lost to the passage of time.

The abundance of women's diaries seems to challenge some feminist critiques of writing as a male domain that provoked quandaries about personal identity in nineteenth-century women. Early feminist theorists followed Freud in suggesting that the pen is a metaphorical penis. They contended that the very act of writing itself—not simply publication of a woman's writings—can be interpreted as transgressing gender norms, regardless of what the author chose to write.⁶⁹ That theory would not expect women of the South, where gender codes were firmly embedded in class and racial categories that made them more rigid than they might have been in a more fluid society, to have left such a rich written legacy, and yet they did.⁷⁰

Some nineteenth-century women wrote diaries in order to grapple with their experiences, symbolically manipulating and reimagining the circumstances of their lives and thus asserting their control over psychological challenges posed to them by crises they faced. For them, diaries became vehicles for proving to themselves that their intellectual power could overcome a feared external reality. Their diaries reaffirmed the value and strength of an inner self. Because diarists selected which experiences to write about, they could shape their record of events and of themselves. In that process, they also strengthened and reaffirmed their own identities. Thus, diaries could prepare individuals to confront challenges from the outside world, from within their social milieu, and from their own emotions.[71]

Other theorists posit that it may have been the private nature of women's diaries that made them appropriate for what nineteenth-century Americans sometimes called the private sphere, the ideal realm in which women could best function without earning social opprobrium.[72] These works, produced in such abundance by Southern women, did not challenge their authors' womanliness. Southern women's Civil War diaries demonstrate that the boundary between what was called "women's sphere" and that of men was more porous than either rhetoric or a quick look suggests. Certainly, women were not called to serve in military units or in political office. However, Emma's diary is one example of how the political debates that maintained the Confederacy and supported it in what it called a war of independence entered and sustained women's realm. By repeating and discussing those political arguments in their diaries, women brought the manly world of politics and war into their private worlds. Some women understood these writings to be treasonous in the Union's view, something that might prove reason enough for the author's arrest and even execution by people to whom Emma referred as "the enemy," should they be found.[73]

Diaries that voiced those Confederate ideals also described ways in which Southern women shouldered previously "manly" duties of overseeing the labor of field slaves and navigated ways to protect their property from theft by hungry soldiers. In Emma's diary, the description of her own such actions indicates that she believed she exhibited the courage appropriate to wartime. Most Southern white women who took on responsibilities previously seen as outside their sphere understood themselves to be acting to preserve their society, not to challenge it.[74]

White women who voiced their support for the Confederacy and echoed its political arguments and ideals in their letters and diaries also understood themselves to be continuing a tradition that emerged in the revolutionary era. As the new republic took shape, it needed men to enact and defend its ideals and women to teach these concepts to the nation's sons. Historians have labeled the descriptions of women's duty to the new nation that were voiced in newspapers, political rhetoric, and advice manuals as "Republican Motherhood."[75] That attitude toward women's duty was echoed a few generations later in the Confederacy's political rhetoric, which drew on revolutionary-era discourse to justify what it saw as its own war for independence from the United States.[76] Educated and thoughtful Southern women like Emma were proud to continue this tradition of women's civic importance while simultaneously modeling the piety, purity, submissiveness, and domesticity of the more recent and hugely popular model of "true womanhood" so ubiquitous in mid-nineteenth-century American discourse.[77]

But for Mordecai and other privileged Southern white woman, the "true woman" was a figure who should not be associated merely with the emerging capitalist economic relations that had moved work away from home and divided public and private into separate, gendered spheres of activity. Surely, Emma and her cohort agreed, the South's slave society was far more humane than the North's industrializing one in providing a place for each type of person in a well-ordered hierarchy. So, despite condemning the "barbarous" treatment of slaves by some owners after Nat Turner's rebellion in 1831, Emma believed the slave system overall to be humane.[78] This attitude was part of the Southern nationalist critique of the North. Southerners may have admired the attributes of "true women," but they believed their own society better able to produce and protect these icons of femininity. Women's diaries demonstrated mastery of such language and social codes. Their authors required a bit of spare cash to purchase the paper and ink, the sense of a valuable point of view worth expressing and preserving, and an ease of linguistic self-expression that drew on some amount of education. For those reasons, keeping a diary demonstrated Southern white women's prerogatives even if they did not own a single slave and even if they did not see writing a diary as a political act available only to the privileged.

Emma lived her entire life as part of the master class, and she relished the literary life it afforded her. She not only wrote in her diary but also read literature in both French and English and translated a French play she had enjoyed reading, apparently *Le mariage au tambour*, which had first been produced in Paris in 1843. She hoped to see her translation performed onstage in Richmond.[79] Theatrical performances of European plays and music enlivened much of antebellum American life, North and South, enriching social life through public performances that wove together scenes from highbrow drama or opera and lowbrow entertainments like comedy, juggling, and minstrelsy. Rosina's given name suggests that her parents may have enjoyed performances in Richmond of Rossini's comic opera *The Barber of Seville*, whose heroine carries that female variation on Rossini's own name.[80]

Despite high regard for literary mastery in the South, the enjoyment of written language was both the province of whites and a highly gendered phenomenon. During the antebellum era, it gradually became illegal throughout the region to teach slaves to read or write, further underscoring the links among literacy, self-expression, and mastery.[81] Even though many parts of the antebellum South lacked public schools, by 1840, the rate of Southern illiteracy had dropped to roughly 9 percent among white adults. By 1840, women's education, often obtained in special academies for girls, changed its pedagogical goals from spoken achievements, such as rhetoric, to mastery of written composition.[82] Many mothers who kept diaries intended them to be gifts for their daughters because their diaries conveyed life lessons specifically useful to women. Indeed, daughters were trained in diary writing as a means of cultivating appreciation of "dailiness and ordinariness" because their "lot in life is the quotidian."[83] That custom of older female relations leaving written advice for younger family members may have contributed to Emma's later decision to give her wartime diary to her niece.

Another factor contributing to that decision might have been the burgeoning propaganda war of the Lost Cause. Through diaries, memoirs, and other published writings, Southerners generated what became known as the "Myth of the Lost Cause," the idea that they had not primarily fought to defend slavery but instead to defend nobly their states' rights against the power of the federal government in matters such as "tariff disputes, control of investment banking and the means of wealth, cultural differences, and conflict between industrial and agricultural societies."[84] Perpetuators of this mythology, such as the Richmond journalist Edward Pollard, whose 1866 book *The Lost Cause* gave it a name, asserted that the North unjustly, aggressively, and cruelly subjugated the South and that Southerners lost the war because the North had more manpower and guns and was a "merciless power." The superior society—the one defending its constitutional rights, which was more virtuous and blessed despite its defeat—was the South. The Lost Cause provided white Southerners with balm for their wounded psyches and served as a way to justify ongoing structural racism in Southern law and custom. It was also appealing to white Northerners who prioritized sectional reconciliation over racial justice. After Reconstruction ended in 1877, Southerners promoted this vision of the Civil War across the entire United States through literature, pageantry, monuments, theater, songs, and eventually film as well.[85]

Emma's diary reflects attitudes entirely consistent with those ideas. The wounded Confederate soldiers she encountered in a local military hospital were "pure, highminded noble men."[86] She wrote confidently about the abilities of the Confederate military. She measured men according to their perceived gentlemanliness, a style of behavior that could be depended on to protect her and other Southern white women from harm. George Fitzhugh, author of the 1854 volume *Sociology for the South*, described Southern women as people who "naturally shrink from public gaze" and, "like children, have but one right and that is the right to protection."[87] A Southern gentleman would recognize his responsibility to provide that protection. Protection was also the key to white privilege.[88] By displaying the behaviors that indicated her status as a respectable Southern woman,

Emma earned that protection. Especially for an unmarried woman without a male protector, personal safety depended on proper womanly deportment according to conventional Southern expectations and standards.

Northern men, on the other hand, raised without those social codes, could be dangerous. When Emma was forced to confront Union soldiers—Black and white—she considered herself brave. There were two possibilities. The soldiers were either "ruffians" who did not understand her manners, race, and gender as signals of her gentility and indicators that she deserved protection or "gentlemen" who did understand those codes and responded to her in ways she trusted would protect her. Her own sense of bravery and pride in her own personal accomplishment were revealed in a letter she wrote describing how she succeeded in obtaining protection from the Union officers occupying Richmond and its environs at the end of the war. That she placed a copy of this letter into her diary exemplified the diary's use as a place of safety and a bulwark against the troubled times through which she was living.[89]

EMMA'S CIVIL WAR

Emma and other refugees aimed to escape the dangers of advancing armies, but in May 1864, Rosewood lay closer to the action than did the home Emma left behind in Richmond. General Ulysses S. Grant had taken command of Union forces that March and soon began coordinating battles that would weaken the South's military on several fronts. While Union forces kept Lee's Army of Northern Virginia engaged for the next year, they also confronted Confederate forces in Georgia, Louisiana, Arkansas, Mississippi, Missouri, Tennessee, South Carolina, and North Carolina. During the months before Emma left Richmond, white Southerners rejoiced in a series of Confederate victories at places like Plymouth, North Carolina, and Fort Pillow, Tennessee, where General Nathan Bedford Forrest committed one of the most striking atrocities of the war in massacring hundreds of Black Union soldiers after they attempted to surrender.⁹⁰ On May 6, Rosewood echoed with the sound of gunfire. Emma and Rosina thought they were hearing the Battle of the Wilderness, part of Grant's Overland Campaign to capture Richmond, destroy Lee's army, and force his surrender before Lee could move south to reinforce Confederates fighting against Union general Sherman in Georgia. Those at Rosewood saw the bright flames from soldiers' campfires against the dark sky that evening, but they were probably too far away actually to have heard the Battle of the Wilderness.⁹¹

The mid-May fighting near Rosewood changed ordinary life. At first, it seemed a fascinating adventure, especially since the inhabitants of Rosewood, like all their friends and neighbors, followed army movements closely and saw Lee as a sort of secular saint.⁹² The day after a battle, Emma proposed that the family "should visit part of the scene of yesterday's encounter." She was surprised at the obstacles in their path. "We found many difficulties to our progress, trees fallen across the roads, dead horses—and finally were frightened by seeing a body of Cavalry moving some distance ahead of us, whom we feared might be Yankees, so we turned from our attempt." Violence had changed the natural landscape, too. "We saw some large trees topped by cannon balls, & others badly cut by them," she noted. The scene included "a good many people in the woods looking for plunder," which might include soldiers' gold charms for good luck or protection given by their families as they left for war. Scavengers may have sought cash in a soldier's pockets or simply a decent pair of boots. There were also more "dead horses & ... badly cut up roads." Perhaps Emma expected even something more dramatic, because she "saw no evidence of the hard fight which took place there only yesterday."⁹³

When the two women drove into Richmond to bring Rosina's daughter, Augusta, home from school, however, they "passed on the road some large bodies of Cavalry & one of Infantry—everything looked indeed like War." Emma described how "weary soldiers were lying within the batteries wrapped in their blankets, all over the wet ground," adding, "a courier passed us, riding up the road at full speed."

As they approached Richmond, they "met parties of ladies & little girls, with servants carrying refreshments to friends at the Batteries."[94] These sights fit their expectation of the South at war: active soldiers in uniform, women serving food, and servants—as Emma always referred to enslaved people—carrying heavy loads. Regardless of the war and difficulties getting into and out of the city with fighting nearby, Augusta seems to have continued attending school fairly regularly until just before the fall of Richmond, illustrating the importance of girls' education to middle-class white Southerners in general and the Mordecai family in particular.[95]

In early June, military action came so near to Rosina's farm that her son John arrived home for a twenty-four-hour break. He simply appeared at the front door, washed up and put on clean clothes, ate what Emma described as a good meal, and slept until the next morning. "He was the picture of a dirty Con. soldier, but looked well in point of health. I at first took him for one of our soldiers come to ask for milk & did not recognize him till he said Howdy Aunt Emma! We rejoice to have him, tho' only for a day and night," Emma recorded with pleasure. Comforting as John's visit surely was for his mother, sister, and aunt, his stay did not mean military tensions were easing. "He brought us news that the Yankees are spreading over the upper country" of Virginia, Emma wrote.[96] The following morning, John returned to his unit. Rosina's other sons, Willie and George, similarly came and went. Both spent time at home recovering from leg wounds that kept them from military service but not from social visits or from running a business gathering the oat tithe from local farmers and bringing it to Richmond. With the Union blockading Southern ports and Southern railroads in disrepair, the Confederacy instituted a tax on income but allowed farmers to pay it in crops, based on one-tenth of their total production. Appraisers estimated, under oath, the quantity, quality and value of the produce and collected it, work that Willie and George found they were able to do while out of combat.[97]

Everyone at Rosina's farm heard the sound of battle. Emma soon learned to identify the reverberations made by different kinds of artillery, and she remained alert enough to troop movements to identify when noise came from pickets (the advance outpost of a larger force) or from the heavy cannons meant to launch munitions far beyond the range of the infantry's small arms. On July 4, Emma expected to hear Union soldiers celebrating with gunfire and fireworks, but all remained quiet. Near the end of her diary, on April 19, 1865, she noted the guns firing at frequent intervals all day in honor of Lincoln's funeral.

During the battles of 1864, the noise of gunfire and rumors of victories and losses both permeated Emma's diary. She heard talk of a Union victory at Chancellorsville, sixty-five miles north of Richmond, and, later, a rumor that Union general Ulysses S. Grant had been killed. The sound of cannon fire from the nearby Battle of Spotsylvania Court House disturbed the farm. Confederate general J. E. B. Stuart stalled the Union advance at a battle at Yellow Tavern, only about a mile from Rosewood. Emma pasted into her diary a letter from a friend who lived almost within the battle area because it richly described her precarious experience. As Union general Benjamin Butler marched his men to Richmond, federal forces approached the city from different directions, and Confederates successfully attacked Union forces eight miles south of Richmond at Drewry's Bluff. Emma noted it all. Although Union forces outnumbered the Confederates, Southerners usually knew the terrain, and many Union soldiers simply protected long supply lines. Moreover, Northerners typically enlisted for three years, and by 1864, many battle-trained men turned their sights toward home. Thus, neither side felt their victory was assured, and Virginia remained a noisy, contested territory for several more months.[98] As for Rosewood, "Heavy cannonading and rounds of musketry," east of the family, continued for more than an hour, Emma complained. "We know nothing but... [hear] firing all around us and that our pickets have been withdrawn to the inner lines of defense, which leaves us in the enemy's lines."[99]

The fierce fighting in May 1864 frightened Richmonders, whose city alarm bells called out the local militia. At that moment, the

Confederacy could muster only fifteen thousand troops and a temporary assemblage of government clerks serving as militia to defend Richmond and nearby Petersburg. Cadets from the Virginia Military Academy were sent into action, probably in the Shenandoah Valley 135 miles away. By the end of June, Petersburg was under siege, yet the struggle to control the city did not end until the following March, when it finally fell to Union forces. Fighting continued on and off near Petersburg until April 1865.[100]

Emma tried to remain calm despite those nearby battles. On May 7, 1864, she described, "Loud firing of both cannon & musketry commenced briskly between 4 & 6 o'clock—don't know where the fight was, but not very far off." It was to be a noisy evening. "A heavy thunderstorm with abundant rain stopped the firing for short time. Continued after the storm abated until dark when Rose went to bed." Gunfire and thunder dominated the evening. All the while, Emma wrote, "I sat knitting in the dark till 9, when I went to bed too, after committing our household to the care of the All Powerful & felt no fear." Despite the brave words, she could not sleep, but she ascribed her sleeplessness to diet rather than the noise of the cannon, writing, "I had taken a cup of tea which kept me awake until near 12, but my thoughts were tranquil & full of trust. R. was asleep all the time."[101] Whatever her real mental and emotional state, her diary entries recorded only an appropriately courageous and faithful frame of mind throughout that fateful year.

Were those truly her reactions? By ascribing her insomnia to a cup of tea rather than fear, she may have been trying to write herself into the calm and confident mental state she hoped to achieve. Perhaps she wanted a record of bravery in this written document. Diarists often reread their creations, and a diary also could be read by anyone who knew where to find it, who stumbled upon it, or who received it as an inheritance. Each of Emma's many assertions about her personal belief in the superiority of the Southern way of life or her loyalty to the Confederacy may have been for an imagined audience or possibly to build her own courage in the face of danger.

The noise of battle and the rumors of victories and defeats constituted a vivid thread of personal war experiences with soldiers that run throughout the diary. Soldiers tramped by and came to Rosina's door for food, her well for water, her farm for a cow, her henhouse for eggs and chickens, and, ultimately, her barn for her horse. At the end of September, Emma listened to loud cannon firing all night as Union forces tried again to capture Richmond. Her brother George, visiting from Raleigh, brought news the next day that the Union had fallen back instead of pressing the victory. The city's alarm bells rang all day, he reported, yet Emma wrote that Richmonders felt little fear. She felt secure enough to travel to the city to stay with relatives for the next three days in order to attend synagogue for Sabbath and Jewish New Year, or "Roshashannah," services from Friday evening through the weekend.[102] Whenever Emma returned to the city, she noted that although the war had pushed her to leave, it drew in many others. Newly arrived bureaucrats, soldiers, opportunists, refugees, prisoners, and jailed civilian Unionists nearly tripled the size of Richmond's prewar population of roughly forty thousand.[103]

After mid-October 1864, the fighting moved away from the Richmond environs as Missouri, Kansas, Alabama, Tennessee, South Carolina, Georgia, and even Florida became battle sites. Even when there was no fighting near Richmond or Rosewood, the war pervaded every aspect of life for people living in the area, including women's standard domestic tasks of sewing and cooking. Like most Confederate women, Emma sewed almost daily, adapting old clothes to new seasons and mending them to be worn again. Knitting socks for soldiers became a patriotic activity for many Confederate women, and Emma knitted while waiting for trains, on daily outings, and during social visits with other women. She became so adept that she could sew in the dark. Augusta and other young women also braided wheat straw for summer hats, and when Emma gathered wheat straw for a young woman she knew, she reported, "All the Southern girls make straw hats for themselves, which are very pretty, and many for gentlemen."[104]

Food shortages were the most pressing concern. Union gunboats blockaded Southern ports so that no cotton could be sent to foreign markets and no goods could be imported. This had a devastating effect on the Southern economy, especially because, decades earlier, economically dominant white Southerners had made a fateful decision to produce cotton at the expense of other crops, including food. Thus, the Union's blockade not only prevented the South from selling its cotton but also left the South with insufficient access to the food it had, by then, grown accustomed to importing. Prices for basic foodstuffs tripled and then tripled again. By the fall of 1862, flour cost $16 a barrel, potatoes $5 a bushel, and butter $1.25 a pound. April 1863 saw bread riots in Richmond, and Richmond's civilians pillaged the food that was designated for the military and stored in local warehouses.[105] Rosina was generous to passing soldiers who asked for food, but she also directed her slaves to build pens to keep her chickens, hens, eggs, and cows safe from men who came to the farm and took what they could. The well on the property was a major attraction.

Food shortages affected every Southerner. Few meals contained much meat. One woman Emma met got her daily allotment of protein from butter. Emma and her neighbors made "coffee" from ground wheat seeds. "The Blockade makes us very ingenious and independent," she remarked of the daily economies she and her neighbors practiced.[106] Her diary was full of descriptions of meals, notable for their relative plenty and tastiness despite the blockade; it was good to live on a farm that could produce its own food. Never did Emma comment on whether food did or did not meet the requirements of Jewish dietary laws, but it is clear from her descriptions that she frequently ate meat and milk together and ate proscribed catfish and pork when it was available as well. She did, however, express pride in the tale of Richmond brothers Ezekiel and Isaac Levy, both Confederate soldiers who abided by Judaism's gastronomic rules and "never eat . . . forbidden food."[107]

The centrality of food to Confederates' daily concerns is evident in the frequency with which Emma wrote about it. She typically recorded not only her visits to neighbors, family, and friends but also what she ate while there. Clabber (Emma called it "clauber"), a kind of yogurt made from soured milk, became a feature of most of her meal descriptions. Soon after she settled in at Rosewood, the minister of Rosina's church came by, and although Emma described him as a "kind, amiable" man, she did not record anything he said. Instead, she noted that Rosina offered him tea, muffins, clauber, and milk for supper. "Who would desire better fare in the most bountiful times?" she commented. In her mind, the meal proved Rosina "a good economist" and "one of the rich poor people."[108] As a slave owner, Rosina could hardly be counted as poor by many of her neighbors, but since she owned only a small number of enslaved people, she was still far from wealthy by Southern standards.[109]

The next week, Emma found that the Richmond newspapers were "full of the heartless depredations of the Yankees in the lower counties. Sheridan's Cavalry, the same that threatened Richmond in such force, two weeks ago, are destroying everything in the country, leaving families but one meal of food to subsist upon." Rosina's farm remained in far better circumstances despite these nearby battles. On May 29, Emma described the "excellent dinner of nice fried chicken, asparagus, boiled onions & rice, with a dessert of cool clauber." These details reveal not only her worries about food scarcity but also the ways in which meals marked time in her daily routines. Food also became an integral part of the visits Emma made to Richmond and to neighbors in the countryside around Rosewood. When she visited cousins in the city in June 1864, she brought them a large basket of peas from the farm. Three months later, she visited a neighbor to watch workers "crushing Sorghum and making syrup of the juice by boiling in huge kettles. This is our substitute (and a very poor one) for molasses, & with some, for sugar."[110] Visits to friends and family usually included at least some food, offering a taste of a different cook's talents—often the talents of an enslaved woman—and, as food became scarce, a chance to preserve the food at home a bit longer.

Almost daily, Emma reported on the visitors welcomed at Rosewood or the visits she herself made to neighbors, including Rosina's relatives who lived nearby. Visiting was a central part of Southern social relations, providing the setting for companionship, business discussion, and religious conversation as well as meals. Brief calls were part of daily life in towns, for men as well as women, and family visits could last anywhere from one night to several weeks or months, especially for unmarried women or widowed parents.[111] This freedom to visit was one of the privileges of whiteness, though enslaved people, too, often found ways to spend time with each other even when they did not live in the same households.[112] The word "visit" appears seventy-nine times in Emma's diary, revealing the importance of the activity to her life even—or perhaps especially—during wartime. These visits provided more than the interesting companionship so valued in country life. They also brought war news that either assuaged or exacerbated the worry uppermost in everyone's mind. Whether from personal experience or, less reliably, from hearsay or accounts from newspapers, war news became the preeminent topic of conversation.

The first visit in Emma's diary was her return to Richmond for the Passover holiday week shortly after she moved to Rosewood, a return that helped ease the transition to her new living arrangements. She stayed with relatives in town, members of her uncle Samuel Myers's extended family. "By all I was most kindly greeted, & I was gratified at the unvarying regret expressed at our family having left Richmond," she recorded with some satisfaction. She wrote, "I was gratified . . . at the kind invitations I received from various friends to pass days or nights with them whenever I could." Emma appeared on their doorsteps frequently over the coming months. Other Jewish holidays brought her to Richmond for synagogue attendance and for long visits at the homes of family or friends, making them emotionally rich events. Yet war news remained uppermost in everyone's minds. She reported about her extended holiday visit in October 1864, "The pleasure of my visit was damped by the unfavorable news from the Valley, which filled me with uneasiness about our boys there." Rosina's sons were then fighting as part of Confederate general Jubal Early's army, and almost all of its artillery was lost. "And as they belong to that, it seemed impossible that they should escape either being wounded or taken prisoners," Emma fretted. Upon returning to Rosewood, however, she found that one son, Willie, "has come home with a slight wound, & he reports having left John safe in Camp, while George, with about twenty-five other men, had escaped capture by fleeing to the mountains." This was excellent news indeed and especially reassuring to Rosina.[113]

Other visits brought Emma the company of other women. On one October day, she traveled into town to shop and returned to find "pleasant Miss Patsey Storrs here on a visit, [and] nice Mrs. Stockdell." The women "spent the evening talking & untangling the long fringe of [Emma's] black crepe shawl, which was matted together with Spanish needles," Emma "having jumped into a bush of this weed on getting out of the cars." Rosina especially valued the women's presence and asked Mrs. Stockdell to move in. As Emma noted, "Rosina has been suffering greatly, she tells me, since I have been in town." Perhaps Emma's frequent trips to Richmond prompted Rosina to find another woman to take up residence at Rosewood. Emma reported Rosina's "wonderful efforts" but added that she seldom spent an entire day out of bed, making companionship especially important. Mrs. Stockdell soon joined the household.[114]

When the Confederacy asked its women to visit military hospitals, it thus adapted Southerners' customary patterns of visiting to answer the needs of the moment. The Confederacy urged women to donate food to military hospitals, which Rosina, no doubt thinking of her own three sons in uniform, readily did. On May 13, Emma and Rosina brought sweet milk, buttermilk, and biscuits to a nearby military hospital. Emma proudly recorded that the matron, Mrs. Lewis Webb, was "delighted" to get them.[115] As summer went on, they added strawberries and sweet cream to their deliveries to the hospitals that were hastily created in and around Richmond. The enormous

Chimborazo hospital was under the supervision of another Jewish woman, Phoebe Yates Levy Pember, but Emma and Rosina visited only the smaller hospitals nearer the farm.

Their visits were about more than food, though the supplies they brought from the farm were most welcome. Women in both the North and the South also helped to tend the wounded. Richmond was full of injured men, who filled beds in fifteen different local hospitals.[116] After a visit on May 18, Emma noted that she remained "at the Hospital till 3:30" and that "many [wounded men] had been removed since yesterday; some to other hospitals, some to their repose." At the hospital, she encountered "ladies untiring, men very grateful; say they cannot fight hard enough for such ladies." The wounded soldiers' gratitude and the sheer need at the hospitals kept Emma returning, as did seeing that she was not alone in the work. Other women also brought food and spent time at the bedsides of the wounded men. "Many delicacies brought, in spite of the great scarcity & enormous prices," she observed.[117]

Women's work at hospitals changed the public understanding of women's nature and abilities and laid the foundation for women's increased political power after the war. In the North, civic leaders established the United States Sanitary Commission, a private agency created by federal legislation in June 1861 to support sick and wounded soldiers. It raised funds primarily to establish, staff, and support hospitals set up across the North, along with the Union's eleven hospital ships. The Sanitary Commission raised $15 million for food, bedding, medicine, and other supplies. Northern women energetically supported the Sanitary Commission by raising funds, and some also assisted in military hospitals. Among them was Clara Barton, the founder of the American Red Cross, who was inspired by the illustrious example of Florence Nightingale in the recent Crimean War.[118]

Confederate women also raised funds for military hospitals. For example, Rosalie E. A. Moses, a Jewish woman in South Carolina, sent the proceeds raised at a concert to the military hospital in

Richmond.[119] Nearly all of the fighting took place in the South, where buildings were quickly adapted to hospital use, and Southern women were loudly urged to assist in caring for the wounded. Representatives of the Confederate Congress meeting in Richmond visited Emma's synagogue, Beth Shalome, for donations and encouraged women to visit hospitals.[120] The congregation's women also met daily in the synagogue's basement to sew, knit, and make clothes for soldiers and convalescents.[121] Because the Richmond area saw so much fighting, the first, hastily constructed hospitals were swiftly replaced by bigger and better hospital buildings.[122] Emma joined hospital staff and other local women in distributing food to patients, visiting with them, and, occasionally, providing hands-on medical care. She visited several different hospitals, including one associated with St. Francis de Sales and run by nuns. The nuns did not appreciate ladies' presence on their wards, and although they were pleased to receive food donations, the nuns limited visits to fifteen minutes, discouraged women from spending too much time at one bed, and discredited their judgment. When Emma closed a window next to the bed of a patient shivering under a thin blanket, a nun reopened it. The women working as paid nurses at the Confederate hospitals were torn between appreciating the help that volunteers like Emma could provide and fearing that such ignorant volunteers, no matter how good their intentions, might prove an actual menace to their patients' well-being.[123]

At other hospitals, "lady visitors" were welcomed more readily by overworked matrons, and Emma took pride in volunteering. She began by doing simple tasks, like helping one soldier bathe with cool water the stump of an amputated limb. She distributed the fresh food she brought and provided simple companionship to the wounded men. She saw such work as her own way to support the military effort and described it in language that revealed her sense of having done something momentous for the Confederacy. One day, for example, she visited Rosina's wounded cousin Lawrence Young at Seabrook Hospital: "I . . . spent the hours from 9:30 A.M. to 3:30, most incessantly and interestingly occupied in attending to as many as were in my reach, making Lawrence Young's cot my . . . headquarters." She wrote, "Well may ladies devote themselves to attending . . . to their poor comfort. . . . I am thankful to be strong enough to help to nurse you." Clearly, Emma felt both noble and brave, recording, "I nearly fainted while assisting a surgeon to dress a wound today, but I got over it by sitting near an open window when no longer needed."[124] She also helped to arrange for one soldier to have an enslaved boy tend him each day.

Emma's devotion to hospital work was sincere but short-lived. Within weeks of her first visits, she noted the deaths of some soldiers she had cared for and admired. This experience weighed on her, and by the end of June 1864, she was only dropping off food donations at hospitals and no longer spending time inside. Finally, by August, she stopped going altogether, in part because the cost of food had risen and Rosina was less able to spare farm produce. Her faith shaken by the sights and sounds in the hospitals, Emma never mentioned them in her diary again.

EMMA'S RELIGIOUS WORLD

Unlike hospital work, religion was a consistent theme throughout Emma's diary. The diary became the prime location for articulating her religious convictions, recording her prayers, and noting her acts of piety and worship. It seems to have been the single site at Rosewood where her Judaism was visible, if only to herself. She usually wrote her diary entries in her room, rather than in Rosina's parlor, which otherwise held the typical Victorian primacy of place as the gathering site for reading, writing, conversing, visiting, and developing the religious and intellectual life of individuals and families.[125] But it was Rosina's parlor, as it was Rosina's house, and Emma never claimed to make it her own. For this reason, she generally restricted all her other Jewish activities to her room as well. Her Richmond house may well have had a mezuzah affixed to the outside doorpost, but it is highly unlikely she ever considered putting one on the door to her room at Rosewood. The doorpost, too, belonged to Rosina. Emma's room became the place for reading her Bible and prayer book on Sabbath mornings, along with writing her religious and other thoughts into her diary. She veiled her Judaism from outside view. When she joined the others in the household, she did so as a white, Southern woman and a relative, focusing on the common bonds they shared rather than the Jewishness that made her distinct.

It was not surprising that Emma kept her expressions of Jewishness mostly to herself when she was at Rosewood. On more than one occasion, she modulated her behavior to preserve her welcome. When Rosina doubted rumors that Lee's army had won a victory at a battle they could hear from the farm in May 1864, Emma rebuked her for "hug[ging] Worry with the closest affection." Rosina responded with affronted silence. The two women did not speak until the next morning. Emma apologized at breakfast but felt she needed to do more to soften Rosina's attitude toward her. The following day, she accompanied Rosina to church and complimented the minister's sermon. It was the only church attendance noted in her diary, and she clearly went with Rosina to smooth over the incident. "If I do not keep the friends I have I shall indeed be bereaved," she wrote.[126] Emma saw little conflict between remaining quietly loyal to her own Jewish beliefs and practices and also accommodating Christian beliefs while living at Rosewood, just as she needed to accommodate Rosina and the other members of the household more generally.

The diary became Emma's private place for recording her Jewish thoughts and actions. More than thirty times she documented her thoughts of God. She thanked God for rescues from danger and for recoveries from illness and wrote as an incantation against evil, "may God confound their counsels and destroy their machinations."[127] She prayed for strength to endure the hardships of the future, accepted deaths as God's will, and invoked God's protection. She noted each time she spent Saturday mornings in her room at Rosina's reading the Jewish Sabbath prayer service and the weekly portion of the Bible. Most Saturdays she withdrew from everyday activities and gentile companions who might lead her to forget the sanctity of the day. Similarly, she recorded each time she prepared to travel to Richmond in order to attend synagogue for a Jewish holiday and stay with her Jewish relatives in town. She never wrote in her diary during these travels and may have left it behind in her room at Rosewood; she did not need it when she was in a Jewish space.

Though Emma found ways to honor her Jewish commitments, particularly on the Sabbath and holidays, she does not seem to have spoken much about them to others in the household, all of whom were Christian. Instead, the diary seems to have functioned as the home for her Jewish identity, thoughts, prayers, and practices. Just as a home is a place where its inhabitants can perform religious observances, place ritual objects, and express their spiritual convictions, Emma filled her diary with evidence of her religious life. Her words turned the blank book into a religious object and a home for her Jewish spiritual expression. "I still feel undismayed, & pray God to enable us to endure whatever awaits us in the way of evil, with fortitude, and to receive with humble gratitude what may await us in the way of success," she wrote soon after moving to Rosewood.[128] Placing the diary in her room at Rosina's, Emma created a marker of her Jewish space within Rosina's residence and lent her room the penumbra of heritage and comfort traditionally at the heart of Jewish homes.[129]

The blank book that Emma used to create her diary had no religious significance; it was an ordinary, secular object. But it became a religious entity as she inscribed her thoughts about the divine, about Jewishness, and about Jewish holidays, Jewish behaviors, and Jewish ideas into it. Because Judaism is practiced in homes as well as in synagogues, Jews have long imbued ordinary, domestic items with Jewish meaning and in that way made of them religious articles. For example, dishes are ordinary objects, useful in any home, but when they are designated for use only for either dairy or meat by families who gather for kosher meals, they become inflected as Jewish objects. Emma's writing transformed the blank book into a place for her to express her feelings and thoughts, and the Jewish content of her entries made of the diary a kind of Jewish home.[130]

Scholars of religious ritual have long understood that objects are made religious by the ways in which they are used. In the early years of the twentieth century, the sociologist Émile Durkheim explained that the fundamental work of religion is to identify the sacred and separate it from the profane. The ethnographer Arnold van Gennep then pointed out that these categories are only meaningful in relation to each other. An item, concept, image, or feeling becomes sacred only in relation to something else that is profane, and the two realms coexist together. Building on this work, the anthropologist Jonathan Z. Smith later argued that a place or item or feeling becomes sacred by focusing people's attention in a distinctive way. Further, the ritual that results when people use an item with that kind of focused attention may restore order to a world that feels out of control. By setting certain texts apart and repeatedly using them in a more focused way than others, people make them into religious objects and instruments of ritual that allow for a different experience of the world to counter ordinary experience.[131]

Each of those ideas helps explain how Emma made her diary into a Jewish object. Her references to God, prayer, and synagogue expressed her attempts to focus her mind on a source of order and protection: Judaism. The realm of the sacred stood apart from the frightening worldly realm she inhabited, and her religious activities, including her Jewish writings in her diary, moved her into an orderly, protected domain, if only in thought. Moreover, by placing that diary, along with her Bible and prayer book, in the room designated for her private use at Rosina's, she marked the room as a Jewish space, if only in her own mind.

Thus, Emma's diary became a location that she could see as Jewishly sacred because it underscored her location at the boundaries of the Christian household where she was living. It held her views on the ways in which the larger meaning of her chaotic world should be understood. Her entries gave her religious beliefs the power to order her world by framing and explaining it in religious terms, and they signaled a new religious ritual whereby the act of writing itself created the ordered world that appears within her diary. The chaos and fear in her experience of the Civil War—abandoning her home, hearing the noise of nearby battles, coping with food shortages, warding off thieving soldiers, dealing with the collapse of Confederate currency, and, especially, coming to grips with the end of slavery—prompted this turn to religion within her diary. With each day of the fateful year that she spent at Rosina's, the diary framed the chaos around her. It ultimately became a resource for imagining the stable, divinely sanctioned world she craved. She made the blank book into the religious item she needed it to be, one that provided consolation and familiarity.

Like all religious writing, Emma's diary mediated between her own experience and the world around her. Her writings on holidays and Sabbaths enabled her to participate in the Jewish communal activities appropriate for religious occasions, in spirit if not in person. Her diary writing practice enabled her to feel that she participated in the creation of what Durkheim called a collective (Jewish) consciousness.[132] As one example, on June 10, Emma wrote, "I had intended visiting the Hospitals today, but on consulting my Heb. [Hebrew] Calendar, I found it was the 1st day of Pentecost, so I remained at home to observe the day as well as I could by reading the services, and reminding myself of my peculiar duties as an Inheritor of law given to us by Him who said 'I, the Lord, change not.' Blind & foolish are those children of Israel, who persuade themselves that the laws given to them by the Unchanging One, for them & their descendants to observe forever, are not binding on them."[133] Such religious language gave Emma a more personal way to frame her sense of place by locating herself in the Jewish community over which God watched. Her diary entry also inscribed God's rules and promises to Jews into her most private space.

In Emma's room were not only her diary but also a Bible and a prayer book. She never identified which versions she read, but there were two possibilities. There is no record of Emma learning any languages other than English and French, so it is safe to assume that she read English translations. The most widely distributed English-language Bible in the United States was the King James Bible. However, a better option was available to her. By the time she moved to Rosewood, Emma would have had access to Isaac Leeser's 1853–1854 English translation of the Bible directly from the Hebrew. Leeser arranged the books of the Bible in the classical Jewish way, with three sections: the Torah (Pentateuch), Prophets, and Writings. His 1848 English translations of prayer books used by Jews accustomed to both the Spanish-Portuguese (Sephardic) or German (Ashkenazic) prayer traditions also would have been accessible to Emma, who was probably most familiar with the Sephardic rites in use at her synagogue.[134]

Isaac Leeser, who by the time of the Civil War was one of the most prominent Jewish religious voices in the United States, had strong ties to Richmond.[135] Immigrating from western Europe in 1824 at age eighteen, he first sought out his uncle, the Richmond merchant Zalma Rehine. Leeser spent five years in the United States working for Rehine, during which time he also studied English and assisted at the Mordecai family synagogue, Beth Shalome. In 1828, his rebuke of an antisemitic newspaper article appeared in the *London Quarterly* and was reprinted in the local Richmond press. His eloquent and informed defense of Jews and Judaism caught the attention of Philadelphia's historic Jewish congregation Mikveh Israel, which offered him the position of hazan, the congregation's religious authority, teacher, and worship leader. Leeser had developed a close friendship with Emma's father, Jacob, who enthusiastically recommended him for the job.[136]

Leeser moved to Philadelphia in 1829. From his base at Mikveh Israel, he launched an illustrious career of translating, writing, teaching, and publishing, while also leading the congregation and personally advising local and national Jews on all matters pertaining to Jewish life. He founded the first Jewish publishing house and edited and published *The Occident*, a monthly, nationally circulated Jewish periodical that ran for twenty-five years. Leeser remained fond of Richmond, corresponded with friends and family there, and visited frequently. He also retained the racial views he had absorbed from his time living and working with Southern Jewish slaveholders who both defended slavery as the natural order and believed that it was beneficial for the enslaved. Although Leeser claimed a studied policy of neutrality toward the sectional crisis in *The Occident*, the historian David Weinfeld has shown that Leeser viewed abolitionism in an unfavorable light and probably shared many Southern Jews' paternalistic feelings toward supposedly inferior Black people.[137] Emma is very likely to have read his translations of both the Hebrew Bible and the daily prayers while spending time in her room, and they might have been all the more meaningful to her because her family knew Leeser personally and shared many values with him.

In the antebellum South, religion was much more than faith. The largely agricultural society relied on religion for entertainment and social life as much as for pious comfort. "Religion provided a good deal of interest," the historian Anne Firor Scott has explained. "Revivals, lengthy meetings, and 'love feasts'—one day revivals—bulked large in otherwise uneventful times. The state of one's soul, and the souls of recently deceased neighbors, was the subject of reporting to friends."[138] Those activities embedded descriptions of biblical events, admonitions, characters, and phrases into Southern culture. In the crisis of war, Southerners found new occasions to use the Bible and more ways to apply biblical imagery to the daily events in their own lives. Southern Jewish and Christian women alike enthusiastically used this language before and during the war. They used the Bible to help deal with the traumas of war and relied on religious language for explanation and consolation. As noncombatants during the Civil War, women found that prayer served a vital role in obtaining divine safeguarding for those who were left at home without male protectors, and they also prayed for protection for the military forces who were defending them on the battlefield.[139]

Studies of Anglo-American Jewish women's writing in the nineteenth century have revealed a common pattern whereby Jewish women wrote themselves into their contemporary culture by substituting the ideas, images, biblical quotes, descriptions of rituals, and life-cycle events drawn from Christianity with those rooted in Judaism. Images, tropes, characters, quotes, and stories from the Hebrew Bible replaced comparable elements from the New Testament in Christian women's texts. As one example, heroic maternal images such as the "Mother in Israel" or the biblical figures of Sarah, Rebecca, Rachel, Jochebed, and Deborah appeared instead of Mary. Jewish women writers thereby created cohesive identities as American or British women who also exemplified the broader ideal qualities of womanhood. These literary techniques appeared in published works by such Jewish writers as Britain's Grace Aguilar and the Southerners Penina Moise and Octavia Harby Moses, all of whom were very likely to have been familiar to Emma, and they demonstrated to readers that Jewish women fit contemporary ideals for women.[140] Emma utilized these techniques in her diary. Her statements of faith and prayers to God for protection from the invading enemy mirrored those found in writings by Christian Southern women, but she wrote those lines as a Jew with Judaism's understanding of God.

This commitment may have been particularly important for Emma to reassert throughout her life as so many of her siblings turned to Christianity. She continuously affirmed her ties to Judaism. She wrote to her sister Ellen in 1839, "[Everything I have] read on either side of the question [of religion] convinces me . . . of my duty to adhere to the religion of my forefathers. My mind is made up." When she attended synagogue on Yom Kippur after writing those words, she felt firmly and enthusiastically committed to living as a Jew.[141] A short time later, Emma established a Sunday school for the children of Beth Shalome under the auspices of the synagogue's Ladies Auxiliary and served as its superintendent. She successfully attracted financial support for the religious school not only from the Jewish community but also from the wider Richmond community through a series of annual Hebrew School Fund Balls.¹⁴² Her model was the Hebrew Sunday School founded in Philadelphia in 1838 by a group of women led by Rebecca Gratz. The first of its kind in Jewish history, the Hebrew Sunday School afforded women the opportunity to teach Judaism in a public institution and to shape its curriculum. In addition to providing religious education to a broad swath of the city's Jewish children, including girls, the school dramatically furthered the women's own knowledge of Judaism. As a result of the women's duties in the school, religious leaders like Isaac Leeser and Sabato Morais, Leeser's successor at Philadelphia's Mikveh Israel, paid special attention to their religious education and carved out time to conduct a special class for the Hebrew Sunday School teachers.¹⁴³ Emma was part of this nationally influential phenomenon. In 1845, she produced a volume titled *The Parents and Teachers' Assistant; or, Thirteen Lessons Conveying to Uninformed Minds the First Ideas of God and His Attributes*. She never put her name to the volume; but her family made her authorship known, and the book was widely adopted in Jewish Sunday schools.¹⁴⁴

Emma typically referred to "God" rather than using a Hebrew term from Judaism for the divine, such as "Adonai" (my Master) or the phrase often used in English translations of Jewish prayer books, "King of the Universe." In the nineteenth century, few American Jews understood the Hebrew language, and Isaac Leeser, among other Jewish religious leaders, began delivering synagogue sermons in English.¹⁴⁵ As a result, the differences between Judaism's and Christianity's spiritual expression diminished even as Jewish women recast some religious language, especially in their published work. There is little observable difference in the correspondence between Emma and her Christian relatives and acquaintances. Her Christian niece Ellen wrote in a letter describing her desolation at the Confederacy's fall, "I do not murmur at God's will," despite also feeling "utterly cast down at our failure."¹⁴⁶ Emma expressed similar feelings in similar words. The kinswomen consoled each other in religious language they could share, underscoring their bond both as relatives and as defeated Southern women. The Mordecai clan, much like other Southern Jewish families, muted Judaism's distinctiveness by sharing the faith language used by most Christian Southerners regardless of denomination. This religious discourse included Jews in the broadly shared religious inflections of Southern culture.

The sense that Jews and Christians shared a similar faith found physical reinforcement when Jews attended church. The historian Shari Rabin has explained that throughout the first half of the nineteenth century, American Jews occasionally found themselves sitting in the pews of a nearby church, drawn there by curiosity, a desire for fellowship with their gentile neighbors, or the aesthetic pleasures of singing hymns (some drawn directly from the book of Psalms in the Hebrew Bible) and viewing the architecture of what was often the loveliest building erected in a small town. Emma's father, Jacob, had sometimes attended church in the small town of Warrenton, though he stopped doing so when rumors of his incipient conversion began to swirl.[147] Her sister and brother-in-law Rachel and Aaron Lazarus regularly attended church in Wilmington, North Carolina, in order to shore up their social standing in a community that had no synagogue.[148] While Christians often delighted to see them and expected the visits to result in conversion to Christianity, the opposite often happened. Jews who went to church more often came away convinced that faith in a man—Jesus—was misguided. Emma shared this conviction, though her sister Rachel was greatly affected by her churchgoing and Christian friends and later converted on her deathbed.[149]

Emma believed that Jews awaited a future that would lift them out of their dispersed, powerless status and restore God's "light" to their community. Like many Jews of her era, she blamed dispersion on Jews' own failings. Only loyalty to their faith and obedience to God's laws would earn their restoration. Some individuals achieved the faith and character that could inspire others on to greater religious dedication. Emma's diary acknowledged one such individual, Isaac Levy, whose family belonged to her Richmond synagogue. When Isaac was killed in a battle near Petersburg in August 1864, Emma eulogized him as "an example to all young men of any faith, ... a true Israelite without guile—a soldier of the Lord & a soldier of the South." Ideal religious behavior for Christian and Jewish Southern soldiers should be no different, in Emma's view. Because Jews aimed for and achieved similar ideals, there should be no prejudice voiced against them. Yet her use of the phrase "an Israelite without guile" pointed to a widespread need to counter commonly heard slander against the Jews. As Emma continued praising the Levy family using the stock phrases that people often turn to when dealing with death, she described them as "full of Faith and Hope and Submission," three virtues highly prized in the nineteenth-century United States, especially among Southerners coping with wartime deaths. But Emma's next comments showed that Jews had a particular reason to aim for those goals. By achieving them, Jews could even earn their restoration to Zion. "If all our people were like that family, we would already arise & shine for our light would have come," she concluded.[150]

While nineteenth-century American Christians and Jews alike pointed to biblical references to explain the current historical moment of Jewish exile, they emphasized different reasons for the diaspora. In the broadest strokes, Christians typically pointed to Jews' refusal to accept Jesus as their savior, while Jews highlighted their insufficient devotion to God and Judaism's laws. But the finer points of that discussion easily could be elided to underscore Jews' and Christians' shared common Southern culture. Southern Jews like Emma constructed comfortable places for themselves while never quite forgetting the troubles that antisemitism could bring.[151]

THE SHADOW OF ANTISEMITISM

Early American Jews found a remarkable degree of freedom and acceptance in the antebellum United States, a welcome change from their European experiences.[152] In North and South alike, no laws restricted their movements, determined where they could live, or limited their economic activity. Those freedoms were unknown to the era's Jews living in the broad central and eastern areas of Europe, where most nineteenth-century American Jews had been born. As the South had fewer tradespeople and merchants than the North did, there was less competition for Jews familiar with those types of labor. Comparatively, the US South was indeed a "happy land," as one Jewish Southerner named it.[153] Nonetheless, anti-Jewish prejudice permeated nineteenth-century American culture.[154] Many Southern states limited government offices to Protestants, and some restricted Jewish land ownership well into the 1800s.[155]

Negative ideas about Jews emerged from two different sources. Christians learned about Jews from the Bible and generally understood the New Testament as showing Jews' responsibility for the crucifixion of Jesus, despite its order by a Roman court and enactment by Roman soldiers. Religious antisemitism, even when couched in an apparently gentler form of Christian supersession that assumed Judaism was an inferior predecessor, was potentially a real threat in a Confederacy that defined itself as a Christian nation.[156] In the North, abolitionists often measured the individual nineteenth-century Jews they encountered or read about against biblical figures in both Old and New Testaments and found them wanting, another form of religious antisemitism that preferred to think of Jews of the past rather than Jews of the present.[157] Just as potent as explicitly religious prejudice, antisemitic ideas drawn from medieval Europe also linked Jews to nefarious business practices. Medieval Jews were banned from most craft guilds, farming, and other profitable economic enterprises because they did not share the majority religion. Forced to live and work apart, to dress in distinctive ways, and to be subjected to different laws than Christians, Jews became objects of both conjecture and contempt. They were also resented for the few economic niches they were allowed to occupy, such as moneylending. In the United States, Shakespeare's *The Merchant of Venice* was frequently read and performed, and the term "shylock" entered common parlance to connote a dishonest, grasping Jew.[158]

An additional form of prejudice against Jews also emerged in the nineteenth century, and the tensions, fears, and rumors that swept the country during the Civil War fanned its flames in both North and South. Referred to as "ontological antisemitism" by Walter Sokol, this concept asserted that the Jew's very being was inassimilable to Western society.[159] Many Northern newspapers identified any Jewish purported wrongdoer by both name and religion and distrusted Jews who became famous, even if they had converted to Christianity. For example, when representatives of a European banking firm led by a Baron Erlanger negotiated a loan to the Confederacy, the popular magazine *Harper's Weekly* attacked Erlanger as a Jew, despite the fact that he had long ago converted to Christianity. The press wove a web of fantasy linking the Rothschild banking family to Erlanger and concluded that all Jews must be pro-slavery.[160] Antisemitic writers in the Northern press often argued that Jews aided the rebels, usually through financial trickery.

Antisemitism also drew on widespread anti-immigrant feeling. In the twelve years between 1848 and 1860, the United States' Jewish population tripled, growing from 50,000 to 150,000, mostly composed of newcomers from Germanic central Europe.[161] Although this migration dramatically expanded the country's Jewish population, it was dwarfed by the millions of other people who arrived from Germany between 1820 and 1870.[162] This large influx, joined by similar numbers of immigrants from Ireland, fueled xenophobic sentiment, especially in the North. When Irish immigrants were among those in New York City who rioted against the draft, they fanned the anti-Catholic and anti-immigrant sentiments bubbling across the Union.

Though new Jewish arrivals in the South barely made any difference to the population there, the Confederate version of antisemitism blamed them for wartime food shortages and other economic stresses. The Confederate congressman Henry Foote contended that "if the present state of things were to continue the end of the war would probably find nearly all the property of the Confederacy in the hands of Jewish Shylocks."[163] Judah P. Benjamin, an attorney and United States senator from Louisiana who served the Confederacy as both secretary of state and secretary of war, became a focal point for this expression of antisemitism. Many Southerners assumed Benjamin to be dishonest and self-serving because he was Jewish, regardless of the fact that he had married a Catholic woman and become an enthusiastic slave owner.[164] One contributor to the *Richmond Enquirer* argued that God could not answer Confederate prayers because a Jew held high office in the new government's cabinet. Just as in the North, the Southern press accused Jews of disloyalty and shirking military service.[165]

Some gentiles assumed that Jews avoided military service because very few ever encountered a Jewish soldier in the field. Jews loomed large in the imaginations of Bible-reading Protestants who constituted the majority of Americans on both sides, yet few had ever met a Jewish person. The "mythical Jew" was hard to find in real life.[166] In fact, the national Jewish population was so small that although a high percentage of Jewish men did serve, few soldiers noticed them. The total US population in 1860 before the war was roughly thirty-one and a half million people. By contrast, the combined Jewish population, North and South, totaled approximately 150,000. Between eight and ten thousand Jews wore the Union blue, and more than five hundred Jewish soldiers died in the war.[167] Because most Jews had settled in the North, Southern Jews constituted only 0.2 percent of the Confederate population. The total number of Jews living in the Confederacy was only between twenty and twenty-five thousand people. Something like two to three thousand served in the Confederate army, including nearly one hundred Richmond Jews, a high percentage of eligible Jewish men but a tiny fraction of the more than one million Southerners who wore the gray.[168]

Accusations that Jews shirked military service appeared in the Confederate press as they did in the Union press, but a much louder charge against the Confederacy's Jews was that they were manipulating the South's economy. Merchants in general were accused of extortion, with Jews as the chief evildoers.[169] These allegations left Southern Jews on the defensive. When Jefferson Davis declared March 27, 1863, to be a Day of Fasting and Prayer for the Confederacy,

M. J. Michelbacher, religious leader of Richmond's Ashkenazic synagogue, Bayth Ahabah, delivered a sermon pointedly denouncing those who profited by and exacerbated the general scarcity, even though he must have known that his congregants were no more responsible for the wartime scarcities than any others were. Although Emma belonged to Richmond's other congregation, she probably read Michelbacher's sermon, which was published in the daily papers and then in pamphlet form.

Michelbacher's published sermon illustrated the ways in which the Jews of Richmond and the South more generally constantly had to guard against antisemitism. "I have come to the unbiased conclusion that you have fulfilled your duties as good citizens and as men who love their country," he wrote. Those who charge that "the Israelite does not fight for his country" are both "ignorant" and "evil-disposed toward our people." He highlighted examples of Jews' bravery in combat from the current number of them serving in Confederate military forces. He noted that they were praised by Generals Lee, Johnston, and Jackson and traced Jews' fighting spirit and bravery as far back as David slaying Goliath. Moreover, he pointed out, charitable Confederate Israelites "brought comfort to households . . . [where previously was] misery." After dispatching the charges of cowardice and selfishness, Michelbacher turned to the problem of speculating in consumer goods and extorting the citizenry with high prices. He pointed out the accusation itself was very unlikely. If Jewish merchants charged too much, customers would simply buy from shops owned by Christians. Moreover, hoarding goods in order to drive up prices would risk both time and money, something Jewish merchants would not do. Thus, Michelbacher argued, "the cry against the Jew is a false one." He concluded with a lengthy prayer for the congregation's protection and, by extension, that of the Confederacy itself, urging God to shield them from the plan of "our enemy" to incite "our man-servants and maid-servants to insurrection."[170] Overall, Michelbacher's sermon defended Confederate Jews against the charges of profiteering, underlined their patriotism and sacrifice, and offered prayers for the preservation of a social order built on slavery. It revealed the worldview of Confederate Jews when the social stresses of war made them vulnerable to attack from both the Union forces and antisemitic fellow Southerners.

Tempers easily flared during wartime, and antisemitic sentiment intensified everywhere. *Southern Punch*, a Richmond weekly with which Emma was probably familiar, published antisemitic content throughout the war, castigating "the dirty greasy Jew pedlar" and the "Jew Yankee" as the worst kind of capitalists exploiting the wartime economy.[171] There were a number of very public antisemitic incidents throughout the South. When poor quality uniforms made their way into the Union military, Jewish suppliers were blamed for providing "shoddy" goods. This accusation led to General Ulysses S. Grant's notorious 1862 order expelling Jews from the military district over which he presided, which included parts of Tennessee, Kentucky, and Mississippi. Fortunately, President Lincoln immediately countermanded the order, which never really went into effect.[172] In one Georgia town, some soldiers' wives stormed a Jewish-owned shop and took what they wished at gunpoint, accusing the owner of amassing fortunes while their husbands fought for their nation. In Talbotton, Georgia, where in 1862 the Straus family was the only Jewish family in town, a grand jury condemned all Jewish merchants. The Strauses responded by packing up to move elsewhere. The townspeople were shocked: they were fond of the family. Antisemitic expression had become so much a part of standard language that the local gentiles hardly thought of how it might affect the actual Jews living in their midst.[173]

Thus, antisemitism was alive and well in the mid-nineteenth-century United States, including in the South. Long before the Civil War, well-informed American Jews like Emma were all too aware of notorious examples of antisemitism elsewhere in the world, such as the Damascus Affair and the Mortara Case, both of which the Jewish community of Richmond publicly protested.[174] In the former, a mob attacked a Damascus synagogue in 1840 following accusations that Syrian Jews had murdered a Capuchin monk and his servant to obtain blood for Passover matzahs. In the latter, in 1858, Jews worldwide protested the Italian police's decision to turn a young Jewish boy over to the Catholic Church on the testimony of a servant that she had baptized him as an infant. Both highlighted for American Jews the importance of guarding against antisemitism and mounting communal action to oppose it.[175]

The undeniable existence of antisemitism, however, does not seem to have been a major concern in Emma's considered decision to dedicate herself to the faith of her fathers, nor did it seem to be the primary factor in her siblings' decisions to convert to Christianity. The fundamental fault line in the antebellum and Civil War South, the one that mattered most in both daily life and social and economic structures, was not religion but race. The scholars Leonard Rogoff and Jennifer Stollman, for example, suggest that the racialized system of antebellum slavery allowed Jews to feel white through their relationships with enslaved people, protecting them from antisemitic racial questioning.[176] As long as Jews were seen as white, they were on the right side of a society fundamentally built on slavery and racism whether or not they owned slaves themselves, as most of the Mordecai family did.

RACISM AND THE SOCIAL ORDER OF THE SOUTH

Like most white Southerners, Emma believed not only that the system of slavery suited the inferior abilities of Black people but also that it was actually beneficent because owners took care of their slaves when they were babies, ill, infirm, old, or otherwise unable to work.[177] When she heard about slaves following or joining the Union army on its way through the South, she was certain they must have been kidnapped. Surely they would never have chosen to leave. She had held these beliefs all her life, and they pervaded her diary. She deplored the excesses of cruel slave owners but never questioned the overall system and resented abolitionist and Union attempts to remake the social and economic world of the South.

It is an open question what "cruelty" meant to Emma in the context of slavery. She spent most of her adult life in an urban environment where she lived intimately with the enslaved people who labored forcibly in her household. That was also the situation at Rosewood, where Rosina saw her long-term relationships with the slaves she owned, most of whom were closely related to each other, as familial. Emma shared this attitude toward Rosina's slaves, with whom she was long familiar. That kind of intimate domestic slavery did sometimes have the effect of reducing the outright violence that undergirded the entire system, a violence that Emma and Rosina in any case both condemned as not only immoral but also counterproductive. They prided themselves on taking good care of their slaves, providing ample clothing, food and housing, and personal care. When Emma heard that her slave Sally, hired out in Richmond, was ill, she went to visit her and brought extra food, blankets, and medicine.[178]

That dynamic allowed Emma and Rosina to congratulate themselves, sometimes explicitly, as benevolent slave owners who acted in the best interests of those who were too feeble and childlike to take responsibility for their own lives. It may be that some of their slaves acknowledged this treatment; one formerly enslaved woman wrote to Emma a few years after the war in an apparent expression of goodwill.[179] But that in no way altered the fundamental horrors of slavery, including especially the constant threat of sale. At any moment, even the most "benevolent" owners could sell any of their slaves for any reason.[180] Emma's sister Ellen did in fact sell her long-time personal maid Abby, with whom she felt so close that she had illegally taught her to read and write. When Ellen began to fear that Abby was exerting a bad influence on her own children, all of whom had automatically by law become Ellen's slaves upon birth, she resolved the situation by selling Abby for $550.[181] Emma herself had also sold slaves in the years before the war. When she could not convince an enslaved man named John to stop running away from the

Richmond house, she asked her brother George to buy him and bring him to George's large Raleigh plantation, where he might be more controllable as a field hand than he was in an urban environment. Left unspoken was the greater likelihood of violence inherent in that sort of control. Emma sold another unruly slave, Aggie, as well, reporting to her brother Samuel that "it was quite a relief to be rid of such a disagreeable piece of property." At no point did she question her right to control the lives of the enslaved. Ellen and Emma's unhesitating resort to disciplining and selling their slaves demonstrates the historian Stephanie E. Jones-Roger's point that women were just as involved in the literal business of slavery as men were.[182] The domestic, indoor spaces of slavery were as fraught and tense as were the agricultural, outdoor spaces, generating a "war within" Southern households that, as Rosina's slaves were about to demonstrate, belied any paternalistic notions of harmonious relations.[183]

For all of Emma's self-congratulatory benevolence, she repeatedly exerted her power over enslaved people and remained a slave owner during her time at Rosewood. That status enabled her to contribute to the household in a manner that demonstrated both her white authority and her ability to perform in the manner expected of a member of the master class. On November 2, 1864, "a cloudy & cold day, with rain, hail, & snow," she brought her slave Moses Norrill, who was hired out as a bricklayer in Richmond, to Rosewood to repair Rosina's fireplaces. Emma wrote, "I sat in my room working all day as there was no fire downstairs, & Rose . . . [kept] to her bed all day." Norrill restored warmth to the house. He returned to Richmond to continue working for wages paid to Emma, and she was pleased that she had brought something of value to the household.[184] He, of course, had no choice in the matter.

A number of episodes in the diary clearly reveal Emma's racism. At Rosewood, the enslaved people generally slept in the house rather than in separate quarters, which was not so unusual on small farms, but they generally slept on floors in the kitchen and storage areas rather than in beds. On one cold winter night, this situation led to an accident. "Fleming, the little cow boy, slept on the kitchen hearth last night and his bed clothes caught without blazing & burned one of his feet quite severely," Emma recorded in her diary. "He discovered 'twas his foot in de fire' in time to save the rest of his person." But Emma had little sympathy for the boy. The injury could keep him from work, and so she believed it likely to have been a ploy, even though she could plainly see his burned foot. "This negro trick gives trouble & inconvenience to more than himself," Emma concluded. She determined to solve the problem by quickly getting him well enough to work. "I have undertaken his treatment, & apply a plaister [sic] of castile soap, and steep the linen bandages with a dilution of creosote 5/6ths water, which proves very soothing and efficacious." Emma provided medical care to the best of her ability, but the incident had little effect on her conviction that most slaves played a "negro trick" to get out of work.[185]

As another example, Emma seemed to find calm reassurance on a "sweet little ramble in the woods ... after breakfast" on a May Sabbath morning. While gathering "honeysuckle, laurel, lupin, and other flowers," she judged the scene before her, which included not only flowers but also young, enslaved boys who were tending their owners' cows, as "tranquil." She saw the boys as "happy, careless little beings" who were "as free as Robin Hood's men 'under the green wood tree.'" To her, this supposedly idyllic scene confirmed the Confederate claim that Southern society followed natural law because it placed each type of person in a hierarchy of rights and ownership on the basis of race, gender, and class. Like many Southerners, she agreed that because their society preserved categories apparently based in nature—and nature was created by God—they must be earning God's approval. The North, she believed, was utterly cruel because white children starved on the streets and African Americans could not successfully compete against whites for jobs in a supposedly free labor market. Defending Southerners like herself, as well as the South's socioeconomic order, she insisted, "Our ruthless invaders do as much injury to the poor negroes as to their owners."[186] This sort of comparison of North and South masked the structural violence of Southern society in the name of Confederate nationalism.

And sometimes the inevitability of violence within slavery appeared even in what Emma saw as the tranquil environment of Rosewood. On June 11, 1864, she at first noted that "nothing of remarkable interest occurred today" but then admitted, "a very disagreeable affair with the servants has disturbed us much." She typically used the word "servant" rather than "slave," particularly when writing about African Americans she knew personally. By her account, Rosina's "little henwife, Georgianna, . . . had to call upon Sarah, her mother, to assist her with the young chickens—upon which, like all negroes who have not sufficient employment invariably do, [Sarah] complained of being overworked, and gave her mistress so much impudence as could not be allowed to go unpunished." In response, George, Rosina's son, took control of the matter and promised Sarah "a proper chastisement if there was any more such conduct." The families, white and Black and living under the same roof, soon took sides. "The disaffection extended to Cyrus, [Sarah's] husband, with whom George had recourse to blows," Emma lamented.[187]

Cyrus defended his wife but found only violence in response. A situation that began with a laboring child asking for help resulted in her mother's chastisement and her father's beating. George Mordecai, the white male authority figure, ruled. Even at this small farm where slaves and owners knew each other well—Georgiana may even have been named after George, though by whom is unclear—white authority overruled Black familial bonds. Emma thought the entire conflict distasteful because it challenged her view that Southern slavery suited slaves as well as masters. It also disrupted slaveholders' widespread claim to family feeling for their slaves, a myth that surely was not shared by enslaved people themselves.[188] Her description of the event revealed her contempt for Black slaves, her inability to see the world through their eyes, her sense that a quick resort to violence was regrettable but appropriate when dealing with them, and her fundamental lack of trust of enslaved people.

EMANCIPATION COMES TO ROSEWOOD

Throughout Emma's year at Rosewood, she was terrified by the prospect of losing the respect and protection that her place in the Southern social order afforded her. But eventually she had no choice but to confront the challenges of the end of the war and its aftermath. Defeating the Confederacy required capturing its capital, and federal armies returned to Richmond in late March 1865.[189] A friend from Richmond walked out to Rosina's farm to warn the women that the armies of both North and South were heading their way. On April 2, Emma learned that the Confederate government, along with all the Confederate troops in Richmond, was to be evacuated that evening, and she responded with "dismay, . . . grief, . . . and appalling terror and dread of every conceivable outrage and injury & insult."[190] Noise from explosions of powder magazines and gunboats shook the house's very foundations, and Emma and Rosina tried to determine the best plan for themselves and, especially, for young Augusta. Many Southern women feared assault or rape at the hands of Yankee soldiers, and these concerns were uppermost in the minds of all three women.[191] Believing the farm to be in the armies' path, they decided to escort Augusta to the city to stay with friends, to take along some household valuables to Richmond to be secured in bank vaults, and to retrieve flour and other items that were previously stored there but were now needed at Rosewood.

Emma set out for the city with Augusta, but the closer they came to Richmond, the more frightening the scene became. Government warehouses in Richmond stored tobacco slated for sale, and others stored gunpowder and arms for military use. In order to keep three tobacco warehouses from the advancing Union soldiers, Confederate general Richard Ewell ordered them burned to the ground, telling the fire department to be on standby in case the fire spread. The fire was set in the early morning of April 3 as Ewell and his forces left the city. The wind shifted and much of the city caught fire, creating a conflagration far beyond the firemen's ability to control.[192] Gunfire and flames lay ahead of Emma and Augusta, who were warned against going on by the fleeing Richmonders they encountered on the road. Augusta panicked and begged to go home to her mother. Emma decided to trust a family she met en route who advised her of the peril, and she placed her valuables into their care. Remarkably, the family proved trustworthy, and Emma retrieved all the items a short time later.

The burning of Richmond signaled the Civil War's end almost as much as did General Lee's surrender to General Grant at the Appomattox Court House on April 9. Because Union soldiers, who by then occupied the city, put out the general conflagration, minimized looting, and maintained some semblance of social order, Richmonders began to think they might survive defeat by the hated and feared Yankees, whom they had demonized during the fighting.[193] Even Emma entertained at least some positive thoughts about Yankees under those circumstances.

A year after Emma began the diary, as the bulk of the Union army made its retreat from Virginia, she recorded a description of the campground where Grant's "immense army" previously had been. "Not a tree or fence or blade of grass—the ground as hard as a brick yard," she wrote. Moreover, the "fortifications" were "immensely strong & extensive, . . . and the numberless huts lately occupied by the Yankees . . . show[ed] their vast superiority to ourselves in numbers as well as in . . . resources." Both Emma, outside Richmond, and her niece Ellen, ensconced near Raleigh, North Carolina, remarked with wonder at retreating Union soldiers who filled entire roads as they marched northward "occupying the whole day." The sight impressed both women with the strength of Union forces and suggested the futility of the South's military effort against them.[194] It also fanned the flames of the victimhood and martyrdom they already felt as vanquished Confederates.

The biggest shock Emma faced was suddenly encountering African Americans who did not recognize her authority as a white woman. Two Black soldiers made off with Rosina's only horse, and a "hired negro boy . . . went off without asking." The "boy" quickly exercised his new freedom to choose not to work, but Emma still thought in terms of the old system that held authority over him and so viewed this as an act of insubordination. Cyrus, Rosina's longtime enslaved man, felt a responsibility toward his family's well-being in this new situation, so he initially continued to work in the fields. But Emma and Rosina "felt no assurance that he would continue faithful," which they took personally. One of the soldiers who absconded with Rosina's horse was an "insolent looking negro, dirty and ragged," who told the women to hand over any saddle they might have and "be quick about it." His orders were to "take ev'y horse & saddle outside de lines," as Emma wrote of the event. By writing in a manner that reflected the speech patterns and accents of Blacks but not those of whites, she ridiculed African American speech. His "insolent look" possibly indicated that he did not show the fear of a white person that she had long considered the proper demeanor for Black people.[195]

Rosina reluctantly gave the soldier the only saddle she owned, but Emma "felt convinced that" he had "no authority for his conduct." In her universe, no Black man could possibly give orders to a white person, male or female, so "after thinking the matter over," they "began to hope it might be possible to get redress." Rosina was sick, her sons had returned to active duty, and Augusta was too young to travel by herself. With little choice in the matter, Emma spent the next few days conquering her own fears as she decided to go to Richmond to Camp Lee, to "state the case to the officer in command there, and see what could be done." Success depended on finding white men who were "gentlemen"—in other words, men who would protect her—despite being Union soldiers. She vividly recounted her experiences during these few days in a letter to her cousin Edward Cohen, who had been serving in the Confederate army in North Carolina.[196]

As Emma made her way to Richmond, accompanied by Rosina's young slaves Mary and Georgiana, she came across both white and African American men in Union uniforms. The streets were "black and blue" with "negro soldiers" and mixed crowds. She found the numerous African American Union troops especially disconcerting and reported that one soldier, "the blackest man" she had ever seen, was "extremely insolent" to her. He accused Emma of saying something negative about President Lincoln and "cursed [her] horribly." Then he went on to say, "You haven't got things here no longer as you have had them; don't you know that? Don't you know that?" To Emma, his language was utterly "blasphemous." Her comment reveals both the intensity of her emotional response to his remarks and her view that God sanctioned the Confederacy's social order. His rebuke of that order did more than refute the authority she presumed she had. It contravened God's plan for her world.[197]

Emma overcame her distaste and fear and spoke "in a courteous manner" to the first Black officer she met, who proved helpful. Yet as she walked through Richmond's wrecked streets to meet a second officer, she "never in [her] life had felt so proudly defiant," she told her cousin. She saw African Americans "in places where a negro was never seen before" and came across others "drunk & sober" celebrating the Union victory. She also saw the physical chaos from the recent fire and explosions, which had ravaged the cityscape. More than eight hundred buildings had burned, devastating the city's business district.[198] All was, to her mind, dirty and disorderly. Despite having to pass through a "nasty crowd," she met no actual "rudeness" and was herself "studiously polite and dignified." She found her way to the officer in charge, "made known [her] business as succinctly as possible," and obtained his assurance that the horse would be returned to the farm. Then she met up with Mary and Georgiana, whom Emma had sent to her niece Caroline's house with a note, and the three made their way back to Rosewood. Rosina's horse was returned soon thereafter. Whatever Emma might have thought of the Union soldiers she met, especially the Black soldiers, they kept their word to her.[199]

Once the war was formally over, it became impossible to avoid frequent encounters with Union soldiers in the area around Rosewood and Richmond. Rosina swiftly moved to turn her farm crops into more than sustenance for her household. In mid-April 1865, a few days after Lee's surrender, she arranged for produce from her farm to be taken to Richmond and sold to Union soldiers still stationed there. This type of trade became the only way for most Southerners to obtain United States currency. Confederate currency had become useless, and Union soldiers were always eager for fresh food. Emma's cousins living on Broad Street in Richmond earned cash by renting a room to a "Yankee Officer who boards & lodges with them. He is gentlemanly and they have become quite reconciled to him," Emma noted with some surprise.[200] Her relatives had found a way to obtain usable currency while carrying on the South's genteel graciousness toward white, well-mannered visitors.

The most fundamental crisis at Rosewood was that soon after Emma's adventure in Richmond, the household slaves began to leave. "The servant question," as Emma called it, became urgent as emancipated people realized that they had new choices to make now that the Union was in charge. Change was quick to arrive. Like many other slave owners, Rosina grieved when the people she had depended on and to whom she was emotionally attached left her home. Emma described both Rosina and Augusta weeping at the prospective loss of the young slave Mary, whom they insisted they loved. Mary's mother had died when Mary was still a baby and had asked Rosina to promise never to "part with her," a euphemism for selling her, a promise Rosina had kept. Such promises were irrelevant now, though. Mary's father, who had been enslaved elsewhere and was now a free man, wanted his daughter to live with him in the home he planned to establish and came to get her within days of the war ending. Mary "got up as usual, ... took out her bed—and never came back." Both Mary and Georgiana had usually slept on the floor in Rosina's room, "as comfortable as any children need want to be," according to Emma.[201] They probably did not see it that way, however, and as the historian Thavolia Glymph notes, mattresses and bedding were among the items newly freed slaves most often took from their former masters' homes in the chaos of postwar days.[202] What bed did Mary take when she left Rosewood? Was it floor bedding that she slept on? Emma's wording is unclear. Her comment that Mary and Georgiana were "as comfortable as any children need want to be" seemed to defend slaves' sparse bedding, such as a pallet of woven straw. A bed complete with a frame, mattress, pillow, and linens would not have elicited an assertion that it ought to have been enough for them. Now Emma and Rosina, like slaveholders across the South, realized that they had misjudged the people who had been their slaves. The newly emancipated would not stay if there were better options elsewhere.

Rosina's longtime slave Cyrus had gone to Richmond to hear a proclamation ending slavery read aloud on the courthouse steps. "All the land belongs to the Yankees now," he reported, and they were going to divide it up among the "colored people."[203] At Rosewood, the actual separation moved gradually as Cyrus tried to determine what would be best for his family amid rumors of various economic opportunities. Slave marriages had had no legal standing in the antebellum South, but, like Cyrus and Sarah, enslaved people frequently managed to create long and stable family relationships. Cyrus was now making decisions as the free male head of his family. He and Sarah left Rosewood in mid-April 1865. Lizzie, one of Cyrus's daughters, wanted to leave with her parents, but her husband, Phil, preferred to stay with Rosina as hired help. Lizzie was pregnant with her own child, which complicated matters. Rosina liked Lizzie very much and hoped she would stay and work for wages, but ultimately she and Phil left as well. Georgiana, another of Cyrus's daughters, stopped coming to work in early May.[204]

The departure of Cyrus's family left Rosewood "very badly off." Although Emma was quite healthy, she faced the reality of doing her own housework with grim shock. On Saturday, April 15, 1865, a day when she typically would have spent the morning in her room reading the Sabbath prayers, she complained to her diary, "Felt stiff and sore with my unaccustomed labours of yesterday. Rosina too felt miserably."[205] It was a new world for Emma, one more familiar to the poorer Southern white women who labored without slaves or the Northern women who could not afford paid servants to assist them. Enslaved women commonly worked as long as eighteen hours each day, and even if Emma worked half that time, it would have been an entirely unfamiliar experience for her.[206] She, Rosina, and other white Southern women they knew searched urgently for newly free Black women to take over household tasks, especially the cooking. The white women's difficulty in securing cooks reveals how free African American women navigated the sale of their labor and negotiated the terms of their work and payment. They sought to be paid by task rather than by the hour in order to gain greater control over their labor and time.[207]

Southern culture provided few ideas to help Emma cope with this new problem. Because physical labor was something done by enslaved people, work was less prestigious in the South than in the North, where industriousness was understood to be the centerpiece of the productive economy for free labor.[208] By contrast, white Southerners of means touted an ethic of leisure that promoted the gracious living they desired. For them, the popular saying "idle hands are the devil's playground" was more likely to be applied to slaves rather than themselves.[209] This concept of gentility, especially for women, was a core feature of Confederate nationalism.

Casting about for household workers, in May 1865 Rosina and Emma turned to orphans. Many white Southern children had lost their fathers during the war, and impoverished mothers had no choice but to place their children in orphanages. These institutions then hired some children out as either day laborers or apprentices.[210] Emma hoped that Anna Lewery, a girl from the Richmond orphanage, would fill part of the gap left by the loss of household slaves, some of whom were also quite young. Things did not go well, however. Emma lamented, "I have been doing drudgery for the greater part of the week—assisted unwillingly & inefficiently by a little white girl from town, who is so miserable at being in the country, that she thinks of nothing, but how to get home again." Her desperate hopes that Anna would remain did not blind her to the fact that the girl was obviously "unhappy & lonesome," even though Emma had every reason to pretend to herself that the girl would be content at Rosewood. White children, even if they were poor orphans like Anna, had choices about their labor that slaves had not enjoyed. The girl "doesn't intend to stay," Emma wrote. Perhaps consoling herself at the loss, Emma added that she "does not seem to be very competent." Emma and Rosina next found "a temporary" to work in the kitchen for the time being, but they had no assurance that the future would hold any better news for them. Rosina was "miserable at present trials & apprehensi[ve] of future ones," full of fear that she may never "have any servants on any terms again." Such a fate would not only mark a significant loss of class status but also present very real physical challenges. For Rosina, a chronically ill person who needed the care she received from the enslaved people who maintained her farm and household, their loss generated panic. It was more than a matter of class identity and ownership—it was a physical need. Therefore, at Rosewood, "the servant question" became especially urgent for the white women left behind.[211]

The turmoil over household labor did not abate. Not even Emma's usual refuge in nature could bring calm. May 11, she wrote, was a "day of rare beauty, following a stormy night—The air so clear, & cool, the sky so blue, & the slopes of the leafy woods so green. The birds are numerous and the air is filled with their warbling." But the beauty did not soothe her; instead, it sharpened her sense of the tumult inside the house. While outdoors the loveliness of the natural order prevailed, indoors she found "no beauty, no enjoyment, no harmony." The social order that had been built on what Southerners viewed as natural distinctions no longer held. "Rose has had two days of nervous suffering & mental torture," Emma wrote. The household was "still unsupplied with servants," and they had "no definite prospect of getting any." To make matters worse, Emma did not feel that she received enough praise for her labors. "My efforts do not meet with the only compensation I desire for them," she wrote in her diary, "the satisfaction of knowing that they afford one ray of comfort, or are in any way appreciated."[212] She felt that she was being utterly selfless in shouldering duties formerly performed by slaves. It is difficult to imagine that any amount of appreciation would have compensated her for that indignity.

Soon after the soldiers lay down their arms, Emma heard of "decent white women" selling food or other goods to Union soldiers in Richmond. She soon began to do so herself, taking advantage of her connections and proximity to the city. On May 4, 1865, she detailed her efforts, writing, "I took in a gold thimble, and some gold trinkets to sell if possible, as I cannot bear to be without any money though I do not require much. I thought I would go into the cake business myself. I sold my gold for nine dollars—bought ½ Gal. molasses, and two lbs. flour, and some soda for sixty-two cts., & with this I have begun trade."[213] She did not explain who actually did the baking of those cakes or where she learned which items would be needed in their preparation. For all her discussion of meals during her year at Rosina's, Emma never indicated that she noticed the effort that went into creating them, much less that she had any kitchen skills herself. Yet, at the close of the war, she seemed completely confident in her ability as a baker. Just as she seemed surprised at the physical toll on her body after a full day of household labor, so she may have simply assumed that a well-made cake would be easy to produce. Perhaps she assumed she would find a servant who could bake well. Or perhaps her assertive language bolstered an insecure confidence. She wrote nothing more about the enterprise in her diary and instead remarked on the simpler effort of preparing Rosina's freshly picked strawberries for market. Who picked them is unclear.

Determined to obtain cash through marketing food, Emma leapt into Richmond's chaotic postwar economy only a year after writing about the evils of capitalism and the benefits of slavery in her diary. Although plantations and large farms garnered Southerners' admiration and idealized their values for both economic and social order, Emma had spent her adult life among Richmond's shops. Moreover, most Southern Jews lived in urban centers, where they labored in a variety of businesses, usually as merchants who bought and sold goods arriving in the port cities, whether on wagons rolling into town from farms or on ships docked in harbors. Trade was far more familiar to them than farming was. Richmond's Jews were tailors and bank cashiers, saloon owners and watchmakers, tobacco growers and sellers, and more.[214] Emma could point to many members of her synagogue who earned their livelihood through trade, and she now proposed to join them for a way out of the dire economic circumstances in which she and Rosina found themselves.[215]

Occupying Union soldiers continued to seek food at Rosina's farm, but thanks to Emma's negotiations in Richmond, she was in possession of a "protection paper" from Union general Godfrey Weitzel that required the soldiers to pay for what they took. Many white women in Richmond appealed to Union military officers for such passes, which in theory could provide a modicum of protection for their property and persons.[216] Emma wrote about one occasion: "About 12 o'clock three armed Yankees came round the house in a boisterous manner, trying to catch our fowls—I went out, though frightened, taking the protection paper with me, and remonstrated with them. At first they professed to disregard the paper, but on my reading it to them, they thought it best to withdraw, but we did not contrive to save a hen which one of them, who had kept out of the way, had found in George's hen-house & took away."[217] The search for food occupied everyone in the South, former slaves, Confederates, and Yankee military alike. Fortunately, she wrote, "no other disturbance occurred, and our nights are always quiet, thank God." Yet composure remained elusive. She turned to faith to try to achieve it, writing, "though our thoughts about all that we are separated from are harrowing, I leave all in God's hands & endeavor to keep close under the shadow of His wings." Nonetheless, she confessed, "both Rose & I have lost flesh in the last two weeks—I keep strong & well, but she feels very feeble and sadly depressed."[218] Between the departure of the slaves, the constant fears of confiscation of property and food, and the general gloom of the comprehensive defeat of the South, Emma concluded her diary amid anxiety and fear.

Head q'rs M. A. Forces
Richmond, Va.
April 7th 1865

Pass the bearers
Dr. M. S. Taylor and
Miss Mordecai through
our lines to their homes.
Good for to-day only.

G. Weitzel
Maj. Genl
Commdg

Pass signed by General Weitzel, April 7, 1865. (Courtesy of the Southern Historical Collection, The Wilson Library, University of North Carolina at Chapel Hill)

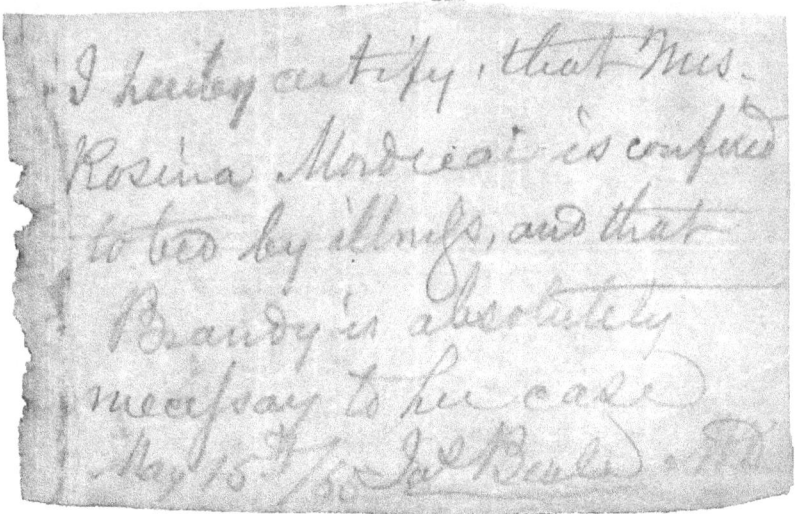

Permission to buy brandy for Rosina Young Mordecai, May 15, 1865. (Courtesy of the Southern Historical Collection, The Wilson Library, University of North Carolina at Chapel Hill)

EMMA'S LEGACY

During the last months of the war, Emma took no pleasure in keeping her diary, perhaps because it recounted a year of growing disasters both at home and on the battlefield. Unfortunately, the record is incomplete because when Emma returned to the diary to copy it in 1886, she found that the section from mid-December 1864 until early April 1865 had been destroyed by insects and mice. It does seem that she had been struggling with making regular entries during the final defeat of the Confederacy because on April 13, 1865, she wrote with resignation, "Thinking I may here after regret it, if I yield to my aversion to the task, I resolved to continue my narrative."[219] At that point, she reviewed recent events in detail so that the diary could catch up with itself. She also placed a few other documents she had saved into the back of the book, turning it into something of a scrapbook about the Confederacy's final year. First was the written permission scribbled on scrap paper that authorized her to purchase brandy for Rosina's use, an act requiring approval by the local military authority then governing the area around Richmond. Two other handwritten documents—also scrawled quickly on torn bits of paper—permitted her to travel in and out of Richmond without worrying about Union soldiers blocking her route. Those items attested to her ability to convince the occupying forces that she posed no threat to their effort to maintain order. General Godfrey Weitzel, a German-born Union army officer, judged her harmless and provided the permits she needed.

She also copied into the diary two letters, one she wrote to her cousin Edward Cohen and one she received from Ellen Mordecai, her niece in Raleigh, that provided descriptions of especially chaotic and dangerous events, including confrontations with Union military forces. By supplementing her diary with these documents, she placed her personal account into the greater context of the events swirling around her. Like many others, she had strongly resisted entertaining the idea that the South might lose the war, thinking that the blood sacrifices of battle surely meant the Confederacy would prevail.[220] The South's collapse ended her confidence that as a white woman she could count on protection. It also forced her to learn skills foreign to her, such as earning money through business and negotiating with free Blacks for their labor.

Finally, several months after Emma stopped making daily entries, she added copies of two newspaper articles to the diary. One, "The Last Six Days of the Grand Old Army of Northern Virginia," written by the British politician and journalist Francis Charles Lawley, was first published in the *London Fortnightly* and was reprinted in the *Richmond Whig* on October 24, 1865.[221] Lawley had been a member of Parliament and was disgraced in a banking scandal. He relocated to the United States in 1856 and years later became a correspondent covering the American Civil War, crossing through the blockade to Richmond and reporting favorably on the Confederacy. His account delineated the military wisdom of the venerated General

Robert E. Lee and contrasted it with the wrongheaded command of the Confederate military commander Jubal Early, who ordered his hungry soldiers to burn eight hundred wagons of food belonging to the Union army. Two days later, when the surrender was signed and those same Confederate soldiers became prisoners, the Northern occupiers lacked sufficient food to feed them.[222] The second article, published in the *Richmond Whig* a few days later, described the postwar legal and financial troubles faced by the local railroad. It attested to the economic chaos that busied Southern courts with legal actions as businesses sought economic redress for the financial failures in the wake of the war. In this case, the railroad that Emma often rode publicized its legal and financial difficulties that resulted from contracts it had signed before advancing armies destroyed miles of track, overturned hundreds of acres of land, and burned its cars. The article aimed to quell rumors of company malfeasance whispered among Richmonders anxious for familiar access to transportation.[223]

All these documents placed Emma's individual domestic experiences in the larger wartime and postwar context. They expanded and supported her effort to frame her own personal experience within the events of the larger world. Together they added new dimensions to the personal picture of the fall of the Confederacy that Emma painted in her diary. Still, she was ambivalent about the diary, which reminded her of the worst time of her life. She seems to have stopped writing altogether within six weeks or so of the war ending. This pattern was not unusual for Confederate women diarists, others of whom also closed the chapter on the defeat by ending their diaries.[224] It is not entirely clear exactly when Emma stopped writing because, after she did so, she put the diary in a drawer and left it untouched for decades. Time crumbled some pages; insects ate others. Yet, even though Emma claimed that she wrote only from a sense of obligation to do so, the document as a whole reveals great care and deep

Last page of Emma Mordecai's 1864–1865 diary. (Courtesy of the Southern Historical Collection, The Wilson Library, University of North Carolina at Chapel Hill)

and some ochra. Aunt Tempie staid a few days not long ago, with cousins Sally & Crizzy. Their servant had just left them, and they had not one – but a very good woman who was living on the lot, did their cooking little enough it was – They are pretty well & quite cheerful, tho' feeling as we all do, the bitter change – and as cousin Sally said, it is the country not the individual adversity that she mourns. Susan Raynor looks thin & badly – she has been sick – has had a summer of harrassing care & pressing anxieties. Martha Mordecai is getting on tolerably – has had plenty of trouble – little Patty is very delicate. Poor Emily died a short time ago – a good, faithful creature. Most of the servants there have been horrid – Lucy good & faithful, and one or two others right good. ××× Write to me and tell me how you are all getting on. ××× My very best love to Rose, Susta, & the boys and all the folks in town. Excuse this miserable affair of a letter, & write when you can & feel like it, to your aff. Ellen –

Copied August 5th 1886. at 1219. Broad St. Richmond

emotion. And however mixed her feelings were, she took the diary with her when she moved back to Richmond after the war and never discarded it.

Perhaps reflecting the important place that the diary had come to occupy in Emma's own sense of her past, in 1886 she copied it in order to preserve it and also pasted the extra documents into the new diary book. From time to time, she added notations in the margins explaining whom individuals later married, what illnesses they died of, and other items of interest to the relatives and friends who might read it at a later date. When Emma recopied what remained of her diary into a fresh, blank notebook with a hard brown cover, she perhaps had begun to show it to some of the people around her who would have known those individuals or their descendants. Popular interest in remembering the war and the Old South was growing among Southerners as the generations that fought in the war and directly experienced its hardships began to pass on. Southern diaries offered the nation a different view of the past than the one proffered by the many memoirs produced by victorious Northerners.

It is possible that when Emma revisited her wartime diary and decided to recopy it, she was mirroring the efforts of the many other Southern women who took up the cause of memorializing and vindicating the Old South. She probably noticed the previous publication of Civil War diaries, many of them by women. Judith Brockenbrough McGuire's *Diary of a Southern Refugee during the War* appeared as early as 1867, as did Sally Brock's *Richmond during the War*. The Confederate hospital supervisor Phoebe Pember's *A Southern Woman's Story* was published in 1879 in both New York and London and indicated broad popular interest in war memory.[225] Pember's memoir might have been of particular interest to Emma as the work of another Southern Jewish woman. Perhaps those volumes prompted her to unearth what remained of her own work, even if she had no intention of publishing it.[226]

The publication of an ever-growing number of Southern recollections of the war illustrated the ongoing reach of the Lost Cause, a mythology popular not just in the South but also throughout the rest of a country eager to heal from its wounds, even if that meant backing away from any commitment to racial equality. In the South, the devotion to the past grew with each passing year and effectively became a civil religion.[227] Rebecca Bettelheim was only a child when her family moved to Richmond in 1869 in order for her father to become the first ordained rabbi of Richmond's Congregation Bayth Ahabah, but she later recalled, "The war was still the chief fireside and table topic; bitterness towards the North was expressed in almost every breath."[228] Confederate nationalism did not die upon Southern defeat.

Frequent commemorations provided ample opportunity to hold onto the past. As just one example, Decoration Day, a holiday focused on tending the graves of fallen soldiers that morphed into Memorial Day, began among Confederate women in the days following the war, including Jewish women.[229] In 1869, the *Richmond Dispatch* published a notice that on Decoration Day, the women of the Hebrew Ladies Memorial Association invited all residents of Richmond to join them in establishing a Jewish cemetery and monument in honor of the "myriads of [Jewish] heroes who spilled their noble blood," expressing their hope for later years: "when the malicious tongue of slander, ever so ready to assail Israel, shall be raised against us, then, with a feeling of mournful pride, will we point to this monument."[230] Unsurprisingly, given this very public notice about a specifically Jewish memorial initiative, as early as 1869, there already was a general Confederate memorial in Richmond's Hollywood Cemetery. After Reconstruction ended in 1877, Jim Crow legislation instituted restrictions on Black labor, finances, and civil rights, and whites regained supremacy across the South. Myriad memorials, commemorations, speeches, and texts lionizing the past justified those restrictions. Richmond was the center of many of the earliest public commemorations of the Lost Cause. The Robert E. Lee statue unveiled to great acclaim in 1890 was but the first of numerous memorials erected to the major figures of the Confederacy along the city's Monument Avenue.²³¹ Richmond became, and remains, a central site of intense contestation over the memory of the Civil War.²³²

Women played a key role in creating the culture that lionized the Lost Cause, and the United Daughters of the Confederacy (UDC) extended that "memory" of a mythological era of Southern gentility, peacefulness, honor, and order across the country. To counter the voices of victorious Northerners, in 1894 women in Tennessee who descended from Confederate soldiers organized to memorialize their ancestors and promote their view of the Old South, especially the myth of the Lost Cause. The UDC raised funds to erect the monuments to Confederate military figures like Lee and Thomas Jonathan "Stonewall" Jackson that stood throughout the South into the twenty-first century. During the war, some of the young women who later founded the UDC had spent the war years at Southern female academies, where their lives were relatively stable. Their comparative isolation and protection permitted them a rosier picture of wartime than most Southerners experienced. Many of these women became teachers after the war, and, as UDC members, they also vetted history textbooks for schoolchildren to be sure that school accounts of the antebellum South and the war itself conformed to the organization's perspective. They tapped into a widespread desire among Southerners to burnish the image of the prewar South and to soothe the psychological wounds inflicted by the devastation and loss, still painful decades after the war's end. Only six years after the UDC's founding, it counted seventeen thousand members; by World War I, it claimed almost one hundred thousand.²³³

The historian Drew Gilpin Faust has pointed out that the work white women did to survive the war and maintain Southern culture ironically transformed them from people who functioned within a protected social space into individuals able to navigate conflict and surmount challenges on their own. As they adjusted to life without male protection because such a high proportion of Confederate white men served in the military, they learned new skills, whether they wanted to or not and regardless of how much they may have resented having to do so.²³⁴ The legacy of those new skills made the UDC a formidable and effective organization.

Although the UDC has no record of Emma ever formally joining the group, she shared its perspective and its goals.²³⁵ For the rest of her life, she maintained Confederate values—including a belief in white supremacy—along with a love for the way she had lived before the war. In 1896, two years after the UDC organized, she donated a desk that had belonged to her brother Samuel to the Confederate Museum in Richmond.²³⁶ And that same year, Emma gave the entire recopied diary to her great-niece Patty Mordecai, who had been only six months old when the first shot was fired on Fort Sumter. Patty, whose given name was Martha, was the daughter of Henry Mordecai, the son of Moses Mordecai, Emma's oldest half brother, who had died when Emma was only twelve years old. Patty would carry on the family history. Through its transmission to her descendants, Emma tied her family to its past. The UDC promoted and renewed general interest in the South's account of the war, and Emma's diary provided Patty with tangible evidence of her family's experience.

At the turn of the twentieth century, reminiscences about the past, the momentous war, and its destruction of the South's slave society continued to capture the imagination of many Americans, and even more diaries appeared in print. The diary of Kate Stone, whose family "refugeed" to Texas after the 1863 Battle of Vicksburg, was published in 1900. Sarah Morgan, who lived in Baton Rouge, Louisiana, kept a diary of six volumes, all of which were published in 1913. Most significant of all was the 1905 diary of Mary Boykin Chesnut, whose husband was a member of Jefferson Davis's cabinet, which offered an inside view of life at the head of the Confederate leadership.²³⁷ The hugely popular 1915 film *The Birth of a Nation*, based on a novel about the launch of the Ku Klux Klan in Tennessee in 1865, brought idyllic visions of the Southern plantation and its purported white gentility and Black submissiveness to a broad audience and developed an even larger market for narratives that recounted a beloved South's destruction by the cruelties of a vicious war. *The Birth of a Nation* was so popular that

Emma Mordecai's tombstone (Courtesy of Find a Grave, www.findagrave.com/memorial/31871327/emma-mordecai)

President Woodrow Wilson screened it at the White House and, infamously, referred to it as "like writing history with lightning."[238]

Though Emma continued to correspond with a wide network of relatives and friends throughout the South, relatively little is known of her later life. She became a schoolteacher after the war and taught in several Southern cities, including Wilmington, North Carolina, and Columbus, Georgia.[239] The 1900 United States Census showed her living as a boarder in the home of the Misses Gay in Augusta, Virginia.[240] Emma passed away in 1906 at the age of ninety-three, an event noted in the necrology of the *American Jewish Year Book*, which identified her as an educator and a writer.[241] Thirty years after her death, Patty Mordecai decided to include the diary among the extensive collection of items the Mordecai family descendants agreed to donate to the Southern Historical Collection of archival materials housed at the University of North Carolina at Chapel Hill. The documents arrived in five bundles in Chapel Hill from 1939 through 1956. A new, younger generation of Mordecais, including Patty's own niece, may have decided that professional conservation could protect the family's documents from the insect infestations and crumbling paper that had destroyed some of Emma's wartime work. Today, the large Mordecai Family Papers Collection includes almost two thousand items, and Emma's 1864–1865 diary has been digitized.[242] The fate of the diary and the Mordecai family's papers reflect their own sense of who they were. Originals of their documentary legacy reside in the nation's major storehouses of Southern documents, where family members, very few of whom still identified as Jewish, placed them, while copies of some Mordecai papers are also preserved at the Jacob Rader Marcus Center of the American Jewish Archives in Cincinnati and at the American Jewish Historical Society in New York City. The Mordecai documents are integral to American Jewish history, but, like Emma's Civil War diary, they belong to the South.

The Civil War Diary of Emma Mordecai, April 1864–May 1865

A NOTE ON THE TEXT

This text derives from a transcript of the copy that Emma Mordecai made in 1886 of her own 1864–1865 diary. Parts of the diary had been destroyed by insects, mice, and the ravages of time, as Emma noted in her copy. Both the 1886 handwritten copy of the diary and the typed transcript are part of the Mordecai Family Papers (Collection #00847) at the Southern Historical Collection at the University of North Carolina at Chapel Hill. The transcript preserves spelling, punctuation, syntax, and grammatical idiosyncrasies found in the 1886 diary copy, as does the text reproduced here. Questionable text from the transcript was checked against the 1886 diary copy. Apparent dating inconsistencies have been indicated in brackets. As Emma copied her diary, she added parenthetical comments of explanation or identification of people and places, which are italicized here for clarity.

DIARY. MAY 1864. KEPT BY EMMA MORDECAI AT ROSEWOOD. NEAR RICHMOND.

On *Thursday, April 18th* I left our house on 6th street, for the last time. Sister Ellen & Brother George had departed early that morning, leaving my nephew George, alone at the house. There were still remaining a few articles of furniture to be sent away, after attending to which George & I came away & at 3½ came out to Rosewood in the cars with Augusta when her school was out. I felt strange without a home anymore, and very still & quiet, tho' not overcome with depression—the reverse, however, of all excitement. Rose had prepared most kindly for my reception, and my room was the picture of neatness & comfort. She received me very kindly, but we made no demonstration or professions to each other. I only know that my inward resolve and humble prayer was & is that I may make my residence with her, for as-long as it may last, a blessing & not a torment or inconvenience to her. There was a time when I should not have doubted this, but the longer we live, the more we doubt ourselves, & now I am not certain—I only hope.

The following week I went to town to spend the Passover with my kind cousins, returning at the close of the festival, the time having been spent very satisfactorily, attending the services at the synagogue, and visiting many of our friends whom circumstances had prevented my seeing before we broke up. By all I was most kindly greeted, & I was gratified at the unvarying regret expressed at our family having left Richmond, & at the kind invitations I received from various friends to pass days or nights with them whenever I could. I returned to Rosewood on Friday 30th. George, meantime had returned to the Army, & Gusta (who went out with me, after school) & I found Rose alone, & pretty well, considering she had been exerting herself over much in many ways. I was soon resettled. The weather continues as it has been all the spring, very cold for the season, making fires necessary except for a few days while I was in town. This brings me to the beginning of my Diary, which in spite of some experience and all resolutions to the contrary, I have concluded to commence.

May 1st

Brother George arrived—having come on to attend to some business—He looks well and considering the times, seems very cheerful. He spent a quiet, resting evening after his journey, & went in the next day with Gusta, in the cars, when she went to school. Caroline came out with them in the afternoon—We waited dinner for them & had a pleasant family meeting, & a good deal of amusement reading some letters they had brought out to me, one from the unfortunate B.D.L. a hopeless lover full of hope—expecting when the war is over to make known his now ill-suppressed feelings for "Miss Myers." Poor fellow!

May 3rd

Brother George left us, intending to start home the following day. Caroline and I walked with him & Augusta, who went in to school, over to the R. road. Weather clear & fine, but still very cold for the season. There had been quite a violent hail storm the evening before. We had a pleasant walk there and back. Undertook to make a "zone" belt for Caroline and worked at it all day—succeeding pretty well, but disgusted at my want of skill—Rosina went to bed with one of her bad headaches, at ten, and kept in bed all day, first writing a long letter to George—Had a pen made at the back of the kitchen to put the cows & calves in at night, if possible, to keep them from being stolen. Everything is a prey to thieves in these disturbed times. Mr. Cohen took us by surprise by walking out in the afternoon. He too had a headache, ditto Caroline, also Augusta, so we were not particularly brilliant. Had a right pleasant evening however.

May 4th

Tried to keep Mr. Cohen to take an early breakfast with us, but he had an engagement in the City for 8 ½ & our eloquence was wasted. He started off soon after six in a brief walk, Caroline & I calling to him as he went down—We found the cow pen had been made just in time, as the thieves had been to the barn after them last night, & not finding anything else, took two of Cy's hens, Spent the day helping Rose alter Gusta's summer dresses—feeling entirely unequal to the task of working on my own. Mrs. Young came over & sat an hour or two with us—invited us to spend the next evening with her. Gusta brought Caroline pleasant letters from Nan Devereux & Maria Burgwin. Nan mentions that an acquaintance of ours, Perry de Leon, at the taking of Plymouth, last week, had captured "with his bow & with his spear" a Massachusetts negro soldier, whom he keeps as his own, & makes him call him "Master"—This is good, & quite tickles a southern sinner.

Read a little to Caroline after dinner in "outre mer"—Before sunset, she and I took a sweet little ramble down to the dear old Rocks—Dogwood in white bloom, & everything looked lovely—Met Mr. Gardner coming over from Spring Farm—he staid all night with us—Brought no news but that the two great armies are approaching each other, & the City ripe with rumors that the great battle had begun. God help us, & destroy the machinations of our enemies.

May 5th

Spent the day mostly in washing Caroline's splendid suit of long, thick golden hair, and in examining and arranging with her help a trunk full of things belonging to poor sister Caroline—A saddening & fatiguing occupation. Rose meantime was helping Deborah, a seamstress, in altering & making over Gusta's summer dresses, work that has been going on all the week, with great expedition and success, no young girl in the Confederacy will be more prettily or amply supplied with an outfit for the summer, tho' not one was bought for her—About sunset Caroline, Gusta & I went over to Westbrook to spend the evening—Beautiful weather & pleasant walk. Saw camp fires up in the woods near the turnpike—Pickett's division wagons were moving up the turnpike to the new camp—Soldiers soon came swarming to the well to fill their canteens. The fires looked beautiful as the evening advanced, & the stars shone with uncommon brilliancy. Mr. Gardner & Mrs. Young's brother, Dr. Braxton, a very amusing man, were at Westbrook. We had real coffee for supper, and a repast, altogether, that would have done credit to the most abundant times. After supper we had some sweet music. Gusta played, & Mrs. Young, who sings delightfully, gave us some of her choice songs. Later, we heard great shouting from the new Camp. The gentleman said they had never heard our soldiers so noisy—ascertained that the poor fellows were ordered back to Chaffin's farm, whence they had just been moved. In a short time the last shout died away, & the noise of their wagons ceased. The Yankees were said to be coming up James River in transports & gunboats, & landing about 5 miles below Chaffin's Farm—All of us felt excited; Mrs. Young very uneasy & fearful—Her brother laughed at her unmercifully, & when she said she was full of fear, he drily remarked. "Well, that is a very good thing to fill up with, in these serious times". Mr. Young walked up to the turnpike to learn what he could from the soldiers; found but three or four by the camp fire, out of the two thousand who had been there an hour before. After he got back we started home, it being now past eleven. Mr. Gardner walked home with us & staid all night. Found Rose, who had felt too unwell to go with us, asleep & undisturbed so we kept silent & retired quietly.

May 6th

Caroline returned to town where she has been living with her aunts, since we broke up on 6th St. near Lee,—I walked with her & Gusta to the R. Road. Beautiful morning & pleasant walk—Felt anxious all the morning to hear from the Army. Gusta brought news when she returned from school, of a victory over Grant yesterday at Chancellorsville. Felt grateful for this, but with such sadly tempered joy, do we hear of our successes—We do not know who may have fallen: we know that many have, dear to others if unknown to us. It is said that the great battle is being fought today; also that several of our Genls. fell on yesterday. As I sit by my open window this lovely May morning, with the quiet green slopes of the little hills stretching down to the beautiful water; nothing heard but the tinkling of the cow bells as they snatch their last browse for the evening, & the twittering of the birds, how unlike is the scene before me, to the frightful onslaught, the carnage, & the thundering of the artillery that are at this moment going on, less than fifty miles from us. It is utterly impossible to realize the fact, & our quiet composure under such circumstances is an unsolvable problem of human nature. Rose felt much agitated on hearing the news, but soon recovered her composure. Her three sons, in the Richmond Howitzers are there.

Saturday May 7th

Passed off very tranquilly in this quiet spot, but we feared to let our thoughts wander to the army; not that we doubted for a moment the success of our troops, though we heard of the Yankees landing in numbers below Richmond. In the course of the morning got cheering accounts from the army. A note from Caroline in which she says "News of a victory—1500 Yankees killed at Chancellorsville—Great battle expected to day." Spent greater part of the day reading, while Gusta worked on a drawn muslin bonnet she is making for herself, and Rose was busy with various jobs. In the afternoon Gusta & I walked over to Westbrook to see Mrs. Dallam. Had rather a stupid visit. Heard that a Yankee Monitor, in looking for torpedoes down the river, succeeded in finding one was blown to atoms. Heard too, that Cole Thompson Brown, the noble & loved commander of our boys, was killed in the battle of yesterday. He leaves a wife & many devoted relatives to mourn his loss, besides the men whom he commanded & by whom he was so beloved & honored. Mr. Gardner came out about 8 o'clock & brought us an Extra, full of good tidings from all quarters, but all feelings of triumph are repressed by the certainty of the cost of our victories in the lives of our brave privates & noble officers. Mr. Gardner brought a report that the Yankees were advancing on the Mechanicsville turnpike, & that the alarm bells were ringing in town for the Militia to turn out. We felt no alarm but went to bed & slept quietly. Beauregard & Pickett & other brave Generals are near with their forces and the whole community feel so assured of success, that instances of fear or misgiving, in man or woman are very rare.

May 8th

Beautiful day. Took a stroll by the ice-house & up the pond after breakfast. The woods are indescribably lovely. Gathered wild honeysuckle and dogwood & dressed the flower pots when I came back. Spent the morning writing letters—to Mr. Ben Lazarus, Miss Cohen of Baltimore & Brother George—also a note to "Edward." Don't know how he will take it; think it will plague him a little. Gusta walked to Sunday school at Emanuel church, on Brook Turnpike directly after breakfast and her mother rode to church later. Brought little news home—heard there was no fighting yesterday. Also that on yesterday morning we destroyed another Yankee Gunboat on the river, being too hotly pursued by the Yankees to keep possession, after having captured her. Our men all escaped in small boats. Mr. Walker, the kind, amiable pastor of this Parish, called in the afternoon, but did not stay to supper, though we had tea & muffins, delightful clabber with ice, & cool sweet milk to offer him. Who would desire better fare in the most bountiful times. Rose is & has always been one of the rich poor people—such a good economist.

May 9th

Rose early—breakfasted at 6-½, read Bible, washed up breakfast things, & then took a sweet walk to Laurel Branch. Got some wild flowers & got back by eight, just as Gusta & Mr. Gardner were starting to the R. Road—gave them my letters, came up & changed my heavy shoes and hose, & wrote up my diary to this moment, 9 o'clock. Am now going to set to work with a will upon my dress which I could not begin last week. Night—Was quite successful in making a beginning to my dress—Rose kindly making the sleeves. Spent the morning busily on it, only stopping to read the paper which Mr. Gardner sent out by the ice man—Full of good news from the Army. Everything seems hopeful, but some anxiety is felt about the enemy's approach on the south side of the James. Augusta staid in town all night. Mr.

Gardner who has now taken up his abode with us returned in the cars at 4 P.M.—seemed to feel a good deal of anxiety about the situation of Richmond. The alarm bells were ringing all day & all places of business closed early, the Local Troops being called out. Put up work & dressed at 6 o'clock—Mr.& Mrs. Dallam, and Mr. Young and their children walked over & paid us a visit.

May 10th

9 a.m. Just returned from a walk in the woods. Found the Blue Lupin in bloom, brought some home & dressed the flower pots—heard heavy firing in the direction of the city. The servants say they have heard it when at work in the field, all the morning. The enemy seem to be making an attack on all sides. I still feel undismayed, & pray God to enable us to endure whatever awaits us in the way of evil, with fortitude, and to receive with humble gratitude what may await us in the way of success. 10 o'clock—Mr. Young, (*Rose's brother*) has just called, to inform us that the Yankees are making another raid above us, & to caution us to hide all valuables. Rose is now having the meat in the smoke house taken down to hide. Great apprehensions are felt with regard to the attack on Richmond from the so. side—the enemy is said to be 40,000 strong. The firing continues to be heard here at about the same distance as an hour ago. I have hidden the few valuables I have here, and am now going on with my dress. The rest of the day passed in the most undisturbed manner. We were aware that at any moment the Philistines might be upon us, but we went on quietly with our occupations. Got a note in the afternoon from Mr. Young, containing nothing of a discouraging character, & a newspaper full of confidence for the future, & of success in the west & south. Gusta could not get home from school, as the raid prevented the train on the Fredricksbg R.R. from venturing out—Mr. Gardner was also detained in town all night. So Rose & I were alone—we went to bed about nine, and slept quietly.

May 11th

A beautiful morning—After breakfast Rose & I went into the garden to help her maidens, Lizzy, Mary & Georgianna work the strawberries, which look unpromising for a fine crop. Received a message from Westbrook to the effect that the Yankees were in force three miles from there, & warning the men Cyrus & George to be on the lookout, ready to hide the horse & mule in the woods west of the farm, if they should get here. They had heard cannon & musketry all the morning, in the direction of Hanover Junction. Having finished our work in the garden by this time, Rose had her meat removed from the place she had it in, and hidden under the hen house—then came in quietly & made the best disposition she could of her money and other valuables, some in her pockets & some in mine and then lay down to rest, & perhaps went to sleep. She was sufficiently composed to do so. I resumed my work on my dress, but as we had heard nothing from town since the day before, & wanted to ascertain the truth of the rumors the servants had heard, I took Georgianna & walked over to Westbrook between 1 & 2 o'clock. Found the house locked up—the ladies & children at home. They had heard nothing more than we had. They were having some things put up for themselves & the children, to send over here in case they had to leave the house. Paid only a short visit, & return'd by the breastworks, the creek & the Mill. After getting home lay down to rest until dinner was ready. After dinner resumed work, & Rose finished reading a story she had begun. Loud firing of both cannon & musketry commenced briskly between 4 & 6 o'clock—don't know where the fight was, but not very far off. A heavy thunder storm with abundant rain stopped the firing for short time. Continued after the storm abated until dark, when Rose went to bed & I sat knitting in the dark till 9, when I went to bed too, after committing our household to the care of the All Powerful & felt no fear. I had taken a cup of tea which kept me awake until near 12, but my thoughts were tranquil & full of trust. R. was asleep all the time.

May 12th

Commenced at dawn of day with heavy cannonading & rounds of musketry somewhere to the east of us—this continued an hour or two without intermission—George, the negro boy, who had staid at Westbrook last night, tells us that a number of Yankees were over there all night & that the turnpike is full of them. The firing we hear is over towards the Mechanicsville turnpike. It is now about 8 o'clock, and another thunderstorm is answering the booming of the cannon & the crack of the musketry, which continue but at longer intervals. We know nothing but that fighting is going on all around us, & that our pickets have been withdrawn to the inner lines of defenses, which leave us in the enemy's lines. The cars not running on the Frdsbg. R. Road, neither Mr. Gardner nor Gusta could get home again yesterday. Poor Gusta, I am sure, feels anxious about home. It has begun to rain very hard, & we hear less firing.—9.30. Just after writing the above, a party of our scouts came in to take shelter from the rain. Gave us cheering news. They think we have these Yankees completely surrounded, so that they can only escape by fighting their way out. Genl. Lee too has obtained another victory near Fredsbg. Genl. Fitz Lee is above here driving the Yankees—(*torn out*) that every man in town is under arms. Firing continues loud, heavy & rapid in this vicinity. Picket firing heard very near through the woods. Flaven's artillery has answered peal for peal of ours. Later, same day—Soon after I had resumed my work this morning, another cloud arose & the thunder & the loud cannon kept up an incessant booming, until the cloud was exhausted. The firing continued with great fury until about 2 P.M. After the rain was over, Rose & I walked to the entrance of the Westbrook lane where some of our country Pickets were stationed. They told us the fight was the other side of Mr. Stuarts (*Brook Hill,*) & one of the men said we had but a small force, not more than 600 to oppose a large number to the Yankees. One of the pickets was mounted on a Yankee horse which he had found, completely equipped & riderless. He had too a Yankee gun which would fire seven times without reloading. We got but little information from the men & returned home.

While at dinner a servant of Mrs. Taylor's came over to say that the fight would be resumed in the field at the top of the hill, that her mistress had been ordered to leave her house, and wanted to know what Mrs. Mordecai was going to do. Rose sent her word to come over here, but that she did not intend to go away unless forced to do so, & that she, as yet, had heard nothing of it. The servant gave very discouraging accounts of numbers of the enemy & of their advancing upon Richmond from the Chesterfield side, & that the batteries around us were to be mounted, as we were forced to fall back. It made me feel wretchedly to hear her talk, & it may not all be so, but we must strengthen ourselves to hear the worst. I certainly do not feel brave this afternoon. The firing has ceased since 2, but we do not know the result of this ten hours hard fighting.

Mr. Linton sent us today's paper—Grieved to see the death of Dr. Fisher's son John. He was killed early Sunday morning, in the 2nd battle of Chancellorsville. He has done his whole duty from the beginning of the war, & is a loss to family, friends, & country.

About dusk, Mr. Linton who had been over in the direction of the fight, stopped on his way home to give us the joyful tidings that we had driven the Yankees off, & that they were now beyond the Chickahominy, Fitz Lee still after them. We could hear the distant firing of our pursuing forces. My heart swelled with gratitude for this signal deliverance—Mr. Linton gave the sad tidings of the death to our brave Genl. J.E.B. Stewart! Genl. Gordon lost his left arm. Numbers of wounded are reported, by the servants to have been carried to Brook Schoolhouse & other places on the turnpike, besides those taken to town in ambulances all day. What a cruel, frightful mystery is War! Later a party of cavalry pickets rode up and requested leave to take up their quarters here for the night. They could not stay at the house as they would be sending & receiving reports all night, so they took shelter in the Barn. It was raining hard again. Rose had some coffee (wheat coffee) made & some nice hoe cakes made & sent them a good supper. So ends this stormy, harassing, exciting day. At Westbrook the ladies did not undress nor get any sleep all last night, and spent today, they being not much nearer the fight than we, in dreadful apprehension of being driven from home & overrun by the Yankees.

May 13th Friday P.M.

The Gentlemen who were picketed at the Barn last night, proved to be town people on duty. They breakfasted with us this morning. After breakfast, Rose filled some jugs & bottles with sweet & butter milk and we had the carriage got and drove up on the turnpike to see if we could do anything for some wounded reported to be left at some of the houses there. Found they had all been sent to town, so I proposed that we should visit part of the scene of yesterday's encounter, only a mile beyond the turnpike, but we found many difficulties to our progress, trees fallen across the roads, dead horses—and finally were frightened by seeing a body of Cavalry moving some distance ahead of us, whom we feared might be Yankees, so we turned from our attempt. We saw some large trees topped by cannon balls, & others badly cut by them, & a good many people in the woods looking for plunder—but except these, and the dead horses & the badly cut up roads, we saw no evidence of the hard fight which took place there only yesterday. We then drove to town for Gusta, who had not been able to get home all the week. We passed on the road some large bodies of Cavalry & one of Infantry—everything looked indeed like War. Weary soldiers were lying within the batteries wrapped in their blankets, all over the wet ground. A courier passed us, riding up the road at full speed. Nearer town we met parties of ladies & little girls, with servants carrying refreshments to friends at the Batteries. In town we saw few persons on the streets. We stopped at the Officers Hospital and left with Mrs. Lewis Webb, the invaluable Superintendent, the milk & biscuits, which she was delighted to get. Then drove to our dear cousin's the Myers's on Broad below 12th Street & saw all there, and found them in good spirits. Caroline looks remarkably well, & rejoices that she has not gone & cannot now go from Richmond. All our lines of communication have been cut off by the Yankees— The Fredsbg, Petersbg & Danville R. Rds all injured & the telegrams interrupted. The P. Office closed, stores closed, markets almost closed—Richmond is indeed a beleaguered City. Mr. Cohen came in, while we were at our cousins, from Camp Marion, 4 miles below the City, where he has been on duty since last Friday morning. He is so foot-sore, that he got leave to be off duty & rest till tomorrow. Has been in the midst of the fighting but not actually engaged, his battalion being held in reserve. They lay in the trenches while the shells flew over them. We next went to the Passport Office for a pass to get home. Then to Mrs. Rusts where Gusta's school is, got her & then home again.

After dinner finished my dress—Learned indirectly that at last accounts there had been no casualties among the Richmond Howitzers to which our three boys, William, John & George Mordecai belong; but nothing has been heard from Lee's Army for a day or two.

May 14th Saturday

Cloudy & showery all day. Firing heard all day, heavy & constant, apparently directly south of us: probably in Chesterfield near the Danville R.R.—Negroes report firing at Drewry's Bluff. The day was an anxious one as we could learn nothing of what was going on. After reading my services for the day, read aloud to Gusta while she finished her bonnet, which looks as if it had come from a milliner's. Gusta got a note, written this A.M. from Marion Stuart, on "some Yankee paper, found in the camp down at the Batteries." It is as follows—

"Brook Hill—Saturday A.M. Dear Gusta, Mother asks me to write to you to see if you have heard anything from your brothers. We have made every possible enquiry concerning them but can hear nothing. Please let us know if you know anything, we feel anxious. Oh:

Gusta, the Yankees!—but thank God we are safe. They did not do us much damage, as we had warning of their approach, & sent our horses, meal &c to town: They stayed here from 1 o'clock in the day, until five the next morning. O, such a night!! eight of their pickets guarding our house to prevent our escape. At least 10,000 camped—(*torn*) and we heard their (*torn out*) wagons and artillery (*lost*) by; they took three hours to pass! just think of it. I hope they did not reach you—Did they go to your Uncle John's? (*Westbrook*) We had a severe fight at Yellow Tavern, & then 60 of our men contended against a <u>regiment</u> of <u>Yankees</u>, every inch of ground to our gate, when our men, overwhelmed, retired in good order. I saw a Yankee shot in our yard by the third Linden tree on the left side, by one of the Confederates, in the back. I am very glad I saw it. I can't write all about the Yankees, so much was crowded into that one day & night. Did you know Hutchie Rennie was killed: I feel extremely sorry for his family. I am very much grieved that we lost Gen'l. J.E.B. Stuart in the fight at the Yellow Tavern, but I expect others will be raised up to take his place.

Hoping your mother is in better spirits & that you have good news from your brothers, I remain ever your friend, Marion Stuart. (*Mrs. B. Peterson of West Va.*)

Later in the day Bell Stuart sent another note giving tidings of the safety of our boys, & that Genl. Lee had gained a great victory on Thursday 12th inst. As George Peterkin who came down from Lee's Army yesterday, was the bearer of these tidings we have no reason to doubt their truth, & I got provoked with Rose for not crediting them, & made her angry by telling her she hugged Worry with the closest affection, whereupon she had nothing to say to me the rest of the evening, & I went to bed feeling very unhappy. Used every means within myself to get in a right frame of mind, under these circumstances, & when we met at breakfast this morning, I told her I was very sorry to have made that disagreeable remark to her last night, to which she replied, she had given me as sharp as an answer, & that she was very sorry too, & so ended our first quarrel, all unpleasant feelings having left us both, except that I feel a sadness I did not have before. If I do not keep the friends I have I shall indeed be bereaved.

Sunday [May] 15th

Went to Church with Rose. Heard some excellent remarks by good Mr. Walker upon the present state of things & our duty under them. Began to write to Raleigh after our return & was interrupted by a shriek from Lizzy, "Mas. Georgey's come!" I knew not what to think but feared something terrible had happened to one of the boys. Ran down & saw George and his Uncle John, sitting in the buggy at the door, a crutch was there too—but George assured his mother & Gusta who had rushed out full of alarm, that he was not hurt, and presently he limped in. He was very slightly wounded in the left thigh, and a worse wound having been prevented, by the Minne ball striking on some five cent pieces which were in his pocket-book, causing it to glance round the surface, instead of reaching a bone. He was Hors de combat, however, and, most fortunately had succeeded in getting home at once. Rose was not so far out, in not crediting George Peterkin's report. His company, 2nd Howitzers, were engaged in the hottest of the fight, and there were many casualties among them. Except George, our boys escaped without a scratch & his wound is a fortunate thing, as his health was suffering from improper diet. We may well feel that we cannot be thankful enough. The Thursday's Battle was the hardest of the war as yet—Our loss very heavy, the enemy's still greater. Genl. Lee shines brighter & brighter, God save him! Have heard firing almost all day on the south side. Heard this morning that we had so far foiled all the enemy's attempts in that quarter, & are likely to defeat them. (*I am copying this in Williamsburg—quite a coincidence.*)

May 16th

Passed quietly here—Whitsuntide—Servants holyday. Gusta wished to go to school but there was no accommodation train. Heard firing all the morning. Spent the morning in my room, doing jobs of work. Gusta did the same down stairs. Rosa wrote to Mrs. Wilmer—George read & slept on the couch in her room, & the house was as still as night. The tranquility was delightful. In the evening, Joe Rennie came to see George, loaded with good news of our successes in every direction. Mr. Gardner returned from town where he had been since last Tuesday. Says people in Richmond are inclined to be triumphant, but he thinks it is our duty to humble ourselves in gratitude to God for his merciful salvation. Mr. Rennie stated that we had beaten the Yankees severely in the neighborhood of Drewry's Bluff along the Petersbg R.R. that we had cut them off from their Gunboats, & that Whiting was driving them from below, Beauregard on this side, & our City forces were on their north or river side. They will probably escape as usual.

May 17th

Mr Linton came over to see George directly after breakfast bringing him *Richmond Examiner* of today, full of cheering news. Beauregard is satisfying the people as he always does. The fight on the south side yesterday was very severe & many of Picketts brave men who had survived the terrible onslaught at Gettysbg. last July, fell during a similar exposure early yesterday morning, but they carried the enemy's position, took their guns & a number of prisoners & drove them a mile & a half beyond their stand. Beauregard only commenced operations yesterday morning, & by seven o'clock this much was achieved. Rose heard this morning that her cousin, Lawrence Young, was badly wounded lying at Seabrook's Warehouse, which is now a receiving Hospital. She is going in to see him. I heard yesterday from Cy, who had seen one of our cousins in the street, that they had a badly wounded soldier at their house. He couldn't remember the name. I think it must be one of the Bartons. Gusta went to school this morning, the trains running regularly again. Except in the terrible destruction of private property, the 15,000 mounted Infantry who came down here from Grant's Army last week, under Sheridan, to cut off all communication between Genl. Lee & Richmond, effected very little. All our trains on both sides of the river, being already in working order. "When the Lord is for us, we have nothing to fear". Rose did not get back from the Hospital until 6 P.M. She found her poor cousin, with his leg amputated above the knee, lying amidst crowds of sufferers in the same or worse condition. Such a scene as she described to us! Such sights, such sounds! She & Mrs. Waldrop whom she took with her, had been busy from the time they got to the Hospital, trying to do what they could for the poor sufferers. Other wounded were being brought in all the time they were there, & the surgeons, with arms bare, were busy doing their dreadful work in the yard of the building.

May 18th

The distressing picture given by Rose, of the condition of our brave men, now more prostrate & helpless than infants, & the urgent need there was of help at the Hospital determined me to go in & lend my mite towards alleviating their suffering. I went on the cars taking a supply of buttermilk, sweetmilk, & some other things, Rose sent by me, & spent the hours from 9:30 A.M. to 3:30, most incessantly and interestingly occupied in attending to as many as were in my reach, making Lawrence Young's cot, my centre & head quarters. All that can be said or sung of brave deeds done, & their consequent sufferings borne with noble heroism, would fail to do justice to our southern heroes. Well may ladies devote themselves to attending their couches, & administering to their poor comfort. Pure highminded, noble men! You deserve all we could do for you if our means were fourfold what they are. I am thankful to be strong enough to help to nurse you, & I pray I may continue so while I can serve you. I nearly fainted while assisting a surgeon to dress a wound today, but I got over it by sitting near an open window when no longer needed. Saw Caroline in town, who told me that her (*word missing*) had telegraphed to her to come at once to him in Danville, & she had hurriedly got ready & gone down to the Depot that morning, but was prevented from going by an accident on the road. I hope now he will not insist on her going yet. Mr. Gardner came out with Gusta & me about 4. Spent the afternoon sewing. George mends slowly—Fanny Young paid us a visit.

May 19th

Was spent as yesterday. Called at my cousin's. Heard that our cousin, Willie Mayo had come home with a wound in the body, that there had been more fighting with Grant who had been easily repulsed yesterday—The wounded continue to arrive by every train. Reports of great success in the West.

May 20th

A beautiful day. Gusta, Mr. Gardner & I started at our usual hour for the R.R. but having heard no train go out, and having heard firing in the direction of Fredsbg. the evening before, we hardly expected to meet the accommodation train, deciding to walk on to Camp Lee, if we did not, and this we had to do. The walk tho' on a R.Road was very pleasant. The air was cool, there was no dust, & the profusion of beautiful wild flowers of various kinds on the sides of the road, delighted us all. We gathered the first wild strawberries we had yet seen ripe. At Camp Lee we sat in the shade of a tree, on the grass, until the little car came out. I had my knitting (for the soldiers) & amused myself with it until the little car came out. Got to the Hospital quite late. Found Rose there who had come in with her brother to see Lawrence Young who is doing very well. He has a man-servant of his own who is devotedly attentive to him. Rose and I nursed generally— Many of the patients have been removed to other Hospitals, and more have not arrived yet.—I came in prepared to stay in town till Monday P.M. Left Rose at the Hospital about 3:30. It is hard to leave. One can always find something to do for some poor sufferer. Am staying with my cousins, Rebecca & Ella Myers. Felt right tired when I got to them, and after dinner lay down all the afternoon. Several Regiments, belonging to Corse's & Komper's brigades were sent to Lee today. Two trains filled with soldiers passed us on the R.R. as we came in, and when we got to town the Capitol Square was filled with those ready to start.

May 21st Saturday

Went to Synagogue. Very few there—Our cousins staid at home to assist in dressing Willie Barton's wound (*Son of my 1st cousin Caroline Barton nee Marx*). I took breakfast with my dear friend Mrs. Hannewinkel. Went to see the Hortons, and called at the Officer's Hospital to enquire after Genl. George Stuart who was so low with wounds received at Rapid Ann last week that he was not expected to live. After Synagogue went down to Seabrook's and staid till dinner time. Few patients left there, one poor man died this morning, after a struggle of three days. The ladies continue to be kind and attentive. After dinner lay down & slept. Caroline and her aunts went out, & Rose Newton (*of Norfolk who is making a long stay with them*) to Church.

May 22nd

Very warm. Went up after breakfast to see about Genl. Stuart. He had died during the night. I saw his remains. I could not have believed that anyone could have changed so. Learned afterwards that this officer was a brother of the Genl's, & I had been misinformed. Genl. George Stuart is supposed to have taken prisoner. His death was reported in one of the papers two weeks ago. Went to see Willie Barton at Uncle Moses Myers's. Wound doing well. He is a fine young man, very pleasing in manners. From there down to the Hospital, where I remained until 2 o'clock. Lawrence Young's father & sister Rose, a young girl, had arrived. His mother had been so overcome by the news of his injury that she was unable to leave home. Rosina & her brother, John Young came soon after I got there, with supplies for him & others. Many worn out & wounded men brought in today. Many ladies came in & brought refreshments which we distributed among all and when these gave out, we went round with ice, water, which many of them took eagerly—Poor fellows! So uncomplaining & brave hearted under circumstances which seem enough to prostrate the strongest. Went to dinner at 2—then undressed & rested till six, when I dressed & took a walk with Caroline & Fanny Halyburton. Troops leaving the Depot on Broad St. with great shouting. Mr. Charles Talcot called to tell Caroline he would take her to Danville on Tuesday. He talked so very despondingly about the state of public affairs that he left a most depressing effect on our spirits, until this resolved itself into a fit of rage with all men who took such views, which restored us to our normal condition of resolution & firm confidence.

May 23rd

At the Hospital till 3.—Many had been removed since yesterday; some to other hospitals, some to their repose. Ladies untiring, men very grateful; say they cannot fight hard enough for such ladies. Many delicacies brought, in spite of the great scarcity & enormous prices. Returned to my cousins to dinner. Caroline finished packing to go to Danville tomorrow. Heard that Lee's Army has fallen back to Hanover Junction. A disappointment & source of anxiety to many, many better capable perhaps, of judging correctly, think this indicates no weakness on our part. Mr. Young called for me about 7 P.M. & brought me home. Hampton's Legion are encamped in his woods. Papers full of the heartless depredations of the Yankees in the lower counties. Sheridan's Cavalry, the same that threatened Richmond in such force, two weeks ago, are destroying everything in the country, leaving families but one meal of food to subsist upon. Our local forces are still in the field guarding Richmond, & the city presents a most peculiar & desolate appearance. Stores and most places of business of all kinds, closed; & the most frequented thorough fares look as they usually do only on a Sunday morning. I found George greatly improved when I got back. He has fattened and is in high spirits.

May 24th

Much disappointed in not being able to visit the Hospital today. At last settled myself to work. A perfectly quiet day. No sounds of War reached us. A soldier who came to ask for milk, told us there was talk of proposals of peace being made by our Government. We all want Grant's Army to be well beaten first. Got a sad note from Mr. Cohen in the evening, written from Camp. He is terribly homesick. Poor fellow!

May 25th

George drove me to the Hospital in the carriage, where I staid all day. A storm came up in the afternoon as I was about to leave & I was detained until near 9 P.M. I did not regret it. Some of our brave cavalry men of Fitzhugh Lee's force, who had made a bold but unsuccessful attempt to disperse those horrid Yankees under Sheridan, in Charles City Co. were brought to the Hospital bout dark. Some sick & worn out, some terribly maimed, all suffering. My heart bled for the noble, uncomplaining, all-enduring heroes. I did all I could for them; gave them water, and bathed their wounds—Constant applications of cold water, is almost the only treatment used in gun-shot wounds. One splendid-looking man with fine features & most excellent countenance, was suffering agony in what was left to him of his bold right arm. It had been shattered by a shell, & in this condition he had walked a mile without assistance. This was on Monday evening—on Tuesday the arm was taken off below the shoulder, & on Wednesday (this) night he reached the Hospital after riding up from Charles City Co. partly on horseback & partly in an ambulance. As I tried to give him some relief by bathing the poor stump & placing it in better position, I said, "This is a bad way of getting a furlough", one of his comrades who had come with him to help him, rejoined, "He has got a discharge now". "Ah!" said the noble sufferer, "the worst of it is, to think of our families." I left the Hospital with Rosa Young & her father, who are staying not far from Mrs. Hannewinkels, where I was going to pass the night. Tea was over when I got there, but Mrs. H. brought me up some supper into the parlour. Though I had eaten nothing since breakfast, but a piece of bread, & had been on my feet all day, I felt neither hungry nor tired.

May 26th

Went to the Hospital after breakfast, calling at Pizzinis on my way to get some ice-cream for a poor fellow who wanted some yesterday. Found my interesting Cavalry man still there, still suffering intensely. I bathed his wound. He had a nervous chill. Succeeded in getting him some liquor, which he had drank & said he knew it would do him good. I rubbed his feet, (he had on a clean pair of nice socks) which were very cold. He complained of a most intolerable itching in the hand he had lost, and tried, involuntarily, to rub the spot where his hand would have been, if he still had it. (Many of the men complain of severe pain or discomfort in the limbs they have lost.) He was transferred to another Hospital in the course of the day, & I have lost sight of him as I am constantly doing of those I am interested in. Lawrence Young remains—well cared for by father, sister, friends & servants. I hope he is improving. Pizzini presented to this Hospital today, 4 gals of frozen lemonade, which the ladies took delight in serving, especially to some wearied men, just brought in from the field. There was enough for each to get a saucer full. "Hurra for Pizzini!". Several men were released from hopeless torture & confinement in the course of these two days. "Death came, to set them free"! Bishop Wilmer says that he believes all who die so nobly in this cause, go straight to Heaven. I wonder if he thinks the Yankees who are killed go straight to the other place. Left the Hospital earlier than yesterday, and on my return to Mrs. H's, called at Uncle Moses's to see Mr. Cohen, who had been relieved from present duty in the field. He was out, but came to Mrs. H's after tea, bringing me the first letters I had got since brother George left us about the third of May. Letters from Raleigh, & one from Mrs. Simpson. (Petersbg.) There have been many deaths among young men from Raleigh, but, thank God!, Tom Devereux is safe, after having run imminent risks as courier to Genl. Grimes, & distinguished himself by his constancy and courage. Walker Anderson was killed by a stray shot. His young widow is said to be an example of faith & resignation. No young couple could have been happier than they were. Mr. Cohen sat with us awhile, and when he left us we went to bed. Mr. Han has been quite ailing for some time, but is patient & pleasant, & I feel perfectly at home with these kind of friends.

May 27th Friday

Called at my Broad St. Cousins on my way to Hospital. Heard there many things which made me uncomfortable—such as every body would have to be sent from Richmond shortly. Guards set nightly to give the authorities time to flee in case of danger &c. Some misunderstanding about the account, but it disturbed me, & I felt dull all the morning. Rose came in about 3 P.M., & brought a good supply of buttermilk, which we served out to some newly arrived men. How the poor fellows did enjoy it!—I came home with her, calling for Gusta who had been at Mr. Chiles's some days. Had a pleasant drive home & find the pure air most delightful after coming from the Hospital. Ate a hearty supper of rice bread, fresh butter and cool bonny clauber, & before going to bed, gave my head a thorough, good cleansing, & took a delightful warm bath, not neglecting my Sabbath Eve services. I trust I am not unmindful of my comforts & privileges of which so many are deprived who are far more deserving than I am.

May 28th

A most beautiful morning, took a sweet little ramble in the woods about Laurel Branch, after breakfast. Got honeysuckle, laurel, lupin & other flowers. Grape vines not quite in bloom yet. How tranquil it was in the wooded pasture, where the cows look as if they would tire themselves with grazing, so uncommonly luxuriant is the growth of grass & clover in the woods around. The negro boys who mind them are happy, careless little beings—as free as Robin Hood's men "under the green wood tree". How much better off will they be in the North? Our ruthless invaders do full as much injury to the poor negroes, as to their owners. Spent the day in quiet, grateful rest. It turned very cool and rained in the afternoon. Ate the first strawberries—a few out of the Garden, & some that Fanny Young sent George, but ladies have brought me some to the Hospital all the week.

May 29th

Another most beautiful day; so cool as to make our wood fires quite acceptable if not necessary. Rose & Gusta went to church. George & I staid at home, he reading & I writing all the morning, a very long letter to Peggy Mordecai in Raleigh, in answer to one from her rec'd yesterday. When Rose came from Church, she told us that Lee's Army is very near Richmond. There has been a Cavalry skirmish at Atlee's Station, about six miles from here. Ewell's wagon train was passing Mr. Stuart's, for hours yesterday, going down on the Meadow-Bridge road. The Battle grounds of 1861 seem to be selected by Grant for his next failure, & Genl. Lee is arranging to meet him in his new position. Hear that much of our artillery is in Atlee's Station, & we may see Willie & John here at any moment. Had an excellent dinner of nice fried chicken, asparagus, boiled onions & rice, with a dessert of cool clauber. After dinner George drove Rose and me in to see Lawrence Young & take buttermilk to the Hospital. I carried my favorite patient, Mr. Horton, of Georgia, a breast of chicken, & a slice of bread & butter. Found him less well than when I left him Friday. He ate part of it, & seemed to relish it, but has little appetite. He has much to contend with. Has lost his left foot, and was severely wounded in the right leg. Poor fellow! so brave & so handsome!—with his white forehead, soft chestnut hair, clear steel blue eyes—strait nose & expressive mouth.

Lawrence Young is not thought to be improving. His surgeon, Dr. Montague (*who afterwards married Rosa Young—Lawrence's sister, with whom he fell in love around her brother's cot*), thinks his condition very discouraging. George saw his wound, & thinks it looks dreadfully. He is said to be the idol of his mother. Several of the men had died since I was there on Friday—all were hopeless cases. Many ladies visited the Hospital this P.M. One brought a large basket of strawberries & dispensed them. The poor invalids enjoy them much. On our way to town we saw several families moving with their servants, cattle, horses, and sheep &c to take refuge within the lines of fortification, as we returned, some were preparing to camp out a common, near the road. Ladies & children seated round a camp-fire, while their carts, wagons and a carriage were drawn up round them, with counterpanes arranged so as to make a sort of tent. Families east of the turnpike, (we are a mile to the west of it) have sent everything they can dispense with, to the City, for safety.

May 30th

Beautiful, cool morning, cars not running yet on Fredsbg. Rd. Gusta went in with her uncle John, to school. I could not get to the Hospital. Took a walk in the woods after breakfast. Sewed all the morning mending clothes. Rose felt poorly & lay down most of the time. A perfectly quiet day. No sounds of War. After dinner read a little & took a long nap. Got up & dressed. Mrs. Young sent a large bowl of strawberries, and in the cool of the evening, walked over with the children. Gusta could not get home from school. Willie came about 8 o'clock from Mechanicsville, having ridden ten miles since sunset. He looks well and hearty, cheerful as ever. Enjoyed his home-supper of biscuits & fresh butter, strawberries & cream—So sorry Gusta wasn't at home. We sat up talking until 11—Willie had leave of absence only for tonight. Says the army is camped as close as locusts, along the whole route he came. Does not know what Grant's intentions are, nor where exactly his army is. He says ours is well fed. A ration each of 1 lb. good bacon; also coffee & molasses.

May 31st

Another beautiful morning—less cool than the two last. Willie saddled his horse & rode off about 9 o'clock. We heard some firing before he went. It increased in sound & frequency after he started, but afterwards decreased. George thinks it was on Lee's lines. Genl. Lee is quite unwell and came down with the army from Spotsylvania in his ambulance! He is now in Richmond doubtless directing all things, while Ewell has command in the field during his absence. About noon we heard heavy and rapid firing. George thought it sounded like a general engagement. This lasted about two hours, and then ceased entirely. A picnic party of boys & girls called by to get some water. Foraging wagons stopped for the same purpose. Several soldiers called to get buttermilk. I sewed all day. Rose wrote to Brother Sam in Raleigh. Gusta came home in the cars about five. Much distressed at missing her brother last night.

Two Cavalry-men called this P.M. One left his horse to be taken care of, as he is going on foot to Louden Co. to get another. His brother fell dead in battle from this one and he values him too much to keep him in danger. His name is Wheatley—from Georgetown. George will have the use of his horse, which, though poor, is a very good one, & will soon fatten here.

Rev. Mr. Walker took supper with us. A kind, good, sensible gentlemen. Gusta had a severe bleeding from the nose, with a recurrence of it which woke her in the night. Stopped it by snuffing pulv. charcoal. Came near having a serious fire before bed-time. A barrel which had been used for treating sick chickens with smoke, was put in the hen-house, & was discovered to be on fire by Cyrus, & was taken out in a light blaze.

June 1st

This month has commenced here with the sound of heavy firing, heard constantly from early morning until this moment (8:30 A.M.) The sound seems to come from the direction of the River. We heard yesterday that Butler had crossed to this, (the north) side. No anxiety is yet felt as to the result. George drove Rose & me in to visit the Hospital. A wheel of the carriage broke just as we reached uncle Moses's, where we stopt to leave some milk for Willie Barton. George had to tinker it up well enough to take it to a shop for repair, while Rose went in, and I went to look for someone to take our things to the Hospital. I met a train of empty ambulances going down to Seabrooks & got one of them to come to our cousins for them. Rose & I got in also and rode down in it. We found so many ambulances full of the wounded, waiting their turn to be taken out, that we went among them, and gave all our milk away before we entered the building. There had been no regular battle, but numbers of our poor fellows have been severely wounded in such engagements as have taken place since Saturday. Found Lawrence better than he was on Saturday. Drs. speak more favourably of his condition. George spent the day at the shop getting the wheel mended. Mr. Cohen came down to Seabrooks to bring me a letter from Caroline. The poor child is in Danville sick in bed with sore throat. (*This proved to be dyptheria—from the effects of which she did not entirely recover for years.*) I am so sorry for it. She enclosed me a letter from Nan Devereux, asking her to seek out Col. Clarke who is at a hospital here, wounded, so I left Rose at Seabrooks, about 3:30, to look for him at the Officer's Hospital, which I did without success. Took dinner at cousin Catherine's, & then went to my other cousins, to wait for Rose to come by for me. Instead of that she went up to the Officers' Hos. for me, & went all over it looking for me, and not until near seven o'clock did she come down to our cousins' for me. All this was very vexatious. The wheels were so crazy that we drove out at a snail's pace expecting to break down every minute. Got home at last. Rose worn out. She and George had eaten nothing since breakfast—I finished off by breaking a valuable gallon bottle as I got out of the carriage. A tedious and unsatisfactory & fatiguing day. Heard of the death of Tucker Randolph, a mother's idol, and a fine, brave officer.

June 2nd

A quiet day until after 5 P.M., when heavy firing was heard, which continued until after dark. Rose busy putting up blankets & other woolens, & hunting up some things sister Ellen had written for from Raleigh. I wrote a long letter to Caroline & did some disagreeable jobs. Gusta could not get to the school today. Got a letter from Lizzie Lee in the evening.

June 3rd

The day dawned to the sound of heavy cannonading. George thinks it is a general engagement, all along the lines. It went on without intermission, with tremendously loud and rapid firing until near noon, & then became more distant & less frequent. George became so impatient to be in the field, that he saddled his horse & rode over in that direction but returned very soon with Willie, whom he met coming home. I felt alarmed when I saw them, thinking something must have happened to John, but, thank God! They are all safe so far. Willie had come with his wagons to Mr. Grant's farm after clover, & came home to stay to night. He tells us the fighting we heard last evening was very severe, & that we gave the Yankees a good whipping. He knows very little more than we do of today's operations. As Gusta could not go to school, she has the happiness of being with her darling brother. Mr. & Mrs. Young walked over in the afternoon & brought good news. Today's fighting had been very successful on our part. We had repulsed the enemy in the one attack after another on every part of our lines, & driven them from their positions, with little loss on our side. We had a dinner today that would have cost at least five dollars in town. Delightful fried chicken, onions boiled & fried; asparagus, cold ham, rice, fresh butter & a dessert of a fine large dish of strawberries & cream. Willie fully enjoyed his home dinner.

June 4th

Beautiful sparkling, bright morning. Willie saddled his horse after breakfast and rode off in his post. George went with him & did not get back until night. Heard a good deal of firing all day. Gusta & I took a long and pleasant walk after the boys went. It did the poor child good for she was tearfully sad at parting with her brother, who is the very idol of her heart. She longed to be a man that she might go camp with them, or one of his wagoners, to be always under his orders. We gathered many beautiful wild flowers, & she dressed the vases with them. When George returned in the evening he told us there had been no engagement during the day, only skirmishing along the lines. Our troops had fallen back to their original lines. He saw John who had been in the battle all day. He was unhurt, & looking as well as he ever saw him. Many soldiers have been passing here for some days, in charge of horses, which have either been wounded, or whose riders have been killed or disabled. They were carrying them to a horse-recruiting camp on the river, above Richmond. It clouded up & rained in the afternoon—so cold a rain that fire was very comfortable by night—Rained steadily all night. Our troops in the trenches, in line of battle, exposed to it all the time. Firing continued to a late hour. George told me that he met a train of ambulances, half a mile long, going for the wounded, & saw many wagons, with wounded men in them going to the City when he went with Willie yesterday.

June 5th Sunday

A wonderfully quiet day. Not a sound of war disturbed the stillness—a steady dripping rain fell all the morning. No one stirred out of the house or about it. Rose, George, Gusta & I spent the morning reading & sleeping—It cleared off in the afternoon & Gusta & I took a sweet walk down by the pond, the mill, & the creek, and to the mineral spring. Everything looked lovely and "the leafy month of June" displayed all the beauties. A beautiful golden sunset closed the day. We heard a few distant reports of heavy cannon while we were out. What can our enemies be about, to occasion this ominous silence in the midst of battle-days? "May God confound their counsels, & destroy their machinations."

June 6th

Another quiet morning—Our army and that of our foes are lying in order of battle not ten miles from us. Gusta went in with her uncle John, to school. Not long after she left, Willie rode up & staid all day. Could give us no army news. Spent the day with us quietly, & the evening at the Stuart's. Gusta failed to get home from school.

June 7th

Mr. Linton sent word this morning that the Accom. train would resume running. Willie was told by Mr. Stuart last evening, that Grant had stealthily withdrawn from our front on Chickahominy, leaving only one Corps, in front of Ewell's. Also that Genl. Jones had been defeated in the Valley, and the Yankees are occupying Staunton. Very distasteful news. Willie went soon after breakfast, not knowing what movements might be made in our army, if this is correct information. I walked over to the R.R. being anxious to get to town to see Miss Deborah Couch, my poor Horton & others. Sat down under a tree and knit for a long time, but no train, accommodating or otherwise, was to seen [sic] or heard, so I came back. Got a note from Moses Norrill, saying he was in trouble on account the impressment of negroes, and could not venture out, for fear of being taken up. I wrote a pass for him, & a note to my cousin, Mr. Gustavus Myers, asking him to get him exempted. George then got the carriage, and drove me to town. The soldier's horse, which he drove, gave me some uneasiness, being unused to harness, & rather skittish. We reached St. Frances de Sales, a Catholic Hospital near Bacon-quarter-branch, where poor Horton, had been taken, in safety. I was grieved to find him not only worse, but as was the case with all the patients in the care of these sisters, looking very much neglected. He lay on a cot, level with an open window, opposite to which was another open window—a damp chilling draught of malarious air, blowing over his wasted, scantily covered frame. I remonstrated with the superior, and pleaded for the window to be closed, that he was under, but in vain. The poor fellow was glad to see me & I remained with him as long as I could, & did what I could for him & others in his room. Poor, poor fellow! Horton told me he was in a bad way—that he had been better off at the Receiving Hospital, and gave me to understand that there was nothing but rigid rules & regulations without any feeling in the management here. He has chills too.

George, meantime, took the old crazy carriage to the shop for more repairs to the wheels. I walked to town from St. Frances de Salles. Went to see my servant Sally, Moses' wife—a poor, faithful, sickly creature, & found her pretty well. Then to Miss Deborah's, who had been suffering from Rheumatism, had a kind welcome from her, & a most ecstatic greeting from our good old friend, Mrs. Gibson, who came in while I was there. I next called to see Mrs. Capt. Sinclair, who has been ill for a month with Erysippelus. She looked dreadfully, painted all over with iodine, but told me she was getting better. Next to my Broad-strt. cousins, where I found Rose Newton in bed with fever, and heard that Caroline had had diphtheria, but got over it. Remained there till George called for me, after getting the wheels mended, & came home in terror, as the horse was very restive. Got home to a late dinner, and found Rose rather poorly. On the whole, a very sickly day. Gusta in town.

June 8th

Very cool morning. Rode in with Mr. Young and stopped at St. Frances Hos. to see my poor Horton. Found things more comfortable then they had seemed yesterday, but Mr. Horton still very ill & feeble. Another friend, Mrs. James Blair also came to see him, & sat with him for some time. The sisters did not like ladies to stay long. Went to town from there. Saw Dr. Hughes & tried to make arrangements for him to visit Horton—Went to see Sally, & made arrangements for Walter to go to St. Frances's every day to attend to one of the men in Mr. Horton's room, who wants a little boy to wait on him. Went to my cousins on Broad St. & was grieved to hear that their house had been entered about day this A.M., locks broken, and a considerable quantity of sugar stolen from the storeroom. Called at my cousins on the 12th, for a moment—Found Willie Barton improving. Got a letter from Brother George—quite a sad one. The two Walter Andersons who a year ago, were happy grooms, have perished in Battle. He says that Brother Sam and sister Ellen have improved in heath & spirits.

June 9th

Spent the day at Westbrook after riding in to see Mr. Horton. Rose had some excellent chicken soup made for him, which I took him—but, poor fellow! he was too low to enjoy it, or to take much notice of anything. My heart is sad & my mind troubled about that interesting young man. He has been neglected. With proper care he would have recovered. God has willed it thus, but we cannot reconcile ourselves to such things as we can to death in battle, or to death after all human efforts have been made. I shall never forget the look of patient, despairing, uncomplaining submission to the inevitable that was the constant expression of his countenance. He had no one to attend to him except at stated periods. No one to keep off the swarming flies, or to answer the many urgent requirements of such a sufferer. Comfortless & perhaps without any one's knowing it, he will die. The sisters do not allow any outsiders to remain with a patient but 15 minutes, so I had to leave him after this short time. I shall probably not find him there when I go again. I have prayed for him—May God pardon and take him to Himself.

June 10th

I had intended visiting the Hospitals to day, but on consulting my Heb. Calendar, I found it was the 1st day of Pentecost, so I remained at home to observe the day as well as I could by reading the services, and reminding myself of my peculiar duties as an Inheritor of law given to us by Him who said "I, the Lord, change not". Blind & foolish are those children of Israel, who persuade themselves that the laws given to them by the Unchanging One, for them & their descendants to observe forever, are not binding on them.

I omitted to mention yesterday that Willie took us by surprise yesterday at Westbrook. He came home & finding we were at his uncle's he dressed himself decently & went over. Rose sent for Gusta who was still in town, & Mary Chiles, with whom she was staying, came out with her to stay until Monday. Willie spent the night at home, & returned to camp after breakfast. A wagon train camped in the woods in front of the house today—the headquarter train of Stuart's, now Hampton's Cavalry. Horses are constantly passing on their way to & from the horse-recruiting camp up the river.

June 11th

The weather continues remarkably cool for this season. There has nothing of remarkable interest occurred today, tho' a very disagreeable affair with the servants has disturbed us much. Rose's little henwife, Georgianna, she had to call upon Sarah, her mother, to assist her with the young chickens—upon which, like all negroes who have not sufficient employment invariably do, complained of being overworked, and gave her mistress so much impudence as could not be allowed to go unpunished, and George threatened her with a proper chastisement if there was any more such conduct. The disaffection extended to Cyrus, her husband, with whom George had recourse to blows. After this things quieted off, & I hope this may be the end of it. Gusta, Mary Chiles, & I were out walking when the most disagreeable part of the affair occurred. I was afraid the worry and fatigue would make Rose sick, for she stirred about a great deal all day & has not been well for some time.

Yellow George was sent to this (Saturday's) afternoon market, with 3 lbs. butter, 2 doz heads cabbage, 1½ peck peas, 1 doz bunches onions, & brought back $110.50 one hundred and ten dollars & fifty cents! Butter has been selling at 24 dollars a lb.—He got only 15 for his. I mention this as one of the features of the times.

June 12th

Another remarkably cool day. Gusta & Mary Chiles walked to Church in time for Sunday school. Rose staid at home, having a headache & also to see the Doctor who had been sent for on account of Georgianna whose fever continued. As the day advanced, Rose's head grew worse & by dark was terrible, giving her spasms. She became easier about 9 o'clock. I slept down in her room, & Gusta & Mary Chiles upstairs. Wrote several letters—to Mrs. Simpson, Caroline, & Mrs. Cohen.

June 13th

Weather positively cold. Rose free from pain but too weak and altogether used up, to leave her bed. John took us by surprise soon after breakfast. Gusta had gone to school when he came. Poor fellow! He was the picture of a dirty Con. soldier, but looked well in point of health. I at first took him for one of our soldiers come to ask for milk, & did not recognize him till he said Howdy Aunt Emma! We rejoice to have him, tho' only for a day and night. He took a good warm bath, dressed himself in some of his home clothes, & looked like another man. He then lay on the good old couch & took a long nap. He brought us news that the Yankees are spreading over the upper country, having possession of Lexington & Staunton, and advancing on Lynchburg. A large part of Ewell's Corps have been sent up to deal with them. Rose had an excellent dinner for John, who did ample justice to it. Gusta got home before we had finished dinner, & was delighted to see her brother.

June 14th

Rosina not well enough to get up, tho' better. Gusta staid at home to be with John, who remained until after dinner. She surprised her brothers by having a bowl of nice frozen custard for dessert, and although the weather was so cold that we had been sitting by a fire all the morning we all greatly enjoyed this rarity. But for the high price of sugar this, in the country, would be a cheap dish. John enjoyed it to our entire satisfaction. After dinner he put on his soldier clothes which had been nicely washed & mended for him, packed his knapsack, & with haversack full of buttered biscuits & fine onions, took leave of us & rode off, George going with him to bring back the horse. After they went over to Westbrook to see Mrs. Dr. Chamberlayne who has been there, sick, since last Friday, and took her some of our frozen custard. I never saw anything like thing the dust. It has been so long since it rained, & every road about the country is so incessantly travelled by army wagons & horses, that the ground is perfectly pulverized. But for this I should have enjoyed the walk, for nothing yet suffers for rain but the roads, and the wild-grape blossoms smelled so sweet, & the wheat fields look so green & luxuriant, & the foliage of the woods so rich & fresh. I had an interesting visit to Mrs. Chamberlayne. Fanny (*Mrs. Young*) too was very agreeable, & lost no time in telling me there was good news from every quarter—that Hampton had entirely routed Sheridan in Spottsylvania taking 500 prisoners & a great number of wagons—that the advance on Lynchburg had been frustrated, and that Grant had gone down the river, the imposing breastworks he has been so busy constructing immediately in our front, having been intended only as a blind to cover their movements. Mrs. Chamberlayne gave me some interesting particulars of the remarkable determination & heroism of one of her nieces in Alabama, a pretty girl of nineteen. Miss Emma Dabney, who went alone from Mobile to her father's Plantation, and successfully bringing away 90 disaffected negroes, who would otherwise have been completely lost to them. They are now settled on a Plantation in Georgia. I had a sweet walk home through the field, & by the creek and mill. The sun was just sinking behind the trees, the partridges were whistling out their cheerful "good night!", & a young hare ran along the path in front of me & disappeared among the bushes. I found, where I knew I should, a quantity of my favorite vine, the Erris Jessamine, full of its little fragrant flowers & brought home a handful of it. It always reminds me of my dear brother, Augustus, who died before Gusta's birth, & for whom she was named. He, it seems to me first discovered it, & I owe to him much of the wood lore that is a source of such enjoyment to me. Gusta & her mother were sitting by a good fire when I got back. George did not get home all night. We fear John may have got into some trouble, as he came home without leave, & his company may have moved while he was here.

June 15th

Went to town with Mr. Young in his buggy, taking a large basket of peas to our cousins. About half way between the toll gate and Bacon quarter branch, one of the wheels broke & we were in a dilemma. After much delay & many suggestions, we got the tire of the wheel tied on strongly enough to allow us to proceed with extreme caution to a blacksmith's shop near the branch, where we left the buggy to be mended. Mr. Clash, who keeps a grocery there, lent Mr. Young a buggy to which were transferred to our horse, our supplies of milk, ice &c for the Hospital, & ourselves, & proceeded joyfully on our way to Seabrooks. The buggy had no top, the dust had no bottom, and the sun was intensely hot. While arrangements were being made to this effect, I went to St. Frances de Salles, nearby, to hear of Horton, & to get some things I had left there. Poor Horton, I learned, had lived until the Monday morning after I last saw him—I had not thought he would live as long. When we got to Seabrooks I found many changes since my last visit, & recognized only a few of the men. There were not many there. Lawrence Young's wound is doing well, but his general health is far from good I fear. Finding little to do there, and plenty of ladies in attendance, I left there in the company of Rosa Young & Dr. Montague, who walked with me as far as my cousins on Broad St. where I paid a short visit. (I had left the peas as we drove down.) Rosa Newton is still quite an invalid, and their friend from Georgia, Mr. Barnsley, who has his home with them, had come in from Camp, sick. Had a pleasant visit, for all that, and then went to my 12th Strt. cousins—all well & cheerful there, thence to the Cars & home again.

George had got back. He and John had camped out the night before, the Army having moved, and they did not find the Artillery camp until the night was far advanced. We hear of many more movements of the enemy. Their real designs not well understood, but they have abandoned the attack on Richmond from this quarter. Got a long, sweet letter from Mr. Cohen today. Mine to him that I wrote on Sunday, was as good an answer to it, as if it had been written after reading his.

June 16th

Morning very cool, but found the sun very hot, walking to take the cars & afterwards about town. Went to Miss Deborah Couch's to make arrangements about visiting Camp Winder. Rode out there with Miss Deborah & Mrs. Ballard. Other ladies went in a Hospital wagon & took many nice things. I went with them through the different wards to assist in serving these out to the men. Everything appeared clean & comfortable, & there were fewer patients than I expected to find. Returned from there about one. Went on Broad Strt. & for 15 dollars 1½ lb of sugar, for 5 dollars 2 lbs rice, for 2 dollars 1 lb of wheat to make coffee of. This may in some future day, be read with amazement. Went to see Mrs. Capt. Sinclair while waiting to go to Camp Winder. She is very much improved since my last visit. Paid a pleasant visit to Mrs. Hannewinkel before the cars left. Mr. H. had been very sick since I saw him last, but he was down stairs. Got home very hot & dusty & tired about 4 o'clock. Used water freely and changed all my clothes before taking dinner.

June 17th

Went in again to visit Camp Winder Hospital. Took a bottle of Buttermilk to Mrs. Capt. Sinclair before going to the rendezvous at Miss. Deborah's. Found her greatly improved, & as sweet & pleasant as ever. Got to Miss D's in full time for the Hospital wagon. Many nice things had been sent there for the lady visitors to take to the patients. Large quantities of bread & butter, at least 2 gals. of rice custard, 2 gals. buttermilk, 4 bottles raspberry vinegar, 2 gals. stewed peaches, & some other things. Mrs. Rogers, a pleasant, kind & cheerful woman, who has something cheering to say to all the men, was the only lady out besides myself. It took us nearly three hours to go round to all the patients in the fifteen wards of the 3rd Division, and to serve each with the refreshments we had for them, and we wasted no time. I just managed to reach the cars in time to get home. Heard that Beauregard had attacked the enemy last night & this morning near Peterbg. and driven them several miles. An old lady in the cars, who lives at Ashland and writes in one of the departments in

Richmond was employing herself enroute, in raveling stocking-tops to double and twist for sewing cotton. She told me she was a refugee from Fredricksbg., that she had been stripped of everything three times by the Yankees, "so", she added, you may suppose that I have to economize in every way. She employs her leisure time in plaiting straw & making hats, which she sells according to quality, from 5 to 15 dollars. She eats no meat, but gets butter at 12 dols. a lb. & uses that as the cheapest substitute. Someone gave her an old cow, which gives about three pints at a milking, and on this & bread she lives. She has three daughters in Columbia S.C.; two in the Treasury Department & one married to an Officer. Her name is Goodwin. I felt much interest in her. When I got home I found a number of men at the well, and incessant applications to Rosina for milk & vegetables, wash-tubs, soap, pens & ink & everything else that can be thought of. The dry weather continues. The dust from so many horses passing to & from water & to look for pasture fills the atmosphere. The very woods are full of dust, & it settles over the garden & fields as if they were public roads.

June 18th Saturday

Still very dry, but cool & pleasant in the shade. Passed a day of rest & quiet. The usual thronging to the house all day, but this disturbed Rose no more than it did me. She is so kind & indulgent to our soldiers that she thinks nothing a trouble that she can do for them, & never refuses them anything if she can possibly spare it. One of them left a poor broken down horse here to be taken care of. He had some bad sores, which Rose & I had well washed and dressed, & she had him well grazed in the garden walks. He had U.S. branded on him, but I have no hatred of the Yankee horses. Not so with their riders. Heard heavy cannonading all day, & men who were on guard say they heard it all last night. George thinks the fighting is the other side of Petersburg. Began to cut wheat today.

June 19th

Very cool morning and somewhat cloudy. Applications for milk & for greens commenced before we were up. Most of the onions were stolen out of the garden last night. Depredations of this kind are of frequent occurrence & are to be expected under the circumstances. Rose did not feel well enough to go to Church. Miss Patsey Storrs came home with Gusta from Church to spend a few days. She is one of my father's old pupils at the Warrenton N.C. school, is a lady of the first quality, and a very agreeable, intelligent excellent woman. Willie came home this morning. His battalion is stationed at Chaffins Bluff & has been attached to the local forces under Genl. Fitz Lee. The dust continues to be excessive. George applied to Lieut. Thorn in charge of the neighboring Camp, for a guard to protect the garden &c from further depredations.

June 21st

Went to town this morning, leaving Rose in bed with headache. The sun was so oppressive that I concluded I would not go in again until I was more needed for fear of getting sick with the prevailing malady, and was glad to get home, & to find Rose relieved. The stream of soldiers to the well continue unabated, & they have drawn off the water until it is quite muddy, & the camp being so near produces swarms of flies which equal the Egyptian plague. After dinner I went up to my room & lay down on the couch and read & rested & slept until past 6 o'clock. Mr. Gardner came out and stayed all night with us. George reported for duty, at the hospital today, and is ordered to return to his command at the end of a week.

June 22nd

Weather still very cool in the morning, & all day except in the sun which is very hot. No sign of rain. The hands finished cutting wheat.

This afternoon the Cavalry Camp broke up, leaving us swarms of flies. Worked industriously repairing clothes all the morning, read in the afternoon. The only news today was from a soldier who told us we were fighting Sheridan at the White House.

June 23rd

A very quiet day. Gusta staid in town with Caroline, & I at home—covering my quilted skirt with an old dress of my sainted mother's—thinking much of her while thus employed, and of the beauty of her character, of which, I fear, I do not inherit one trait. Put on a cool dress in the afternoon, & read "Lady Audley's Secret", an exciting but most improbable story. A soldier who came for milk told us that Genl. Lee had gained a great success over the enemy near Petersbg. last evening, storming their breastworks, taking some guns & many prisoners. George went over and spent the evening at Westbrook. This has been the first warm day of the summer—Drought & dust continue.

June 24th

An intensely warm day. Mrs. Young sent for us all to dine with her, it being her birthday, and her mother, Mrs. Carter Braxton, having sent her a nice fat lamb from Chericoke, her dear old home in King William—a very comforting present to her taken in connection with the recent occupation of that country by Sheridan's merciless & unprincipled Cavalry. They took away a number of her valuable Negroes, her carriage horses, and a great deal of her cured bacon, but for a wonder, did not trouble her stock, nor destroy her growing crops. Miss Braxton's maid went off with them, taking with her all her young mistress's most valuable dresses & many other articles. Another woman took from Mrs. Braxton several handsome white counterpanes & much valuable bed-linen-articles which can hardly be replaced during the blockade, or if so, only at enormous cost. But these losses were as nothing in comparison with those of her less fortunate neighbors, many of whom were despoiled of every servant, & every article of food, & every animal, while perfect destruction laid their plantations waste. Yet these people are said to bear their losses with wonderful cheerfulness. Mrs. Dr. Chamberlayne is still staying at Westbrook, & I find her society exceedingly agreeable, & her conversation cultivated and interesting. The day passed without ennui or effort & was very pleasant in spite of the heat.

June 25th

Still hot & dry. Passed the day quietly & not without satisfaction. Rose went in to see Lawrence Young & altho' she paid him a short visit, she did not get back till past 4 P.M. (*The account of her misadventures is written on one of the leaves of my manuscript which are half destroyed by roaches, but I gather from what is left of it, that the carriage broke down & the horse had to be shed under difficulties—the account continues legible thus.*) She got home very well & in fine spirits—much amused with what would have vexed most women to a degree. Mr. Gardner came home with her & staid all night, & a hot night it was!

June 26th

No abatement of the heat and drought nor signs of rain. The vegetables in the garden are suffering much—nothing can grow & some things perish. Gusta went to Sunday School & her mother & George to Church. I finished "Lady Audley's Secret" which is a very interesting tho' faulty book. Mended a skirt and wrote in my Diary. Wrote two long letters—one to Gratz Cohen & one to Ellen, & nearly melted before I had done.

June 27th

(*This day's history so mutilated that it cannot be restored but in part—It seems to have been intensely hot, with a pest of swarming flies. Mrs. Young sent over ice cream which prudence seems to have prevented the full enjoyment of—*) Welcome clouds gathered in the evening, bringing an abundant rain, which revived the face of nature and the heart of man. Gusta staid in town, fearing to encounter the storm.

June 28th

I was quite indisposed last night & this morning but got up and dressed as usual. It has been the loveliest of June days. The rain last night cooled the air, and everything has looked fresh & lovely—no dust, no flies, no heat. I lay on the couch after breakfast, just enough ailing to have an excuse to be lazy. Mrs. Chamberlayne came over from Westbrook & spent the day with us, and we had a very agreeable day, reading, talking, laughing & knitting. Rose mended up George's great coat and blanket, while he went in to the Examining Board, expecting to be remanded to Camp. He returned home to dinner, with another week's extension of his furlough, his wound not being sufficiently healed. Gusta came home in the cars—had staid all night with Caroline, who is again indisposed & had sent for Dr. Peticolas. Rosa Newton also has a return of the prevailing. I cured myself by diet and homeopathic medicine. Gusta's school has broken up for the three months' vacation.

June 29th

Morning clear & bright & so cool that a fire was very acceptable. Felt quite well & had no symptoms of indisposition. Gusta went to town to take her music-lesson, pay some visits & attend to some other matters, intending to stay all night. We heard firing again this morning—hope Lee has attacked Grant. Do not know when the letters I wrote Sunday can leave the P. Office, all communication with the South being suspended by the injury done to the Weldon & Danville roads by the Yankee raiders, the latter being damaged to the extent of 30 miles. No anxiety seems to be felt with regard to supplying our armies, though I do not know from what source they can be supplied. Grant announces that he has commenced the siege of Richmond. John came home today, having walked all the way from Camp at Chaffins Farm. He stopped to breakfast in town and reached here before 9 o'clock. The boys are much disgusted with their present inactive service, attached to the local forces, for which they feel great contempt, whilst the rest of their Corps (Ewell's now Early's) are far on their way to the Potomac.

 Rose had a good dinner & a blackberry dumpling for Johnny which he enjoyed to her entire satisfaction. John brought us the good news of a victory in Northern Georgia over Sherman, communicated by Genl. J.E. Johnston in a concise & unexcited dispatch. The boys (John & George) went over to Westbrook to spend the evening. Rose & I entertained each other with music—mine instrumental, (piano,) hers vocal & instrumental—performed after she had undressed, & was ready for bed.

June 30th

Beautiful cool morning. Rosina & I took advantage of it to pay some neighborhood visits. George drove us, using the soldier's horse, Barber, which behaved so vilely that we insisted on stopping at Westbrook & sending the carriage back to have the horse changed. (*Here my old ms. is again destroyed by roaches, for some lines, but I can extract some meaning from the words left on the mutilated leaves, which indicate that we found Mr. Mrs. Young both at home, and taking a "late breakfast", with good, "something"—that we proceeded on our expedition after the return of the carriage, our route being across the Turnpike, and through the field of action of May 18th of which* *ample signs remained, trees topped by cannon balls, fences gone & fields wasted—I now resume the copying of my ms.*) Still, the country on the whole, looked less devastated than one would have expected to find it. Our visit to Mrs. Gooch, a few miles west of the turnpike, was very interesting. She gave us many particulars of her experience with the Yankees, her place being in the direct route of Sheridan & in the midst of the fighting ground. They took from her every piece of meat, every fowl, every egg, all her corn & wheat, a great deal of old wine—searched her daughters trunk for jewelry which they took—brought their wounded in & laid them on her well-kept floors, used her mahogany table for amputating purposes—left their wounded & dying men in her house, and took off as many of her negroes as would go with them. She showed us large blood-stains on her floors which she finds it impossible to remove. She told them she was not afraid of any, or of all of them—That she never gloried so much in being a Virginian as she did that day. It would take pages to describe all that she told us. We called next at Brook Hill, Mr. Stuart's sweet lovely place, which had escaped injury, and then home—Willie came in the evening.

July 1st

An exceedingly hot day—unmitigated. Very dry except on the surface of the skin where it was anything else. Willie & George went off soon after breakfast to engage the tithe of the oat crop from all the farmers around. Gusta walked up to Brook Hill to spend the day. Rose & I did great violence to our lazy inclinations, she busying herself a long time in the Garden, & I after practicing for an hour or two on the piano, set hard to work repairing my old hoop skirt, which took me until 6 P.M. Then took a good bath, dressed & read the Sabbath Evening Service. The boys came back after dark—George sun burnt to the color of a Peony. Willie was already done, when they started. Rose sent to the carriage for Gusta. We sat in the porch after supper talking.

July 2nd

Heat & drought continue. We think almost with terror of the situation of the troops in the trenches near Petersbg. Their sufferings must be intolerable. The rumours were confirmed today, that we had captured two thousand prisoners from Wilson's and (*name eaten out of M.S.*) raiding gangs, fourteen pieces of Artillery, many wagons & horses—700 stolen negroes, and had routed the whole force. Wilson's mass chest was among the spoils, full, no doubt of stolen spoons &c. Willie continued his tithing business today. George went to town to attend some matters, and saw Caroline who was well, & Mr. Cohen who was at his office, the City Battalion having been disbanded for the present. Gusta staid at home & plaited straw for her hat. After reading the services for the day, I read aloud to Gusta and her mother. A little rumbling thunder gave promise of rain, but the sun went down, clear and hot.

July 3rd

Morning refreshingly cool, but I felt stupid & sleepy & took a long nap after breakfast. Willie George & Gusta went to Church, Rose kept at home by a threat of headache. Heat not oppressive—a little cloudy—hopes of rain, but it did not. Rosina very unwell all day. She exerts herself beyond her strength and suffers much in consequence. Mr. Cohen walked out in the afternoon and staid all night. Looks well & is in good spirits. Willie told us of having seen a man who lives near Spottsylvania C. House, who had been home lately for a horse. He told Willie that his way lay over part of the Battle-field of May 12th, & that on Wednesday last, 29th June, he saw at least 2000 unburried Yankee bodies lying near the breastworks, & in one spot, evidence of their Ambulance Corps having been routed as he saw the bodies or the mere skeletons of wounded men still laying on the stretchers, just as they had left when their bearers were put to flight! An awful fate!—and such is war.

July 4th

We expected to hear sounds celebrating the day, from the Yankee Gun boats down the river, but the morning, as far as we know has been very quiet. Cloudy & pleasantly cool. I walked to the R. Road with Mr. Cohen & had a good long talk with him while waiting for the cars. Willie returned to Camp this morning. Mr. Cohen told us yesterday that Richmond is full of Refugees from Petersbg., & that wagons loaded with their effects are seen on the streets, on which I exclaimed, "Poor Petersbg & poor Richmond! Fredericksbg, Norfolk, & now Petersbg. taking refuge in Richmond, to say nothing of many exiles from Maryland. I can't think how people are to be fed or lodged." No anxiety is felt about the army. There are supplies to last a month already in the City, & in a short time our communications with the South will be re-opened. Petersbg. is at the mercy of the Yankee guns, & can be destroyed if they choose to do it. Gusta & George took a ride on horseback in the afternoon, which the former enjoyed greatly, not so great a novelty to her brother. They looked very pretty & pleasant as they rode off under the trees. Night very cool—No rain yet.

July 5th

Morning very cool & clear. Rose, Gusta & George went to town. George reported at Hospital but his wound still found to unfit him for service. They did not get home until 4 P.M. I spent the morning practicing, writing, & reading "My Novel", which I find a charming book—Gusta sits a horse remarkably well, and is very fearless. She enjoys nothing more than riding—Willie came while they were gone.

July 6th

Drought continues—George rode off with Willie after breakfast to continue the oat-tithing. Gusta to town in the cars, to take her music lessons. Rose, at my request ordered the carriage and about ten o'clock we went to pay a visit to the Rs. Good people but very coarse—visit exceedingly uninteresting. Got back about 12. Rose made a blackberry dumpling for dinner, by a confederate receipt, which calls only for hot water & flour to make the paste. Sally Chiles came home with Gusta. Waited dinner till they came. Boys got home in time to dine at 4:30. Feel very lazy these days & can hardly force myself to do anything. Sally Chiles plays very well & gave us some pretty music this evening.

July 7th

Went to town & spent the day & night. Paid a good many visits & saw many refugee friends from Petersbg. Most families have left the place. Many are camping out between Petersbg. and Richmond. Saw Mrs. WM. Simpson and Mary. Their parents are staying at a place beyond the range of the enemy's shells a few miles from town. Mr. Simpson's health is wretched. Saw Miss Deborah—busy about Hospital supplies. She showed me a letter from Brother Sam dated 16th June, our latest news from Raleigh—all well. Had a very pleasant day and evening—saw Mr. Cohen for a few minutes. Went to see my cousin, Mrs. Caroline Barton (*nee Marx*), who is staying with our 12th Street cousins. She lives in the Valley of Va. and gives us deplorable accounts of the enemy's proceedings there, where they found a garden and left a desert.

July 8th

Rose early & came out in the 6 o'clock train, leaving all asleep at my Broad Street cousins'. Morning oppressively hot. Drought continues. Breakfast was just ready as I got to Rosewood. Sewed a little on a new dress for Rosina after breakfast. Felt very dull today about everything—especially about public matters. Heard in town that the Hospitals, extensive as they are, are filled up with poor wounded and broken down men, & that their sufferings are great. It is also rumoured that the secret expedition of Early's, Imboden's & Breckenridge's Corps, is for the purpose of liberating our 50,000 prisoners at Pt. Lookout. A very hazardous enterprise. Read to Gusta in "My Novel." Prepared some wheat straw for Sue Doughty, a sweet young friend of mine, who wants it to finish a hat she is plaiting for herself. All the Southern girls make straw hats for themselves, which are very pretty, and many for gentlemen. The Blockade makes us very ingenious and independent. George finished getting out his little crop of wheat today, & had it safely put away. He made thirty six bushels, enough to supply the family with flour, and save seed for next year.

July 9th Saturday

Spent the morning quietly & satisfactorily in my room. George & Willie went off on business. Poor Rose was exceedingly unwell all day, but persevered in working on her dress, which we nearly finished. The boys returned quite late with news that there was a rumour of Yankees being a few miles above here. Did not credit it, but felt some uneasiness. They went off about bed time to ascertain the truth, but heard & saw nothing at Westbrook nor on the turnpike to warrant the report. Today has been pleasantly cool indoors—No rain yet.

July 10th

Morning cool. Day exceedingly warm and sultry. Gusta, Sally Chiles & George started to Church—In half an hour they returned, saying Mr. Walker had dismissed the Congregation on account of the reported raid. Rosina very unwell today & suffering—went to bed and got easier in the course of the day. George rode up the turnpike and satisfied himself that there was no foundation in fact for the alarm about the Yankees. I wrote a long letter to Sister Ellen (in Raleigh) today. Heard of the loss of the Alabama. Sunk off Cherbourg in an engagement with the Kearsage. Most of the officers & crew saved by an English vessel. Our friend Mrs. Sinclair had a son on board. Feel anxious about him.

July 12th

Rosina went in to see the Doctor, having spent a night of suffering, George drove her in lying down in the carriage. Willie went off tithing. Gusta, Sally Chiles & I spent the day very pleasantly in various occupations. Rose returned about 6 P.M bringing John home, who had walked up to town from camp with 24 hours leave of absence. Rose stood her jaunt wonderfully, and seemed in better spirits on her return.

July 13th

All three of the boys at home together! Rose had a very comfortable day by lying still on the couch all day. Willie went off after breakfast as usual. We had blackberry dumpling for dinner, made without butter, fat or sugar, except in the sauce. A real blockade invention & remarkably good. John enjoyed his dinner vastly, and had to start off soon afterwards. Gusta loses no opportunity of petting her brothers when at home. I should have mentioned that we had a thunder shower last evening—A very moderate rain but thankfully received. It rained again this evening. Heavy rains below us—light here.

July 14

Gusta & Sally Chiles went to town for their music lessons. George went to report for service, but his surgeon gives him another week at home, his wound though healed over being still tender. Willie away all day, tithing oats. Rose & I had a quiet day at home; she in bed but much easier than yesterday. I sewed & read & knit and saw to matters generally. Got newspapers in the evening—Our forces in Maryland seem at least to be giving the Yankees a terrible scare. Mr. Young called to see Rose in the evening.

July 15th

Rose suffering—sent for Dr. Beale who was too busy in town to come out. Fanny Young came over & sat with us the greater part of the morning. George went with Willie, tithing oats—came home to dinner. Gusta plaited straw, I sewed. John Waldrop, who has a weakness for Gusta, came out after dinner. As we were all standing in the porch after our early supper, it being still quite light, George saw a partridge running along in the upper part of the yard. Willie whistled to it with such a perfect imitation of his note, that the shy bird was decoyed quite up to where we were all standing, very still, watching it—then flew up & perched on top of the well-house close by, where it sat for at least ten minutes whistling its clear bold notes.

July 16th

Weather dry & clear. Willie off tithing. Got home just as we were done dinner, for which I had made a blkberry dumpling, which turned out to be very good. Sent for the Dr. again, & again in vain. Mrs. Waldrop came out in the carriage & staid all night—Splendid news today from our army in Maryland. It seems incredible that we should have so completely turned the tables on the Yankees as for us to be storming Washington, instead of their storming Richmond. Such wonderful news makes us rejoice with trembling. Willie & Gusta went to Brook Hill on horseback & spent the evening. I am so anxious to get tidings of my nephew William Mordecai who is with the Alabama troops near Petersbg., & who will never write, that I not only wrote him a letter today, but wrote and enclosed an answer to it—stamped & directed to myself. (*He got the letter and kept the answer without writing another—saying it was too clever to part with!*)

July 17th Saturday

George rode in before breakfast & got the morning papers which confirm the good news of yesterday. Still Let not him that putteth on his armour, boost himself as he that taketh it off. Early is not yet safely over this campaign. It is a known fact that Genl. Lee has withdrawn from Petersbg. but no one knows whether he has gone to Georgia or to Maryland, whether alone or with a corps of the army. No doctor again today though Rose is still wanting him. Mrs. Waldrop went home, her son still here. Weather very cool and clear. Felt too much excited about army news today, to be able to read my prayers with satisfaction.

July 18th

Dry cool and clear this morning. Mr. Gardner called after breakfast, had no news. Rose still ailing but better. George John Waldrop & Gusta went to Church in the carriage, Willie on horseback. Some neighbours called in the afternoon Mr. Johnson, Mrs. Redd & Miss Betty Redd. Heard that Early had retired from before Washington. Some people are much disappointed and discouraged at this, & blame our Generals for not being sufficiently rapid in their movements, which I take to be unjust, unreasonable, and presumptuous.

July 19

An August fog this morning ushered in a beautiful day. Willie returned to Camp today. The boys much outraged at being put into Cuttshaw's battalion, as it has not attained any peculiar distinction. John Waldrop went home this morning. Gusta read French & English, plaited straw & practiced. I read and worked. Mrs. Taylor, a near neighbour came to see Rose this evening—Told us of a report that Grant was killed. George went to Dr. Ferrils & spent the evening— Heard the report confirmed. Also heard that Genl. Johnson had been relieved from command in Georgia.

July 20th

Cloudy morning. Went to town in cars & got there in such a hard rain that I got quite wet in walking from the Depot on 8th St. to my cousins' on Broad below 12th. Found everybody at home and glad to see me. Undressed & dried my wet clothing. Had a mighty pleasant day, & we all gloried in the rain & were thankful for it—As I could not go out I staid.

July 21th

Cloudy morning. Went out after breakfast to see my maid Sally, who has been sick & is still poorly. Sat some time with her. Got 11 yds of blk. & white Alpaca which Rose asked me to get for a dress for her, & paid $110.00 for it. For twelve yds. of thinner material for myself I paid $120.00. Bought 2 lbs. common brown sugar for 22.00, & an ounce or so of black tea for 4 dollars. Went to Mrs. Hannewinkel's—all out. Called at my cousins' on 12 Street—They were all at home, but look very badly—so fallen away. The times tell upon them more than upon any whom I see though they bear their privations & difficulties with admirable cheerfulness. Sat some time with them, & returned to my other cousins where I staid until three o'clock, when Caroline came out with me in the cars. Found Willie & John at home—George had gone to report again at the Hospital. Dinner was over, but they had put a nice one away for us, with dessert of blkberry dumpling. Caroline played for the boys—we had a pleasant afternoon, & went to bed soon after our early supper. Caroline & I talked until past ten, & then went to sleep. It is delightful for me to have the dear child with me Thursday. We rose quite early as breakfast was to be earlier even than usual for John to get back to Camp in time. George drove him in a borrowed vehicle. Caroline & I then took a delightful walk down to the Rocks, the mill & the creek. Gathered some sweet orice jessamin. Caroline & Gusta spent the rest of the morning practicing, reading French & English plaiting straw & eating lunch. I busied myself getting out garden seed & putting them up. Caroline helped me put up two doz. paper bags for sale. After dinner I lay down and read, & Caroline slept for two hours. Mrs. Young came over late in the afternoon—told us there was a report of a victory over Sherman in Georgia. Willie came to dinner—George later.

July 22nd

We breakfasted soon after 6, & Willie went off directly after. Beautiful cool, clear, misty morning. Caroline and I walked down below the mill, where I read my Bible and knit, while she sketched a rustic bridge over the creek. Weather perfect—had a pleasant walk. When we returned I attended to things generally & put up garden seed. Rosina had a good night & felt pretty well today.

July 23rd Saturday

Another very cool day. Gusta went to town in the cars. Caroline Willie & I sat in Rose's room talking very pleasantly, till it was time for Willie to go. George drove to town for Mrs. Waldrop & Dr. Beale, who of course did not come. Caroline, Gusta, George & I spent the evening at Westbrook—very easy & pleasant as is always the case there. Supper especially good. Got home about 11. Heard today of a decided success in Georgia. Battle still progressing.

July 24th

Dr. Beale came out in cars before breakfast! Found Rosina much better than he expected. Staid about two hours & returned in the carriage. Caroline & I took a long walk after he went. Weather dull. Neither cloudy nor clear, no light and no shade. Very cool and not damp. Strange weather for this season. Willie and George went to Church, Gusta staid at home. Had a good rain lasting all night.

July 25th

Cold enough for fire this morning & indeed nearly all day. Worked at putting up garden seed. Caroline & Gusta employed & amused themselves as usual. Mrs. Waldrop went home after dinner—Rosina tolerable.

July 26th

Caroline & Gusta went to town to attend Lilly Moore's wedding—will stay all night. I put up garden-seed, George helping me. Had an untroubled day. No news of interest.

July 27th

Cool pleasant morning. Caroline & Gusta returned from town in fine spirits, having enjoyed their visit. Saw Mr. Collins from Raleigh. Got a letter from Nan Devereux. Little John had been very sick with typhoid fever, but was getting well when Nan wrote. The Yankees are coming over to the north side of the River in heavy force. News of a victory in the valley, by Early over Hunter, Crook &c. Willie got home to dinner. Rosina had a very uncomfortable day.

July 28th

Very warm—Cloudy but no rain. Spent the greater part of the morning in the Garden, gathering parsnip seed. Rose still confined to the bed but more comfortable. George went to report at the Hospital & when he returned brought letters from Raleigh—The latest dated 13th July—all well. Sister Ellen wrote three of them—one to Rose, one to Caroline, & one to me. She seems very well satisfied. Caroline & Gusta read & sewed & plaited straw and practiced all the morning. Caroline after an afternoon nap, dressed & took a ride with George.

July 29th

A fine summer day, with a fine breeze blowing. Little to record—George got stung by a hornet—Caroline and Gusta spent the morning as usual. I read "Lucille" that beautiful poem to Rosina, & wrote to sister Ellen. Willie out foraging—Gusta & George took a ride in the afternoon.

July 30th Saturday

An intensely warm day. Willie left us for Camp this morning—may return on sick-leave, as he has all the summer been suffering with an ulcer on each leg, just about the ankle on the shin seeming to affect the bone. It gets no better & cannot, the Drs. say, unless he keeps still. Caroline & I spent the day as usual, reading. George spent the evening at the Stuart's. Heard disastrous news from Petersbg.—The enemy sprung a mine & blew up Pegram's Battery. 21 men missing—Also set fire to several houses in the town.

July 31st

Dr. Beale came out in the cars to breakfast. Performed a slight but very painful operation on Rosina. She was very nervous both before & after it, but suffered less than she had anticipated after it was over. I spent the morning in her room, attending to her & reading to her. It has been an intensely hot day. How do our poor soldiers stand it!—Mr. & Mrs. Young walked over in the afternoon, & brought news that our disaster near Petersbg. had been turned into a great triumph. After springing their toilsome mine, & blowing up Pegram's Battery, they rushed into the breach in great numbers, & at first with some success; the negro troops in front, with the cry "No quarter to the rebels!" After a varying contest, they were finally overpowered in the trenches; hundreds & hundreds slain & 800 taken prisoners, including a General & all his staff. Many stands of colours taken & Pegram's Battery recovered. Thank God for this!—Mr. Cohen took us all by surprise about sunset, having returned from his mission to the South sooner than he expected. He is well & in good spirits. Saw all the family in Raleigh. Brought many letters & excellent accounts of everybody. Staid at Ellen's the two days and a half he spent in Raleigh. He staid all night and walked in the morning before breakfast.

August 1st

Monday morning. Intensely warm weather continues. Spent the morning attending things generally. Caroline read & sewed—Gusta plaited straw. Rose suffered little pain & was as comfortable as the heat & flies would allow. We had frozen stewed apples & milk for dessert. Caroline & George took a pleasant ride in the afternoon.

August 2nd

Intensely warm day. Willie came home on business; looks better than when he went away. While we were all at supper in the back porch, who should come striding up with his long legs; but John. All the boys at home together for the second time this summer. John is off duty on account of a painful boil on the elbow. Caroline, Gusta, Willie & George spent the evening at Westbrook. John & I sat in his mother's room, the usual sitting room & talked until bed-time—Rose seems to be improving fast.

August 3rd

Caroline returned to town to-day. Gusta went in with her to take her music lesson & take her thirty yds of straw-plaiting to have her hat made. We continue to get good news from our army in every direction. Had an excellent dinner for the boys today & frozen custard for dessert. They all did full justice to it, especially John, who has been less at home than the others. Spent the evening pleasantly in the front porch, talking with Willie, John and Gusta. George went to Brook Hill to pay a farewell visit.

August 4th

All the boys left home, this beautiful, warm day. George's wound being perfectly healed he returned to Camp with John. Mr. Young came over to tell us that two of his negro boys, small chaps, had run away. Cyrus was all day hunting for them, one being his son, little Cy. He found them in the neighborhood—Rose felt very sad at giving George up, but bore it well, as usual.

August 5th

Beautiful day—Gathered peaches with Mary's & Georgianna's assistance. Very abundant, but very imperfect. Spent the morning thus, & in many household matters, & in sewing. Willie came home for dinner. Rose very comfortable, except for the flies & hornets which are very troublesome. One of the latter stung me on the head severely this afternoon, but a little hartshorn soon relieved the pain. No news & no paper today.

August 6th Saturday

Very Warm. Passed the day for the most part in my room, very satisfactorily. When Willie got home at night, he told us there was a rumour which he feared was true, that Mobile had been taken by the Yankees. News from other quarters pretty good. Rose got a letter from Marx & Julia. The former has established himself at Greensville So. Carolina, at present.

August 7th

Intensely warm—Gusta & Willie went to Church. Heard that Mobile had not been taken, but that three of our unfortunate Gun-boats had been taken or sunk by the Yankee Fleet. Heard, too, that several Corps of our Army were moving from Petersbg. to join Early.

August 8th

The first thing heard this morning was the arrival of George & John, before we were up. Their Battallion has been ordered to the Valley, & they came home on their way to Culpepper C.H.—They had been up nearly all night—marching & riding. They were tired but in good spirits, and are pleased with the change. They are riding as their guns are sent by R. Road, & they have to take up the horses. Willie's legs are still so bad, that he has got the Surgeon's certificate of his unfitness to follow the Army at present, & he will remain at home until they are well. They boys staid till after dinner, which was excellent & which they did justice to, as usual. Johnny said his conscience was clear, for he had come home as often as he could, and staid as long as he could and had eaten as much as he could since he had been near Richmond. After dinner they packed up their horses, took leave & rode off, their haversacks filled with nice biscuit, bread and hard-boiled eggs, & a bag of fruit & onions, the soldiers delight, on a led horse they had to take along. Wrote to Brother Sam in the afternoon, and got a letter from brother George, saying he would be here one day this week. He tells me Annie Devereux has typhoid fever.

August 9th

Pleasant morning hot day—Drought continues though we have promising clouds daily. Gusta finished a pretty straw fan today. Willie made the handle & put it on. Rose not so well today.

August 10th

Did not forget that this was my beloved, prized & lamented sister Eliza's birthday. An intensely warm day. Gusta went in to her music lesson, Willie rode in to the quartermaster's & to get his medicine. I gathered fruit & vegetables—knit, fought the flies & hornets, & panted with the heat until dinner. Brother George came out in the cars with Gusta after dinner. We did not expect him so soon—He looks pretty well. Brought very cheerful letters from sister Ellen. Annie Devereux is quite sick with the fever, but was something better, perhaps, when he left home. Ned Myers came to Richmond with him from Danville, where his headquarters have been for some time. Rose had much company later in the afternoon. Mrs. Dr. Terrill, Miss Redd, and another young lady, & after them, Mrs. Young & the children. All left after sunset, when we had supper, & Brother George, Willie, Gusta & I sat in the front porch talking pleasantly till 10 o'clock.

August 11th Thursday

Went to town with brother George who returned home in the 4 o'clock train, so we saw little of him. I staid with my Broad St. cousins until Sunday morning. The weather was intensely warm all the time, but I enjoyed my visit very much & went to see many of our friends in the heat of the morning, & the heat of the evening, for there was no <u>cool</u> to either. We had a great many hearty laughs, and any quantity of foolishness, the "we" meaning Rebecca & Ella, Caroline & me. Wrote to sister Ellen by Brother George.

August 14th Sunday

Came out in the cars at 6 A.M. with Mr. Gardner whom I met at the Depot coming out. The jaunt was pleasanter than I expected, a friendly cloud protecting us from the sun, until we nearly reached the house. Rose who was better, but still in bed, had a good deal to tell me about a Cavalry Camp that had been formed in the woods near here, and, as usual, had been quite troublesome. They went off this morning. Troops are all pouring towards the Valley & Grant is withdrawing from Petersbg.—There was a good rain out here Friday—very little in town. Some showers today.

August 15th

Cloudy morning—still very warm. Cut out my new dress for which I gave $120 a few weeks ago, Gusta, Rose & I sewed nearly all the morning, tho' R. is still in bed. Gusta & Willie started to spend the evening at Brook Hill—but a thunder cloud turned them back—It didn't rain after all.

August 16th

Gusta walked to Brook Hill to breakfast, & from there went to town with the children, & got home to dinner Mrs. Young & her sisters Mrs. Dallam of Balt., & Miss Braxton of Cherikoke, King William Co., called in the afternoon. Willie, Gusta & I went over after tea, by the light of the moon, & spent the evening with them at Westbrook.

August 17th

Gusta went in for her music lesson—Willie spent the morning at the Stuarts'. News, today, of a fight yesterday 12 miles below Richmond, between several corps of the enemy and a small force of ours, in which were successfully repulsed. Gusta brought me a note from Caroline. Local forces including Mr. Cohen called out & gone down to meet the enemy on this side the river—(*North side.*) Rose had an uncomfortable day, but busied herself sewing in bed & shelling peas.

August 18th

The drought continues said to be the greatest for 19 years. I went up & gathered a good many nice peaches this A.M. Surprised that they haven't been stolen. Deborah, who is working for Rose, with the assistance of the latter, has succeeded in making two nice dresses for Gusta, out of a handsome dressing gown of poor sister Caroline's—A great deal of heavy firing heard today.

August 19th

Went to town to do some shopping. Got a letter from Brother Sam. Annie Devereux is convalescing though still very sick. Brother Lot's family are expected in Raleigh, refugees from Mobile. Ellen is preparing to receive them. After shopping paid some visits & then went to my cousins' to stay until the 3:30 train time came. Had much to tell & to hear. Came home in hard rain, & got ridiculously wet between the R. Road & the house. Rose called for a tub for me to drip in as I came into the house. Willie sat on the porch & laughed at me, & I laughed so I could hardly get along. Came up to my room & changed & dried thoroughly. Then eat my dinner, talked & worked the rest of the afternoon. Willie went to spend the evening at Brook Hill & it rained so that he had to stay all night. So the great drought is at last over, on this Friday, 19th Aug. 1864 which we may call a Good Friday.

August 20th Saturday

Heard of a successful engagement with the enemy, yesterday, near Petersbg. Besides killed & wounded we took upwards of 2000 prisoners. Genl. Lee's head-quarters have been moved the north side. Several engagements have taken place in the course of the week on this side of the River, with advantages on our side. Encouraging news also from Atlanta. Spent the morning quietly & satisfactorily in my room, while the others worked down stairs. I read to them in the afternoon. It rained all the morning—Willie says the effects of this blessed rain are already visible.

August 21st

Damp & cloudy. I spent the morning in my room mending clothes. Took a nap after dinner, and then went with Gusta to see Mrs. Taylor, who not being at home, we went over to Westbrook, where we paid a pleasant visit. Mrs. Braxton was sick in bed but we saw her—also her son Dr. Braxton, a great wag, two Mr. Dallam's, & Mr. George Small from Balt. & Lucy Braxton. The latter with two of the young gentlemen, walked back with us.

August 22nd

A sweet, hazy August morning. Gusta dressed herself in snow-white cambrick & her pretty hat which she plaited the straw for & trimmed herself, & the nice straw fan which she also made, & walked up to Mr. Stewart's directly after breakfast to go with the girls to a picnic at their Grandfathers, (*Mr. Williamson*) given to Bell Stuart on the occasion of her 17th Birthday. I went with little black Mary to look for ripe Elder berries to make blacking & ink of. Went over to my dear old home, Spring farm—Nothing left to look as it formerly did, but the drive up the lane—All passed away like the times & the people I once knew there—I thought of the past and the departed.

Willie returned from the Picnic after dark—had a fine dinner and a superabundance of it. Mr. Williamson was one of the greatest sufferers from the Yankees last May. So we rise—

August 23rd

Helped Rose with her sewing. Willie at home. Reading—unfavourable news from the Army at Petersbg. Fine weather. A letter from John— they were camped on the Shenandoah river, not far from Winchester after a terribly fatiguing march from Culpepper, in which the horses suffered terribly. Letter dated 15th.

August 24th

A most beautiful, Fall-like morning. Gusta went in to her music lesson. I gathered fruit after breakfast & then sewed hard all day on a dress for Rosina. Finished reading a beautiful little French Play, by Scribe, "Clermont". Wish I could read it to my poor blind brother Sol in Mobile. Gusta brought me the sad news of the death of Isaac Levy, a fine young soldier, killed in the trenches near Petersbg. He & his brother Ezekiel Levy, have observed their religion faithfully, ever since they have been in the army, never even eating forbidden food. He leaves a devoted father & mother brothers & sisters to mourn his loss. Rose got a letter from George written before John's, received yesterday. He gives a distressing picture of the country they had marched through. Houses, trees, fences all gone—as if a fire had swept through the country—nothing left but the bare surface of the earth, grown up in weeds & parched with drought. The very beds of the watercourses dry.

August 25th

Another beautiful morning. We expected Ella & Caroline out in the early train to breakfast, but the cars went on without stopping. We cannot account for their not coming. Gusta & I walked over to Westbrook in the afternoon, where we were treated to frozen peaches—and—cream. Willie went to town for Mrs. Stockdale—a relative of Rosina's, who came from Peterbg. to stay some time with her. A thunder cloud rose about nightfall, & we got uneasy before the carriage returned, the night being dark as pitch, the carriage rather unsafe, and the horse very old & weak. By the aid of the lightening they got here safely by nine o'clock, having been from 6.30 performing the journey from the Petersbg. depot—distance about 5 miles. Mrs. Stockdale, refugee as she is, is surprisingly cheerful, & says all the people in the besieged little City are so. They bear their privations & discomforts almost jestingly, and the gasworks being destroyed by the shells, and candles three dollars a piece, most persons do without light, & sit in their parlors, & entertain friends in darkness.

August 26th

Sat in my room working—Mrs. Young & Mrs. Dallam called in the afternoon. Gusta went with Willie to Brook Hill—he to spend the evening, she the night—no news.

August 27th Saturday

Mrs. Stuart came bringing Gusta home, while we were at dinner. Told us of a victory near Petersbg, yesterday, in which three N.C. Brigades of A. P. Hill's Corps. took a whole line of the enemy's works on the Weldon R. Road, killed & wounded a great many & captured 2000 prisoners & 9 pieces of artillery a success unlooked for at this point, having heard that the enemy's works there, were esteemed impregnable.

August 28th

Most beautiful and delightful day. Mrs. Stockdale & Rosina poorly. Gusta & Willie at church. I spent the day reading & writing and visiting the peach trees, which have been robbed of nearly all their fruit. Some of them entirely stripped. Wrote a long letter to my dear young friend, Gratz Cohen, and a note to Mrs. Rennie, asking her to deduct at least one half her charge for knitting three pair of little socks for one of Mrs. Hannewinkel's children, for which she asks 10 dollars a pair! Willie was quite indignant & disgusted at her shamefully exorbitant charge—a person too, not in need. These are times that try men's souls, & prove that some women have none.

August 29th

Beautiful morning—very cool. I spent the morning repairing clothes, & putting together an old barege dress, which I had had washed last week, & which looks very imposing. In the afternoon went with Gusta to pay a visit to Mrs. Johnstone formerly Miss Linton, who lives at the sweet old homestead where she has lived all her life, & which is so quiet & peaceful, that she says she forgets sometimes that the war is going on. We got some peaches and pears. A letter from Brother Sam this evening—Written in good spirit—Annie is nearly well, he tells us.

August 30th

Went to town this <u>very</u> cool & beautiful morning, in the cars. Took in a basket of tomatoes to my 12th St cousins, & apples, pears & peaches to the Broad St. ones. All glad to see me and had a great deal to tell me. Mobile William Mordecai was wounded in the arm a week ago, & had been at Howard Grove Hospital—had been to see Caroline—had got my letter and enjoyed it greatly. Was going to Raleigh, & thence home. I wish very much I could have seen him. Earlier in the war he had been wounded seriously in the shoulder at one of the battles around Richmond, & had been nursed by his Aunt Ellen at our home on 6th street near Lee, assisted by his body servant who had come from Mobile with him & had followed him faithfully as so many negroes did their young masters. I had a delightful visit to town, saw some of my old friends, & made some new acquaintances. Went to see Mrs. Levy whose son Isaac was killed near Petersbg. on Sunday 21st. Was greatly interested in my visit to the family. Isaac was an example to all young men of any faith—to those of his own most especially. A true Israelite without guile—a soldier of the Lord & a soldier of the South—a noble patriot. His parents & sisters mourn for him as those mourn who while full of love, are also full of Faith and Hope and Submission. If all our people were like that family, we would already arise & shine for our light, would have come. Returned home on

August 31st

Learned that Dr. Beale had been out the evening before and performed another operation on poor Rose. She told me she bore it much better than she had the last—thinks he will have to repeat it, perhaps more than once. She seemed to feel pretty well, & was very cheerful. Mrs. Stockdell & I walked over to Westbrook in the afternoon—most beautiful evening and a very pleasant visit. Mrs. Braxton still sick. Family invited us to dinner the next day.

September 1st

Spent the morning, till two o'clock altering a dress. Then Mrs. S & I dressed & walked over to Westbrook. We took our work, and sat in the parlor with Fanny until dinner at five. An excellent dinner to which we did justice. Mrs. Braxton worse today—All seem uneasy about her—& large family over there now. We came away about dusk leaving a new arrival, Mr. Harrison Tomelin. I got a short letter from Gratz Cohen—very sweet—begs me to pay them a visit in Savannah next winter. Perhaps I may—

September 2nd

Another refulgent morning with its intense blue sky & all the delightful features of this delicious season. I busied about considerably after breakfast, & worked on my dress which is never to be finished. The Stewart children called for Gusta soon after breakfast to go with them to spend the day at their Grandfather's— Rosina sat up in bed & sewed all day. Gusta staid all night at Brook Hill. We had peach dumpling for dessert today with creamed butter & sugar sauce.

September 3rd Saturday

Weather cool & pleasant. Staid in my room & read all the morning. Went over in the afternoon to see Mrs. Braxton, who was rather better. Augusta returned with Willie from Brook Hill where he had spent the evening, about 11 o'clock—There is a rumor that Atlanta has fallen—some bad news seems to have been received & suppressed by the War Department.

Sept. 4th

Cool, cloudy morning. Mr. Young called after breakfast in trouble about his hogs, which had got into Mr. Johnson's corn, and were taken up—Willie went over with him to see about it, got the matter adjusted and returned in time for church. The day passed without disturbance—I sat in my room & read & wrote several notes. Mrs. Stockdell & Gusta went to church—Rev. Mr. Walker called in the afternoon and had prayers. Rosina well enough to write to George.

Sept. 5th

Very warm day—Mrs. Stockdell & I walked to the R.R. after breakfast & I gathered my first bouquet of Fall flowers. Miss Morrison who is staying at Brook Hill rode over on horseback to ask Gusta to go with her to Drury's Bluff tomorrow. I spent the day mending shoes, reading & sewing. Rose sat up nearly all day & at the front door with us after supper. Willie, Gusta & I talked pleasantly in the front porch—had a thunder cloud & a cooling rain about bedtime. Something got into one of the chicken coops, killed 8 young chickens and injured the hen.

Sept. 6th

Cool, damp, cloudy weather. Gusta went to town to keep her engagement with Miss Morrison. It turned out a drizzling, snug, August-storm sort of day—reminding me of past times and persons.

Sept. 7th

A splendid fall morning. Willie got a letter from John, written in camp near Winchester, giving cheering accounts of the army. Both John & George are in perfect health, and feasting upon apples, of which he says there is such an abundance of the finest he ever saw, that Lee's army might be supplied with them. Fanny Young came over about noon and staid until dinner time—told some amusing anecdotes. Gusta returned disappointed of her trip to Drury's Bluff—boat not running. Got a note from Caroline in the evening—Bad news from Georgia.

Sept 8th

Another splendid day—almost cold—Rose had a fire in her room—I slept badly last night disturbed in mind. Cannot help feeling sometimes, that I am not living at a home of my own, & think of seeking an independent position. Finished today, a dress I began six weeks ago. Quite successful at last. Better news from Georgia.

Sept 9th Saturday

Cold, cloudy, wettish morning. Rosina in bed all day with a bad headache. Beautiful afternoon—Gusta & I dressed and went to pay a visit to Mrs. Ballard—Had a delightful walk, and a very pleasant visit. The place is very handsomely improved.

Sept. 10th Saturday

Spent the day in my room—not without satisfaction. Rosina better but Mrs Stockdell not well—Had fever when she went to bed.

Sept. 11th

Beautiful, clear, mild morning. Gusta & Willie walked to Sunday school—I took a walk in the woods & gathered some bright Fall flowers. Spent the rest of the morning in reading a MS. of long past experiences. Very, very interesting. A thunderstorm came up before dinner time, & Gusta & Willie stopped at Westbrook until it was over. Got home just as I was sitting down to dinner alone. Wrote to Brother Sam afterwards. Mr. Young came over and Mr. Gardner who staid all night. Mrs. Stockdell quite unwell—had a chill last night.

Sept. 12th

Cold weather for the season. A good fire in Rosina's room. Dr. Terryl came to see Mrs. Stockdell, who had fever all day. Uncomfortable news from various quarters. Everybody wishes that Johnston was reinstated in command of the Army of Tenn. It is rumored that Petersbg. is to be evacuated. Gusta rode over to Mrs. Redd's this afternoon, on horseback, with little blk. Fleming for her groom. I slept little last night—but 3 hours.

Sept. 13th

Beautiful morning, very cold—Willie, Gusta & I took a pleasant walk over to Mr. Saunders' to see them crushing Sorghum and making syrup of the juice by boiling in huge kettles. This is our substitute (and a very poor one) for molasses, & with some, for sugar. Staid there some time, watching the proceedings—The ladies from Westbrook came and made themselves very agreeable, soon after we got back. Gusta trimmed my old bonnet for me & made it look very nice. The news from the armies does not improve, & we went to bed feeling much disheartened about the state of the country.

Sept. 14th

Very cool cloudy morning. Willie went to town to deliver the tithe of the wheat crop, & to exchange five bushels of wheat for a bbl. of flour. Gusta went in to take her music lesson. She bought a pr. of corsets for her mother for 45 dollars.

Sept. 15th

I went to town with my kind friend, Mr. Young and spent two days very pleasantly at my Broad St. cousins' where they are always glad to see me. Saw some of my friends and attended to various little matters. Heard a good deal of discouraging matter with regard to public affairs. Two of our blockade runners have been taken by the enemy's vessels. Wilmington, our only sea-port is threatened, and stirring times are expected around Richmond. The local forces were all called out while I was in town, & orders were issued to enroll a large class of men who have hitherto been exempted from military service. Prices of all kinds of produce or manufacture have advanced. Green tea is sold at 75 dollars a lb. Still, people are undismayed, & I trust in God, and am hopeful and cheerful.

Sept. 16th

Returned from town late in the afternoon. Found Rose busy superintending the preserving of a quantity of peaches, which Mr. Gardner had sent out along with the sugar for doing them. Found letters waiting for me from Brother Sam & Sister Ellen—The latter written from Milton N.C., where she is paying a pleasant visit to our friends, Capt.

Lewis Maury & family. She is delighted with the little town and its people. A letter from Lizzie Lee also.

Sept. 17th Saturday

Passed as usual. Rosina uncommonly active today. Mrs. Taylor & the ladies from Westbrook called in the afternoon. Willie, Gusta & I walked back with them & spent the evening. House full of company—had a very pleasant evening & came home between 9 & 10 o'clock.

Sept. 18th

Rosina poorly. Willie & Gusta walked to S. school—I took a long walk by myself—gathered a quantity of Fall flowers & dressed all the flower-pots. Wrote up my Diary—& a letter to Sister Ellen—

Sept. 19th

Mrs. Stockdell's daughter, Mrs. Harrison, with six children, large & small came to spend the day. They are refugees from Charles City Co. and she told us many interesting incidents of the abominable treatment she received from the Yankees. One of her little girls told me she had been offered a five dollar gold piece by a Yankee officer, if she would let him kiss her, which she indignantly refused. Willie, Gusta & I were invited to spend the evening at Westbrook. Mary Stuart, and several gentlemen from Brook Hill were there, which, with the present Westbrook household, made up quite a party. Had some sweet music, a profuse supper with real tea & coffee—Ice-cream & cake closed the entertainment.

Sept. 20th

Mrs. Dallam & children came for me to walk with them—Gusta spent the day at Brook Hill. Rose felt miserably all the morning but took a drive in the afternoon which did her good. Willie went to Brook Hill, spent the evening & brought Gusta home after bed-time.

Sept. 21st

Gusta went to town in the cars—Rosina drove in to see the doctor, and staid all night. Gusta brought us the depressing news of Early's defeat in the valley, on the nineteenth inst. after a severe fight, lasting all day. We feel anxious about our boys, who are there. I walked over to Westbrook in the evening to hear what I could. All cast down there—Willie quite unwell & went to bed with fever and headache—Gusta, poor child! miserable about her brothers. I lay awake a great deal, full of unpleasant apprehensions—

Sept. 22nd

Got two letters this A. M. One from Brother George. Ned (*Caroline's Brother*) is sick in Raleigh with a severe attack of asthma. Tom Devereux, (*son of my niece, nee Margaret Mordecai*) has had another very narrow escape. In a skirmish in the Valley his horse was killed under him—the other letter is from Gratz Cohen—very interesting but sadly depressed about the fall of Atlanta. We had a fine rain last night—the first for many weeks. Answered my letters—& read "Helen" to Gusta (admiring it more than ever) until 9 p.m. while she made over her hoop skirt—Rose still in town—too damp to send for her.

Sept. 23rd

Willie brought us today rather better accounts of the affair in the Valley. Not so disastrous as appeared at first. Willie had a return of fever—Rose did not get home.

Sept. 24th

Willie sent for the Dr. who lanced his boil & gave Calomel. Gusta went to town for her mother who got home to dinner, seeming much better than when she went in—She had heard from the boys who were not in the battle of Monday.

Sept. 25th Sunday

Splendid day—very cool. Willie had a chill & was very sick all day. Doctor repeated the Calomel. Rose got a letter from George—He too has been sick with fever. His battalion was on its way to Petersbg. when the battle took place. Gusta & I took a delightful walk today & returned loaded with flowers & red berries. John Young came over and brought more bad news from the Valley. Our men gave way in an attack from the Yankees, and <u>ran</u> from a strong position. There are rumors of success in Georgia.

Sept. 26th

Splendid day—Gusta & I took a walk. Willie better. As we sat down to dinner, George rode up! His battalion was ordered back to the Valley, & he being too weak to stand the march was allowed to come home. He is in fine spirits, & will soon be well—His coming is a great relief.

Sept. 27th

Went over to Westbrook & took a walk with Mrs. Dallam. Another beautiful day. Mrs. Young returned with me & paid a visit. Willie missed his chill & is improving. Gusta went in to stay with Caroline till Friday.

Sept. 28th

Weather quite warm. George went to the apple trees & found a man gathering apples. Concluded to have all the winter apples gathered tho' not ripe, as they would all be stolen if left to ripen. So they were gathered & put away. Willie well enough to come down today—looks pale & thin. I spent the greater part of the morning translating a French play which I commenced on Monday. Rosina for the last two days has been able to go to the smoke house.

Sept. 29 Thursday

All last night we heard the sounds of distant, heavy firing. It increased & drew nearer as the day advanced, until afternoon, when it lessened. George went to town and did not return until night when he rode up so quietly, whistling as he came, that I was astonished at the exciting news he had to tell. The Yankees in considerable force had advanced upon Richmond and were within a few miles of the City below Rocketts. If they had been a little bolder they could, at one time, have easily carried our inner line of works, there being no troops but the Artillery within them; but they fell back before the local troops reached the fortifications. George rode down to where our men were firing & saw about 100 prisoners, some of them wounded, and brought in. The alarm bells were ringing all day. He says there was little alarm felt in the city.

Sept. 30th Friday

All quiet today—no sounds of cannon. Willie is sure that the Yankees have withdrawn from before Richmond.

October 1st, 2nd, and 3rd

I passed in Richmond, where I went to attend the Roshashannah services, going in on Friday with Mr. Young. There was a severe tho' not general engagement going on that day very near the city; Genl. Lee attempting to recapture Ft. Harrison near Chaffin's Bluff, and the enemy attempting to take Ft. Gilmer. Both attempts were unsuccessful, leaving us with the exception of the loss of men, just where we were when the day began. Edmund Myers, who was in town, rode down to the Fortifications & returned at night, having seen many ghastly sights—trenches full of dead and wounded negroes—Surgeons busily engaged in their horrible work of amputation in the house of Mr. James Taylor on whose farm the fight took place; while strange to relate, sorghum mill was busy grinding cane & Mr. Taylor superintending the process of making the syrup, as if nothing unusual was going on. Such is War.

Saturday was a very rainy day, none of us out. About 5 P.M. the most terrific & incessant cannonading began & continued till night. It was more terrible in sound, than any that had ever taken place near the City, & all hearts trembled with anxiety, none knowing the cause. I was terribly alarmed & dispirited, tho' none of my cousins felt as I did about it. At night we learned that a large body of Spears' Cavalry were attempting to enter the City, and were kept back by the batteries nearest town, and also that further off our gunboats were shelling Ft. Harrison. It was truly a miserable day, & so was the next, tho' more quiet. Everybody seemed depressed & discouraged to a degree that has seldom been the case and the future seemed without hope, as the present without spirit. Monday was another quiet day, & tho' all places of business were closed & few men seen in the streets, but the old or the disabled, it was a relief to hear no cannon.

Oct. 5

I paid several visits—sad ones this morning before returning to Rosewood. I went to see our sweet friends, Dr. & Mrs. Sinclair, who are mourning for their hearts' idol, Willie Sinclair who was drowned at sea while attempting to reach "The Florida", to which he attached, from an ordnance boat which had been capsized. All the crew were saved but himself, and he too might have been, but he generously threw an oar to which he was clinging, to a man whom he perceived to be drowning near him. His mother is heartbroken. I saw Mrs. DeWitt, whose young brother, John Fontaine, was killed on Saturday, near Petersbg. This war is taking from our country all its noblest, and best young men, and there is scarcely a house in which there is not one dead. I returned home in the cars with Gusta, and was glad to be in the country. Rose seems greatly improved, and Willie & George nearly fit for service again. Rose tells me that Mrs. Stockdell's son-in-law, Mr. Harrison, with his oldest son William were taken prisoners by the Yankees at Craigton, a few miles below Richmond, last Saturday. Mrs. Stockdell does not know this, but is extremely anxious about them. Several pieces of good news reached us today. Sheridan has been driven by Early, still further north down the Valley; a large force, which was threatening us in So. W. Va. has been repulsed; and Genl. Price is advancing upon the enemy in the West, being within 24 miles of St. Louis. Beauregard has been put in command of all our forces in the So. West.

Oct. 6th

Nothing to note down. Weather very warm—Willie having cider beaten. No news of interest from any quarter. I had vertigo & nausea after going to bed—the third Wednesday night that this has been the case with me—Rosina uncommonly well.

Oct. 7th

I was invited to dine at Westbrook to eat catfish soup, saddle of mutton and apple dumpling. Dressed to go, but did not feel well enough to venture after my last night's turn, so staid at home and dined on tea & toast. The boys staid till ten.

Oct. 8th

Beautiful morning. Heard further particulars concerning the treatment of Mr. Harrison & William who were made prisoners at Craigton—the home of his sister Mrs. Christian. They had taken refuge there, some months ago, when driven from Westbury, his plantation of James River, in Charles City Co.—The Yankees drove off all of Mrs. Christian's cattle, and every horse & mule, including those of Mr. Harrison, which he had brought there for safety, in their advance on Richmond last Friday & Saturday. Mrs. Stockdell has not been told of this yet, & as the P. Office is closed, it may be some days before she hears of it. George went to town to make final arrangements for rejoining his command, & had some difficulty in avoiding arrest, as every man who cannot show good reasons for being away from the army, is taken up & sent to the works below Richmond. He learned that a battle was going on a few miles below the City, but we have heard no guns, the wind being in the opposite direction.

Oct. 9th

News confirmed of the fight of yesterday, in which our forces, tho' victorious, were not strong enough to improve the victory. An invaluable officer, Genl. Gregg of Texas fell at the head of his troops. Gusta, Willie & George, walked to Brook Hill and spent the evening—returning by moonlight.

Oct 10th Sunday

Went to town with Mr. Young to spend several days, Monday being Yom Kippur. Remained until Tuesday afternoon when I returned in the cars, after having spent my time with some degree of satisfaction & improvement. The services on Kippur eve were solemn and impressive. Mr. Jacobs delivered a short but excellent discourse. Mr.

Cohen who had got leave of absence from his command, came up to keep the day, walking all the way from Chaffin's Bluff after performing much arduous duty. He looks better than he has done since he first arrived from Baltimore. There has been a great change from the warm weather of last week—a slight frost on Sunday, and a killing one this morning, doing great damage to all the late crops—killing cornfield peas, late corn & injuring the sorghum. Ice was seen in many places in the country.

Oct. 12th

Before leaving town, I went shopping with Caroline to try and get a few articles that Peggy Mordecai in Raleigh had written for. There is scarcely anything in the stores in Richmond; and not one that she wanted was to be found. The weather had moderated & was delightful. Got home at 4 P.M. & found all well. George had started to the valley the day before—two letters had come from John—written in depressed spirit about the state of things in the Valley & around Richmond, but expressing trust in the Divine Power that has brought us out of many critical periods. Willie spent the evening at Westbrook and heard much croaking from an unworthy officer he met there.

Oct. 13th

Beautiful morning. Took a walk after breakfast, and gathered a few wild flowers the frost had spared—did nothing the rest of the day but entertain Mrs. Braxton & Mr. & Mrs. Dallam who walked over & spent the morning with us. Miss Amelia Judkins came home with Gusta in the cars & staid all night. She is a Boston woman, devoted to the south & our cause, is as warm hearted as she is intelligent, & was very agreeable & interesting. Rose had an excellent dinner & we sat in her room all the afternoon & evening (which were dark & wet) talking by the light of the wood fire, to save other light.

Oct. 14th

Splendid morning—walked to the R. road with Amelia & Augusta, and took a beautiful walk back through the woods and got flowers & red leaves—dressed the flower pots, read my Bible & wrote up my journal which I had not done since Friday. Amelia seemed charmed with her little visit to Rosewood, & admires the situation of the humble little dwelling.

Oct. 15th

Went to town with Gusta prepared to stay a week to keep the feast of Tabernacles which commenced that evening. Had a very pleasant visit to town—staying with Caroline at my Broad St. Cousins'. Spent the first day with my other dear cousins, C.H. & J. the sisters Cheerable, as I say they are and in the course of the week besides attending all the services at the Synagogue, I visited most of my friends & acquaintances—dined at Mrs. Hannewinkel's, Mrs. Stokes on Church Hill, Mrs. Gilliam's and Judge Hallyburton's. The pleasure of my visit was damped by the unfavorable news from the Valley, which filled me with uneasiness about our boys there. Almost all our Artillery in Early's army was lost, and as they belong to that, it seemed impossible that they should escape either being wounded or taken prisoners. Willie, however, has seen the Capt. of their Battery who has come home with a slight wound, & he reports having left John safe in Camp, while George, with about 25 other men, had escaped capture by fleeing to the mountains. The victory, in spite of the great loss of artillery, is claimed by our side, as the enemy's loss in men was very heavy & ours but small. Our want of final success & loss of artillery was owing to the superiority of the enemy's Cavalry, which flanked us—forcing us to a retreat, ending in disaster.

Oct. 24th

A beautiful morning—I did some shopping for Rose & wrote a letter to brother Sam, before returning to Rosewood in the cars at 3:30. The woods are looking indescribably beautiful. Found pleasant Miss Patsey Storrs here on a visit, nice Mrs. Stockdell, who is on a visit to town. Spent the evening talking & untangling the long fringe of my black crepe shawl, which was matted together with Spanish needles I having jumped into a bush of this weed on getting out of the cars. Rosina has been suffering greatly, she tells me, since I have been in town. She makes wonderful efforts.

Oct. 25th

Took a delightful walk after writing up my journal & translating a few pages of the French Play I commenced before I went to town, and found some Blue Gentian, a flower I have been looking for all the Fall. Went to work after my return, mending old garments. Miss Patsey Storrs was very agreeable & interesting. She has known our family from childhood, having been educated at my Father's school, in Warrenton, N. Carolina. She lives about two miles from Rosewood, on the other side of the Turnpike. She walked home, after dinner, with her maid, who came for her, & later Rose took a walk with me. No news from our armies today. Weather glorious.

Oct. 26th

Rose walked with (*word missing in text*) down to the old mill. The woods looked more beautiful than ever. Mrs. Young, Mrs. Dr. Braxton (*nee Caperton*) & Mrs. Stockdell who has been on a visit to Westbrook for a few days, called after we got back. Mrs. Braxton played for us—She is a fine performer, & Rose was delighted with her music—She is a lovely, refined little creature, and their visit was quite a pleasant one. Rose is very anxious about George who has not been heard from since the late disaster in the valley, & she fears he is a prisoner. Willie does not think so. Patching today.

Oct. 27th

Mild pleasant morning. Sounds of heavy & continual firing commenced about nine o'clock, & continued all day without intermission. Mrs. Young came for me about 12 today to pay a visit with her to Mrs. Tom Ellis who lives about two miles from here, nearer town. We had a pleasant walk. The woods looked glorious though the sun was obscured. We paid a very pleasant visit, and were treated to an elegant lunch which would have done credit to the best of times. It began to rain & we had to wait for it to hold up, & at last were caught in a hard shower on our return. Rose miserable about getting no tidings from George & is sure he has been made prisoner. Willie came from town with news that a battle was going on below Richmond, but no apprehension was felt about it.

Oct. 28th

Willie walked home before breakfast from Brook Hill where he went to spend last evening, & was detained all night by the rain. He goes to town daily now to attend to business connected with his company, for which he is detailed. He brought letters this evening from both John & George, who are both safe in Camp; the latter having been taken prisoner, and made his escape under cover of the night, over the mountains, where, after a four days tramp, he found his way back to Camp. Rose is inexpressibly relieved. Gusta brought her friend, Alice Robinson (*Now 1886—Mrs. Carpenter of N. Jersey with a family of children*), a sweet little girl, home with her to stay till Monday. The battle of Thursday, below Richmond, resulted in a repulse of the enemy with little loss on our side, but much on theirs.

Oct. 29th Saturday

The girls, Gusta & Alice walked to the Stuart's & returned to dinner. Rose took a walk with me this A.M.—seems better. The news from George is such a relief.

Oct. 30th

Beautiful, delightful day. Spent the morning at my translating work— Willie & the girls went to Church—no news. Took a pleasant walk with them in the afternoon.

Oct. 31st

Went to town with Gusta & Alice Robinson in the cars to do some shopping for Rose. Saw many friends—Hallyburtons, Miss Deborah, Mrs. Dr. Sinclair & others besides our cousins. Caroline went down town with me and had many little things to tell me. Returned with Gusta in 3.30 train. Willie came out with us unknown to us until we got out of the cars. Found Rose lying down resting after having cut off & commenced making her new rag carpet for the dining room.

November 1st

Splendid day. Spent it in helping to make the new carpet. Mrs. Stockdell, Rose and Lizzy, the cook's daughter, whom her mistress is training to be an admirable servant, were the other workers on the heavy job, which we completed by 8 P.M. Gusta brought me a very interesting letter from Mr. Cohen—I answered it tonight.

Nov. 2nd

Cloudy & cold—It rained, hailed & snowed during the day. Moses Norrill (Negro of Norval my man, husband of my Sally), came out

& repaired fire-places. I sat in my room working all day as there was no fire downstairs, & Rose from over-exertion with the heavy carpet had to keep her bed all day. Fleming, the little cow boy, slept on the kitchen hearth last night and his bed clothes caught without blazing & burned one of his feet quite severely. He discovered "twas his foot in de fire" in time to save the rest of his person. This negro trick gives trouble & inconvenience to more than himself—I have undertaken his treatment, & apply a plaister of castile soap, and steep the linen bandages with a dilution of creosote 5/6ths water, which proves very soothing and efficacious.

Nov. 3rd

Another cold rainy day. Busy fitting, finishing and putting down the new carpet, which was not completed until 9 P.M. Rose suffered greatly all day until late bed time. Willie at the Stuart's—Gusta in town—has resumed her school.

Nov. 4th

Rosina no better. I attended to everything, & sewed on my new moreen skirt, mended a dress &c. Willie went to town and completed arrangements for returning to Camp—Love & War.

Nov. 5th

Clear & windy. Willie went away before sunrise. Rosina had such a wretched night tho she determined to go to town and see the Doctor. Gusta rode in with her after breakfast, and returned without her, it being necessary for her to be near the Doctor. Fanny Young came over about 12 and sat until 3. Gusta then practiced and studied her lessons, after which I read "Helen" to her until it was time for us to go to bed.

Nov. 6th

Very cold but clear—Ice on the puddles of standing water. Mrs. Stockdell & Gusta walked to Church. I staid at home and mended clothes, for the wash. Read & slept after dinner—Reading the history of the Georges—that abominable race of men.

Nov. 7th

Pouring rain all day—Gusta couldn't go to school. Sewed all day read to her in the evening. A note from Rose saying she could not come home for some days—fear her treatment is severe.

Nov. 8th

Warm & cloudy—Gusta went to school & did not come home. Spent the day making over an old black petticoat. Fleming's foot improves under my treatment. Mrs. Stockdell spent the greater part of the day in her room. Got a newspaper from Westbrook. War news little but favorable. This is the Yankee Presidential Election Day. Finished translating my pretty French play tonight.

Nov. 9th

Warm & cloudy—sewed all day. Gusta came home—her mother intends returning tomorrow—wrote to Willie.

Nov. 10th

Weather too warm for fire to be pleasant. Mrs. Stockdell went to town to stay several days. Rose came home—somewhat relieved. Had heard from George. Beautiful sunset—clear & cooler. The ground is covered with dead leaves and the autumn glory of the woods has departed.

Nov. 11th

Beautiful day—Westbrook children day spending—no news.

Nov. 12th Saturday

Rather disagreeable morning, but pleasant later, when I took a walk & returned with bunches of red berries & leaves, holly & Blue Gentian. Found Mrs. Young here on my return. She took dinner with us & was very pleasant. A violent wind blew up after dinner & it rained & hailed for an hour. Cleared at sunset.

Nov. 14th

Clear & extremely cold. Ice & sparkling frost everywhere. Went to town with Gusta, and as the clock had stopped, we went to the Rail Road much too early, and had much fun trying to keep warm while waiting for the train. In picking up frosted persimmons I found the numb ends of my fingers restored to feeling—which pleased me, being so purely homeopathic. Staid in town quite unintentionally, until Friday afternoon. Saw many old acquaintances & made a very pleasant new one. Sold some things and bought some. Everybody now sells whatever they do not need. Had altogether a pleasant visit, but passed my time in such busy idleness that I came home quite demoralized. Wrote to sister Margaret & Sister Ellen. Heard the distressing news of our dear brother Sol's having been burnt out, with heavy loss of bedding, clothing & c. Rose better but suffering.

Nov. 19th Saturday

Dark & rainy—Spent the morning quietly but not satisfactorily. Thoughts too wandering. Read aloud in the afternoon. Rosina in bed all day.

Nov. 20th

Rained hard all night. Our poor Soldiers! Without tents & almost without blankets. Willie writes from the Valley that the mountains are capped with snow, & the wind from them very cold. Got a letter from Mr. Small who boarded with us on 6th street. Mr. Young came over in the afternoon & paid us a pleasant visit—Rosina easier.

Nov. 21st

Rained all last night & today—a perfect flood. Gusta kept from school. I wrote all day, copying my translation. Rosina less suffering than she is sometimes.

Nov. 22nd

As it was not raining, Rosa determined to go in to the Doctor. She felt too sick to go, but went. Gusta rode in with her. I spent the day writing—very cold night—snowed.

Nov. 23rd

Clear & very cold. Spent the day by the fire—writing. Rosina & Gusta both in town. Mrs. Stockdell & I had quiet day of it.

Nov. 24th

Still, clear & cold. Mrs. Stockdell & I walked over to Westbrook after dinner—found Fanny alone. Returned after Starlight—found Gusta at home. Finished copying my translation tonight & am more & more pleased with the play (Le Marriage au Tambour) every time I read it. Hope it will be produced on the Richmond stage. Rosina still in town.

Nov. 25th

Writing again—letters & notes. Lovely Indian summer weather, but I was too busy to walk out. Mr. Cohen came in the cars with Gusta—handsomely dressed in a new uniform. He has accepted the commission offered him of 2nd Lieut, in a Southern Regiment, & came out to take leave of me. I was very sorry to hear it. We had a sweet evening together—The comfortable red sofa was wheeled before the big wood fire in the dining room, and Augusta played all her pieces for him that she used to play when he was staying with us on 6th street.

Nov. 26th Saturday

Directly after breakfast this morning I walked with him to the R. Road, & we took many turns under the pines while waiting for the train. I talking and he listening. At last the cars came in sight & we parted. I know we shall both always remember that sparkling, frosty walk, and that sad warm parting. Soon after I got back, Gusta went in for her mother, & I to my room to read. Rose came in the course of the morning seemingly benefitted. The children from Westbrook here all day.

Nov. 27th

Spent the morning arranging & numbering some old MSs. of mine, & in the afternoon John (*Mr. Young, we have been friends from early days*) came over and paid us a pleasant visit. He confirmed the news we had heard through the servants, that his wife's brother, Mr. Armstead Braxton, was killed in an encounter with Yankee Cavalry on 16th inst. His mother, who is very sick, is terribly grieved at his death.

Nov. 28th

Spent the morning repairing old clothes. Got into an immoderate fit of laughter recalling an anecdote that John told us yesterday. It made me laugh after going to bed last night, all by myself—such a laugh is worth recording. (*Wish I had recorded the joke—wonder I didn't 1886.*) Gusta returned from school triumphant having had the courage with the help of some of her schoolmates, to have two teeth extracted which have long tormented her. I went to see Fanny Young late in the afternoon. Had an interesting visit. She seems truly affected by her poor brother's violent death, and gave me the interesting particulars. He lived twelve hours after receiving the mortal wound, & was most kindly attended by the ladies near whose house the terrible affair occurred. Spent the evening reading aloud by fire-light, (all other light is too expensive,) Miss Edgeworth's *Belinda*, with which we are delighted on re-reading.

Nov. 29th

Went to town with Mr. Young who took me to the Penitentiary to have my measure taken for a pair of Calf skin shoes. The price will be 95 dollars, & I shall not get them for six weeks; the shoes made there, being so much cheaper & better than those to be got elsewhere, they are overrun with orders. Spent the rest of the day attending to all kinds of matters—saw several old acquaintances, and fell in with Frank Cameron, now stationed at Drury's Bluff, whom I seized upon and took to see Caroline. The poor fellow is in wretched health and spirits, has withdrawn himself from Ladies' society (so he says,) & I hope my accidental meeting with him, will result in doing him some good. Dined with my 12th St. cousins, and staid all night with Caroline. Had some long talks with her. She had much that was interesting, to tell me about her several admirers. We talked until one o'clock after going to bed. Mr. Cohen removal to So. Carolina is much regretted by all his friends. Got letters from

Raleigh & from Willie. Brother George has been very sick, but was getting well when they wrote.

Nov. 30th

Went to see several old friends, and walked a quantity in a business way. Had a pleasant, interesting visit to town, and laughed enough "to grow fat", but it is surprising how much it tires me to walk on the pavements now. I got home almost broken down. Took a warm bath, and went to bed at eight. The weather for the last three days has been warm Indian summer weather—too warm for taking exercise with comfort.

December 1st

The delightful weather continues—cooler today. I walked over to Westbrook to see Mrs. Young about some matters of hers. A very fortunate visit, resulting in my getting a handsome new Beaver-cloth cloak, which I need, at much less cost than I could get the materials & have one made. This one I gave <u>only</u> three hundred and ten dollars for, & I expected to pay five hundred for one less handsome. It had been made a quarter of a yard too long for Mrs. Young, and was the exact length for me, & she was glad to dispose of it, & I to get it. (*This cloak served me until the winter of /86. When still fit for use & respectable in appearance I gave it to a poor woman—I called it my warrior.*) Had a pleasant walk back by the creek & the mill. Spent the rest of the day patching flnl.

Dec. 2nd

Cloudy morning. Mrs. Young called for me by appointment in her carriage, to go with her to purchase her mourning, and I as usual to attend to a great variety of matters. We were on the streets till past four o'clock, but succeeded in all we went to do. Met Ella & Caroline,

& took them home in the carriage. Fanny Myers is in town, (*from Danville*) but I hadn't time to see her. Lill & Lizzie are staying at their aunt's on 12th St. the rest at Mrs. Tolcott's—Got home about sunset tired & hungry.

Dec. 3rd

Spent the morning as usual, in my room reading. Gusta stayed in town yesterday with Fanny Robinson at Mrs. Wm. H. Haxall's—Returned to day in the cars. Brought the sad news of the death of Genl. Gracie—killed yesterday, near Petersbg. By the bursting of a shell, when there was no engagement going on. His poor young wife, our cousin, (*Josephine Mayo that was,*) has an infant just three days old. She has not been informed of her terrible misfortune—Rose got a letter from Brother Sam—speaking of Brother George's recent illness which seems to have been very dangerous, & that he is better.

Dec. 4th

Splendid day—took a pleasant walk alone—worked hard all the morning—wrote all the afternoon. Gusta dined at Westbrook on her way from Church—Mr. Gardner walked back with her & staid all night.

Dec. 5th

Frosty morning—sweet day—Had some country visitors whom I did not see—Rosina uncommonly well today.

Dec. 6th

Went to town with Fanny Young & did not return till Thursday evening, when Rosina went to see the Doctor & I returned in the carriage. Went to Lizzy Giles wedding Tuesday night (*Divorced and married to Sam Robinson of Georgetown. Now a happy wife & mother—1886).* A motley crowd collected at St. Paul's to see the show. Caroline & Rose Newton went to the party at the house. Saw Edmund & Fanny & the children while in town. Staid both nights with Mary Jane Fulton. Weather Friday & Saturday very bad. Cold, snowy, sleety and horrid for the troops.

Dec. 15th Thursday

Willie Myers & Mattie Paul married at St. Paul's tonight. Gusta went to the wedding & to the party at Cousin Augusta's afterwards, which she enjoyed keenly. I went to town & returned. Heard unpleasant news from Georgia—

(*From this date up to April 1865, the leaves of this Journal have been destroyed by mice or roaches, and converted into paper crumbs—I will fill in the interval by copies of letters, which I think worth preserving as pictures, vividly representing the experiences of the War.*)

LETTER 1ST, FROM MRS. L. P. LEWIS OF MONROE CO. VA. (NEE FLOYD) TO A FRIEND IN RICHMOND.

Lynnside—Sept. 10th 1864.

Dear Mrs. D.
A week or two has elapsed since I received your kind & acceptable letter of Aug. 14th, & I would have replied to it, but we have never had a mail to this place since the Yankee Raid on Dublin in May. We have had to write & receive our letters by "chances", and sometimes when one occurs of sending letters over the mts., the notice is too short, & I have mostly availed myself of them for a hurried scrawl to my absent children. The Yankees have not left me suitable materials upon which to thank you & all my kind friends for the generous & affectionate sympathy each & all have expressed for me, and it goes far to compensate me for all the heavy trials that seem to be gathering about my old age.

After all life's work is over, what remains to us at last, that ever had any real value, but the loves we have known, the affections we have cherished, & the good deeds we have to remember. Thus it is I am neither dejected nor sorrowful under my privations, for Life's best blessing are still intact with me. The enemy could not carry away God's sunshine, & the sweet airs; so with me they could not carry away the affection and remembrances of my heart that have made the sunshine of life to me. My friends have been thoughtful & generous to me in my trials, & my good children so devoted, so tender, so full of every noble and beautiful sentiment & affection that I have almost ceased to regard as a calamity, an event that has brought me such real happiness. It would be impossible for me to give you on any amount of paper I have left, any real idea of all the horrors and outrages we have passed thro' in this valley. Sister Nancy's simple and beautiful letter published in the "Enquirer" would give you most of the details of their Carnival of crime & brutality, but it could not give you more than half an idea of what really happened before us. I actually forgot my losses in the indignation of outraged feeling, and the remembrance of the insult to God and to human nature.—I had read sensation novels & police trials, & many a learned discussion about "human depravity", but never till I saw that compendium of human villainy, Genl. Hunter, had I any distinct idea of what that favourite Puritan dogma meant. You would hardly know our poor, dilapidated house; yet we have tried to set our rags & rubbish in order, & give it some semblance of itself. The furniture was not broken, nor beds torn up, & we have a few sheets and table-cloths left, & such odds and ends of tableware as enables us to take our meals after a fashion. At the last moment a guard was obtained, which secured us the means of living, at least, & enough was picked up in the yard & meadows & fields, to give us to the necessaries of life. Five table-spoons were left, and six tea-spoons, & about a dozen towels—some pillow-cases, & three blankets. The torn table-cloths we have made into towels—have mended up counterpanes & all the bed comforts were left, as far as I can remember. Nearly every likeness in the house was destroyed except those on the walls—every single iota of jewelry sister Nancy & I had was taken fifty or sixty volumes of books taken, every bottle about the house that had anything in it was broken. All my medicines destroyed, all my cooking utensils taken away. I have not in the whole house one single thing that was ever given to me as a token of affection or remembrance.

Everything that had an association or remembrance attached to it is gone. The Gold of Ophir could not give me back my little simple treasures that were so dear because of all the tender & holy affections, & the elevated virtues & associations that were connected with them. You cannot think of what a sense of utter bereavement I sometimes have. What a strange pain it is! But I do not allow myself to give way for a moment. I am cheerful, & full of high hope—neither "humbled" nor "subjugated"; but ready & willing to work to suffer unto the end. It is astonishing how little is necessary for our actual wants; and the requirements of taste & feeling can be readily waived in view of the terrible exigencies of the times & of our country. Sister Nancy, at all times a model of every womanly virtue and every Christian grace, is cheerful too, and entirely resigned to all her trials. Col. Lewis—never luxurious or self-indulgent, has gone to work cheerful & contented to struggle against the weight of years & of trials, and we all make merry over our tribulations. The children are all fat & happy, and run in the sweet air, & pick up a living like the birds, upon apples & other fruits. I was really proud of them when the Yankees were here—They were brave and consistent and proud & enduring, for even little Rush never asked for bread or cried or complained when the little creature was picking up onion stalks, dropped by the Yankees & eating them from very hunger!

That day's remembrance left in these little hearts a seed that if we were to be subjugated today, would bring a harvest forty years hence that would entitle each child to a Yankee Liberia, if knout or halter did not give them an exodus sooner.

We have suffered more dreadfully from drought than from the enemy. Our gardens & crops have been a complete failure, and there is obliged to be suffering in the country before spring. But there is an abundant apple-crop which would compensate Sadie & Joe if they were here for all disasters. I came nearer breaking down than from any other grief, when I saw our dear little pet, "Ruby", (a pony mare,) taken away with all her family, except her poor disconsolate "baby", which was but four weeks old. I thought of all her gentleness & intelligence, and all her care of the sick, & her sports with the children, till I could not keep from a sob or two at least. The poor little colt seemed so utterly disconsolate that it was grief to us all. "Walk-away" left a colt too, a day older than Ruby's, and we have so petted & caressed the little creatures, that they are getting to be rather dangerous pets. The little playthings and one of our grey horses, are whole stock!—Our friends in the Valley are all well and cheerful. Mrs. White did not have her house robbed, and Mrs. Kelly lost but little as she had a nephew among the Yankees who attended to her interests. They have sheep and corn, and some little in the house but not much. Bierne was torn to pieces in his property like ourselves.

Our country is entirely quiet—indeed we have direct intelligence that the whole of "West Va." has been entirely evacuated by the Yankees. God only can tell what is in store for our country, but I am full of hope & trust, and rely on the mercy and the justice of God. Oh if we but save our children, what else do we want? We are fighting & suffering for independence, & I will avail myself of its utmost license to have what fashions I please, & I'll be bound they shall not look like Yankee fashions! As for me, I have turned into Live Oak—I fear misfortune is good for me! Do you see how I have blundered in writing—I have "turned over a new leaf" every time. What a misfortune for my blank book! I would write it over out of respect to you, but I have no time or paper, & I am writing with an old turkey quill I got out of a wing that I had been dusting with. Our Yankee thieves were educated & accomplished—They were men of taste & letters! providing themselves with stationery for "Pencilings by the way", & light reading to enliven the tedium of forced marches. Genl. Hunter gave to understand they had all had the blessings & benefits of the common school system! My good daughters and their husbands insist on our leaving our plundered home & coming to live with them till the war is over, and have offered me everything

I need; but honour & duty require that I shall stick to my own shelter while I have one. I shall stay with it, like the defenders of Ft. Sumpter no matter what the ruin. I shall stand by the Flag of Home, & like a true Indian, (*The Floyds are of Indian descent, & most of Gov. Floyd's children had Indian given names*) will die by the graves of my ancestors. I do not mean to try to do more than live, till God gives us better days. I shall not tempt enemies nor distress friends by taxing their generosity for even the least thing I can do without. I am neither afraid nor ashamed to be poor. Why should I wish to appear other than I am? and why seek rest & ease at the expense of others, even of a good child?

LETTER 2. FROM THE WRITER, TO A FRIEND IN THE ARMY IN N.C.

Rosewood. April 5th, 1865. (Tuesday)

My dear Edward,
I must endeavor to command sufficient composure to narrate to you our experience of the last two days, commencing a little before sunset Sunday afternoon, when, like the crash of a terrible thunder-bolt, the unlooked-for tidings reached us, that Richmond was to be evacuated at twelve o'clock that night!

The two days preceding this had been of exquisite beauty & tranquility. I had spent the previous week with friends in the City, where no apprehensions were entertained of such a calamity. My darling Caroline had accompanied me home on Friday, to spend a week with me in the country, and it would have been impossible for us to have been less prepared than we were for such an awful, crushing blow. I need not tell you that language has no power to describe the dismay, the grief and the appalling terror, produced by such tidings. Lieut. R. J. Moses, who had been lately returned as a paroled prisoner; like a kind friend, walked out to let Caroline know, so that she might return to town before it was too late, our situation outside the lines seeming more perilous than any in the City. A hurried addition was made to a letter that C. had that morning written to you, which he took charge of, & which, I hope reached you. Oh how I have thought of you, and of all our beloved ones in N. Carolina. Our agony was great, but yours I knew must surpass it. We have been most mercifully preserved thus far from injury. Our faith has not been strong enough (is it possible for any faith to be so under such circumstances?) To preserve us from terror and dread of every conceivable outrage and injury & insult, but the result so far has proved that our trust in God's mercy should have been more firm & consoling. But to return. The Carriage being broken, and the servants away as they generally are on Sunday, there was no means of conveyance, & C. was obliged to a walk to town with her escort. I accompanied them for a mile & when we parted at the Brook Turnpike, it was impossible to conjecture where, or under what circumstances, or when, if ever, we should meet again. They proceeded on their way, & I retraced my steps to Rosewood, with what feelings I cannot attempt to describe. The period that has elapsed since Sunday afternoon, should be counted, each hour for a long, long day. It is impossible to realize, almost Impossible to credit the evidence afforded by Sunrise & Sunset, that but two days have passed since. Every sound, every footstep, has sent trembling to the limbs of us three helpless & unprotected females, & made our hearts stand still. And yet, I must say, we have conducted ourselves with wonderful composure. Rosina has been an example of firmness and collectedness, but her delicate frame could not stand as much as her strong spirit, and she has suffered terribly with her head yesterday & last night, but fear of rude intruders would not allow her to keep her bed during the day. This morning she has suffered less. Augusta has suffered agonies of dread. Neither she nor her mother slept at all Sunday night, but though the night seemed interminable, they dreaded the day; who could tell what it would bring forth?—I was astonished at myself. I went to bed, upstairs in my own room, and succeeded in composing myself to sleep—woke again, & slept again. We heard the whistling of engines & the rolling of trains on this & the Danville R. Road almost all night. I wondered if my precious child had left Richmond as I had urged her to do, if possible. I did not know when I should be able to hear anything about her, and my heart ached for all my friends in the City, for our boys in the field whom we knew to be suffering intense anxiety if, indeed, they were yet alive to suffer anything,—We still know nothing of their fate, nor do we expect to know anything for an indefinite time to come. Just before day broke upon this night of consternation, we were aroused by the report of a terrific explosion, which jarred the house to its foundations. I started up, horror stricken, & groped my way down stairs, and got in bed with Gusta & her mother, all terrified & trembling together. We got quiet after a while & began to consult about what we had best do—about hiding valuables, provisions &c. packing away clothes. After much deliberation it was concluded that Gusta should be sent to some friends in the City. Another still more terrific explosion, (these were the powder magazines, gun-boats &c.) interrupted us, and made us start up with one accord. Again we got quiet and poor little Gusta, exhausted with her night of terror fell asleep. Rosina had a barrel of flour at Mr. Gordon's store in town, and a box of very valuable old plate at the Bank, both of which she was very anxious to get home, as we supposed the stores, Banks &c. would be sacked. A trunk and carpet-bag were packed with valuable clothing belonging to Gusta & her mother, & they decided, though I did not like the plan, to send these to a friend in the city, & Rose wrote notes to the same and Mr. Gordon, asking him to send out the flour and the plate if possible. Soon after an early breakfast, Gusta and I dressed ourselves with care, and seated in a covered cart, drawn by a mule, and driven by George, (the servants, as yet, behave as loyally as possible) proceeded to town with the trunk &c. I was to leave Gusta in town, if it seemed best to do so, & to return myself in the cart. As we proceeded along the Military road, we passed soldiers, generally in couples, hurrying away—loaded with whatever they possessed. Some spoke to us—asked if we were going to Richmond and said "you are going to a bad place". I asked of all we met whether the enemy had yet entered. "They were expected", was the answer. We saw smoke, & even flames, although the sun was shining brightly, rising from various points in the City, all the way we went, and heard incessant reports of cannon, or bursting shells. I knew the tobacco &c. was to be burned & the works destroyed, so all this did not astonish or unnerve me. When we got to Camp Lee, the white tents but yesterday occupied by our returned prisoners, were silent & deserted. Two youths, bending under the weight of some tobacco they had found there, were the only living creatures we saw. We stopped at a house a little further on to make enquiries of some women we saw talking to a returned soldier whose home it was. They told us that the enemy had entered the City, & were then on the Capitol Square; that they had come in very quietly. They had themselves been to town that morning—they did not think George would be troubled if he went on with the cart which, they said, he could load with flour and meat &c. that had been thrown open to the people. As there was a possibility of his getting Mr. Waldrop to recover the silver, and George was very anxious to go in and secure some of the stores that they told us were being destroyed and thrown away, I decided to leave the baggage with those people who seemed very kind, & who promised to take good care of it—to let George proceed, (I do not think we could have induced him to go back) and to walk back home with Augusta who felt terrified & was crazy to return to her mother. So these kind people, whose name was Luck, carried the things into the house, and we all separated—Gusta & I walking rapidly homeward—fire and smoke behind us, while the incessant roar of one explosion after another, or of many together, were multiplied by the repeated reverberations from hill to hill, in terrible grandeur. I do not think we saw a living creature along the road, except a crow now & then alighting to feed in the road, and the little birds, which find in this troubled world of ours, an untroubled world of their own. We had met a young negro woman shortly after leaving Luck's hurrying into town. She said without slackening her pace "Missis, you gwine way from dem nasty Yankees?" "We are going home" I replied, "Where are you going?" "I'm gwine to town to hunt up my young mistress—I'll risk my life to get her", and on she hastened. We soon reached home. Gusta was rejoiced to get back to her mother, whom she had left with great reluctance. The excitement prevented our feeling any fatigue, and I set to work as soon as I had told our adventures, packing my things in trunks, with a view to concealing them, but as there was no place to do this, I left them standing in my room, with the keys sticking in them to prevent their being broken open. I next helped Rose put away a quantity of valuable clothing belonging to the boys, which we found good places for, between the bed-cases & the beds, then she lay down and read a number of appropriate Psalms & hymns, while Gusta & I nervously employed ourselves in knitting. The day seemed never ending, but night came at last and staid as long. I slept downstairs. We had been anxious all day about George and the mule & cart, and when we went to bed they had not come, and I felt great regret at having acted as I had done, and that I had not insisted on his coming back with us, for Rosina gave up all hope of ever seeing the mule and cart, or the things we had left at Luck's. I believe Gusta & her mother slept pretty well that night. I told Cyrus, if we became frightened in the night we should ring the bell, & he promised to come in. The fact is, that we are in a state of undefined terror all the time, which is intolerably increased at every usual or unusual sound or sight. Thus ended Monday. The noises from the city ceased after night fall, & the night was quiet. Early next morning Rosa went out to set a hen!—Her composure surprises me. The business of the morning proceeded as usual. Rose's brother came over from Westbrook just as we had finished breakfast, and told us of the destruction to the City on Monday by fires spreading from the Government property which had been burnt by orders from our authorities. All Cary street, all the south side of Main from Rocketts to the Spotswood hotel, rows of private dwellings upon Franklin street near the Capitol Square; (All his flour which was in store on Carey St., all Mr. Stuart's corn, which had been sent in for safe keeping), the Banks, from which the funds, but not the private plate had been removed—so poor Rose has lost all the Beautiful old silver that her father had made out of pure specie, and many valuable trinkets she had deposited with it. Here was a list of losses, for one who had no means of replacing them, cart, mule, clothing, silver & jewelry.—We heard that the enemy were establishing order in the City, had assisted in stopping the fires, and that there was less to apprehend from them than we had supposed. Still we could not but feel fearful, though we went through the usual routine of the morning with outward composure—I again dressed myself with care, and we sat down in the chamber to our knitting—the usual work of Confederate women, but now, Alas! we should have no army to work for, still the employment made us less nervous. Massie, a hired negro boy, went off without asking permission; the first act of insubordination as yet experienced. Cyrus went to work in the field, but we felt no assurance that he would continue faithful. The house was closely shut up. By & bye we were startled by the clatter of horse's feet, leaping the fence by the hen-house. Rosa was lying down, so I went to the door, and saw a negro dragoon, fully armed, galloping round the house, while another, in the woods nearby was calling to him in peremptory tones, to "come away directly", which he did, & joining his comrade, they rode rapidly away in the direction of Camp Lee. We wondered at our escape, and were rejoiced to find ourselves less terrified than we had expected to be, at this dreaded sight. We resumed our knitting, and endeavored to resume our composure. About eleven o'clock we were again startled by the sound of horse's feet in the yard, and again I went to the door. There close by the porch, on a barebacked horse, sat an insolent looking negro, dirty and ragged. On seeing me he said, "You got any saddle here? If you have, hand it out." I called to one of the women servants, to enquire where Cyrus was, and told her to go up in the field and tell him to come. The negro said, "If it's the man dat was ploughing, he told me dey was a saddle here. I done got his horse an' now I want de saddle, so han' it out, and be quick 'bout it." I said, "have you got any paper, or order to get these things?" He said "No, but I got orders to take ev'y horse & saddle outside de lines"! The horse he was on was a newly stolen one. I looked around and said, "Is there any officer with you?" "Yes", he said, "yonder de Sergeant"; pointing towards the garden and in the field, drawn up close against the garden fence, were two negroes in uniform, mounted & armed. Meantime, resistance seeming worse than useless with such a ruffian, Rose had told Mary to carry out the saddle, & he commenced putting it on in great haste asking if there was no blanket to put under it, to which I replied "NO!" Rose crept out then into the yard and in the direction of the "officers", to try and expostulate with them about taking her only horse, but when they saw her coming, they sent her horse off and rode away before she could get near them. I felt convinced that these men had no authority for their conduct, and after thinking the matter over, we began to hope it might be possible to get redress. Our reflections and consultations came, at last, to this result. I determined to go myself to Camp Lee—to state the case to the officer in command there, and see what could be done. There was no one to go with me, so we decided that I should take Mary & Georgiana, two little negro girls, as better than to go entirely alone. I made the children eat something, & did the same myself, and dressing myself with care, proceeded with my little escort, towards the enemy's camp. The day was lovely. We met no one for some time when a white man driving a cart came in sight. From him I got instructions and encouragement, and again I walked on. I had told Rose to pray for me as I set off, and I committed my undertaking to God. Before we reached the outer line of pickets, we saw something moving along the road, looking like a number of persons in a group. On getting nearer we found that a number of negro soldiers in uniform, under the direction of two mounted white officers were removing a cannon from one of our abandoned batteries, to some other point. I hurried on, anxious to get up to them before the officers should ride off. On reaching them I spoke in the courteous manner to one of the officers and asked him if I should be allowed to pass into the lines. He proved to be a gentleman. I told him my object, and he advised me to go to Genl. Draper's headquarters, and he thought I might get redress. We had some further conversation, and thanking him for his courtesy, I passed on. He soon overtook me, as the cannon he was attending to was moving down the lines, and offered, if it would be agreeable to me, to dismount & let me ride, saying "his animal was a very kind creature". I declined this with thanks telling him that I should be afraid. He persuaded me to try it, but seeing I objected, did not insist, but rode slowly by my side, talking very pleasantly, and showing me every gentlemanly attention, dismounting to assist me over several streams that ran across the road. When he got to a place where the cannon he was in charge of had to be turned into another road, he gave his men directions and continued with me—past the pickets, (black and insolent,) into the Camp, and up to the headquarters of Gen. Draper, whom I found occupying one of the buildings at Camp Lee. By this time I had had a good deal of conversation with my escort, to whom, as I discovered he was an Irishmen, I had expressed myself very freely, telling him too, that while his kindness had almost enabled me to obey the precept, "love your enemies", I rejoiced he was not an American, as I should have disliked extremely to be under such obligations to a

Yankee. He said he could sympathize with my feelings as a Southern woman, but advised me to be less open in expressing them, "especially" he added in a lower tone, "when you go before Genl. Draper, who is not of the regular army, and is something of a fanatic". As we parted, I asked him to let me know the name of one who had been so kind to me. He said "Capt. McKee." I told him I should never forget his kindness, & he left me with Genl. Draper, a sleek, dapper, <u>unmilitary</u> looking man, who received me very politely, rose & gave me his seat of which there were only two in the room, and after hearing my statement of the conduct of his men, told me it was contrary to orders; that they belonged to the 5th Mass. Coloured Cavalry, and if I could see their Colonel, (Adams) and identify the horse, it would be restored. This was more than I could undertake to do, so I asked for a pass to return. To my horror he informed me that he had just received orders from Headquarters, most stringent orders, to let no one pass out without a permit from the Provost Marshall whose office was in the Capitol. I asked him if I should be in danger of rude treatment in passing into town. He assured me I need fear nothing of the kind, and gave me a pass to go in. So I thanked him and started off with my little escort. The whole place within the Fairgrounds, late Camp Lee, & now a Yankee Camp, was black and blue with well-equipped negro troops. Cavalry, Infantry and Artillery, all enjoying the "<u>dolce far niente</u>" in various ways. I walked through them majestically; (I never in my life had felt so proudly defiant) and met with no rudeness or interruption. The walk from there to the Capitol seemed interminable; and Richmond could no longer be recognized. Yankee officers on fine horses dashing through Broad Street—the sidewalks thronged with people whom I never saw before, and negro soldiers, drunk & sober. The population of Screamerville looked truly joyous, and delighted with the new order of things. The blockade was at last raised, and Yankee sutlers were bringing in loads of provisions that had become rarities in the Confederacy.

As I advanced down Broad Street towards 6th, the pavement was covered with the plate glass from the fine doors & windows, reduced to powder by the explosions, while rough boards supplied its place. All stores were closed and the streets filthy. Close up against Stebbins's handsome China Store, on the sidewalk, was backed up an immense Yankee Ordnance-wagon—without horses. As I turned the corner of 9th Street to go to the Capitol, as far as I could see towards our war office, the street from curb to curb was ankle deep with fragments of Confederate printed blanks & other papers, while burnt piles of the same were seen in many places. Everything looked full of rubbish and disorder bespeaking Ruin. The once beautiful grounds of the Capitol looked filthy, and was thronged with a motley crowd of native & foreign negroes, where a negro was never before seen, a few white females, Yankee officers riding over the grass plots to the very steps and troubled looking citizens going to and from the Provost Marshal's office. All looked disconsolate, desolate and defiled. I told the little servants with me to go down to my cousins'—to tell them we were all safe and well: to find out whether Caroline had gone, and how they all were, and then to return and wait for me at the middle gate. I should have mentioned that as we were coming into town, Massie, the hired boy, had been seen by Mary, and he told her that he had seen George that morning, hauling things from the Capitol; so I determined to get a permit from the P. Marshal to take the cart and driver home as also the articles left at Luck's. The office is in the old Senate Chamber, and I found my way with the assistance of an acquaintance I met at the entrance. I had to pass through what might well be called a nasty crowd, to get into the presence, but I met with no rudeness, and was, myself, studiously polite and dignified. I asked of two officers seated at a desk, for Gen. Manning. "I am he" said one of the two, a very youthful and worried and busy looking man. I made known my business as succinctly as possible, including the stealing of the horse. He was stern, but he had so much to attend to that I excused his manner. He said it was impossible with the stretch of business then on him, to attend to such matters—that Genl. Draper should have done it; but he gave me the desired permit, and I left him, thankfully. After looking about a little in hopes of seeing George, I took my stand at the appointed Gate, and was soon relieved by seeing the children appear. Mary gave me a note which Caroline had written that morning hoping to be able to get it to me. She said Miss Carrie had pinned it in her sleeve and told her to let no one see it. I will copy it now, though I could not read it then, it was dated April 5th.

My dearest Aunts and A.—I write thinking it possible I may have a chance of sending this before very long. We have been most mercifully protected. Yesterday was truly a day of humiliation, fasting and prayer. But horrible agony of terror as it was for ourselves, it was almost worse to think of you all and others who must be suffering the same, only intensified by suspense. I am thankful that I did not go away. Lieut. Moses after talking it over with me, strongly advised my <u>not</u> doing so. So did our friend Mr. Iglehart. We are all well.—Have a new inmate, (*a Yankee officer*) who is perfectly polite, and a protection—nothing more. We were advised by some drunken soldiers to do this. I trust we may meet before long. I heard from Fanny Halyburton this morning—they are all well. Her father (*Judge H. formerly of U.S. Court*) has gone—their servants are behaving beautifully, and they have been completely unmolested: ours are also doing <u>very</u> well. We are none of us alarmed today except the servants. But yesterday was Pandemonium! If we could only hear who was killed in the awful battle at Petersburg! Do pray let us hear from you as soon as possible. It seems to be decidedly the policy here to be polite to us; even the drunken ones are so. I long to talk to you all—I can't write more fully. Yours devotedly. C.

Oh that music! (Yankee bands.) I next went down towards the burnt district. What a scene of desolation and destruction. I did not go far—I was looking for George & seeing nothing to make it probable he would be in that direction, I turned from the distressing spectacle, and retraced my steps towards Broad St. A man whom I knew, met me and told me that Lincoln was then coming into the City: that the guns then firing were in honour of his arrival. "Then", I said, "it is time for me to go out." There was a roar of shouting in the direction of our President's mansion. I turned my steps towards it, thinking curiosity might lead George there, when to my joy, I saw him at the pump at the corner of 9th Street, watering his mule—the cart to it. I almost ran to him. He had been unable to get a pass, & was anxious to get home. He was just tipsey enough to be foolish and headstrong. I got in the cart, the two children with me, and after indescribably tedious and trying delays, caused by his condition, we at last reached Mr. Luck's, and found our things all safe. I was told that the house, though in the midst of a negro cavalry Camp, had been entirely unmolested, so after getting the baggage, and thanking these honest people, we again proceeded, as slowly as before. We drove on to the outer picket post, (George, regardless of keeping the road, and complaining that I confused him so, was the reason he could not drive right), and were there rudely halted by a powerful, ruffianly negro picket, the blackest man I ever saw, (it is universally remarked that these negro troops are the blackest of their race ever seen here) who demanded the pass. He held it upside down, and then sideways, and at last found out the right way when pretending to read it, for an immense time, he returned it to me saying in his horrid voice, "It's all right, but you must take it to the Lieut. over yonder". This was some distance back, so I got out and walked there, telling George to follow me, but he was too tipsey to be obedient. Well, the Lieut. (a white man) examined and kept it, saying he had to show it, and I would not need it. I walked back to the cart, climbed in, & at last got George to start again. Meantime the Black Ruffian was extremely insolent to me. I was indignant, not frightened, and treated him with sovereign contempt and coolness. As we drove off, and had got at least thirty yards from him, I said speaking to myself, "They are all as ill-bred as old Lincoln himself". To my astonishment he called us to halt. I said "Drive on George, he has no right to stop us". George drove on, whereupon he levelled his musket at us, and cocked it. Still I told George to drive on, that he would not dare to fire, but George was afraid, saying "I seen too much a dey cayins on in town", and the two children, terrified, jumped out & ran up the road. The Ruffian in the meantime approached. I told him I would go and report him. He cursed me, and said, "Well go! What's that you said about Lincoln?"—I did not condescend to reply. He repeated the question with more curses—I remained silent.

George was sobered by his fright, and made up some plausible falsehood in reply, saying in a most conciliating tone, "I ain't hear her say nothing 'bout Lincoln today", whilst I sat still and looked defiance at him. At last I said, (he was close up to the tall board of the cart then) "And suppose I were to tell you what I said about Lincoln, would you shoot me, or would you stick your bayonet in me?" He cursed me again horribly, saying "You haven't got things here no longer as you have had them; don't you know that? don't you know that?" "Well," I said "have you done and will you allow me to pass on?" He continued his blasphemous language; but at last I got George to drive on, & it was over. I was astonished at my own coolness. I felt incensed, not at all frightened. At last, a little after sunset, we reached home. Rosina & Augusta had been in an agony of anxiety about me and the children. The servants had been almost as much so, and such a rejoicing as there was over my triumphant arrival, with cart, mule, George trunks &c. you never witnessed. Rose said she had been praying all day. I told my adventures to eager listeners, and we all thanked God that it was so well over. I had been assured by the officer I had met, Capt. McKee, that no interruption to property, no rudeness to persons would be permitted, and that the discipline was very strict, so we felt less uneasy than we had hitherto done, and passed a tranquil night. So ended Tuesday. It is now Wednesday evening. We have had several frights today, caused by nothing—only we are so easily alarmed—so nervous. Gusta, poor child! does not breathe an easy breath. We hear that Lee has been surrounded, and he and Mr. Davis taken—negro news, but it may true. I feel that it is all over with us, and look to God, who still orders all things. Numbers of servants are leaving their owners. Mr. Young has lost several of his. He also lost by the fire, his law library, his service of china, and eight handsome carpets, sent to town for safe-keeping.

So far the letter.

1865. JOURNAL RESUMED.

April 13th

Last Wednesday afternoon I completed in a letter to Edward Cohen, for the benefit of all my relatives in N. Carolina an account of all that had befallen us since the evacuation of Richmond up to that time, including only three days.

Thinking I may here after regret it, if I yield to my aversion to the task, I resolved to continue my narrative. We spent days and nights in such apprehension, that I resolved to make an attempt on Thursday 6th, to get to some headquarters to try to obtain a guard. Having been so grossly insulted by the negro picket on the Camp Lee Road, I concluded to try the Brook turnpike this time, so I took Mary & Georgiana & set forth. In the lane I found Cyrus & one of Mr. Young's men, sitting idle under the hedge. I asked Cy. if he was not going to work anymore? He answered, "Not until I know who I gwine to work for". I said, "Why hadn't you as lief work for your mistress as for any one else if she compensates you for it?" He said I onderstand she an't got nothin' to compensate me wid. "But" I rejoined "if you work the place, she will have something". "No," he couldn't work on dem terms. He informed me there was to be no more Master & Mistress now, all was equal, he "done hear dat read from the Court House Steps". I asked if he expected "to continue to live on 'Mrs. Mordecai' without working for her?" "Yes" he said, "until I see how things is gwine to work. All the land belongs to the Yankees now & they gwine divide it out 'mong de coloured people". I listened with perfect self command: there was no redress, no refutation—so I left him and walked on, asking Mary if she was mighty glad to hear she was free?—She replied "No m' I just as leave be slave as not". (George who had professed so much joy at getting home with the mule and cart Tuesday night, took himself off with all his effects the next morning.) I found some mounted negro pickets on the turnpike at the entrance of the Lane. They were quite civil, but could not let me pass, so I went to Westbrook & paid a visit. Mr. Young met me at the door—a picture of woe and despair. He had been grossly insulted by some negro soldiers the evening before, who forced him, by putting their carbines to his head, to disclose where he had buried his silver. They had expected to find specie, not plate, and, wonderful to say took off only portions of it, which, still more wonderful fact, was returned by an officer, an hour or two afterwards. But the humiliation could not be obliterated, and almost crazed him. Fanny was more composed than I thought possible. While I was there, Cy sent for his two daughters, Martha & Caroline, who belonged to Mr. Young. Little Fanny came in to her mother's room, terribly distressed that Caroline's father was going to take her away, and she wasn't coming back any more. She cried as if her little heart would break, for Caroline was her little playmate. Her Mother told her it could not be helped, and she must not cry so much about it. So these two, in addition to all the rest of Cy's family have been here, at Rosewood ever since—doing nothing. When I got sight of home on my return from my unsuccessful attempt, all looked so tranquil, that I was surprised to learn from Gusta who met me at the door, that <u>nine</u> of the most ruffianly black demons had been here during my absence, and under pretense of searching for arms, had been all over the house—upturning everything, going into smoke-house, dairy, closets—drawers &c!! Still we had escaped in such a way as to make us thankful for God's protection. They had not torn or destroyed anything in the house. They took off my little work-box, with all its valued contents, gold thimble, little log-cabin which I valued particularly as, with the box itself, they were mementoes of past times and departed loved ones. Also some valuable trinkets—sacred things, from a little trunk in the closet of my room, finding a key on my bench which unlocked it. These things belonged to Mr. Young, and Rose had kept them for him ever since his marriage. We passed the rest of the day & the night in apprehension of further outrages—but nothing happened.

Friday morning [April 14]

Mary got up as usual with Georgiana, (both slept in Rosina's room as comfortable as any children need want to be,) took out her bed—and never came back. Her father—one of the trickiest and meanest of his race—was waiting for her when she went out, and took her away—not even allowing her to take leave of one of the kindest of mistresses. This was a great grief, as well as a great loss to Rose & Gusta. They were very much attached to the child who was both good and useful. Her mother had belonged to Rose, & on her death bed, which her mistress had watched over with unwearied kindness & attention, had made her promise that she would always take care of Mary & never part with her. That day I walked to town with our neighbour, Mr. Taylor, to try and take some measures for restitution, and to make a statement of our grievances. I saw Genl. Weitzel, but in fact accomplished nothing—was only promised that the horse and the articles should be restored if possible. Genl. Weitzel was occupying Pres. Davis's house, which was just as it had left by the family. Even Mrs. Davis's white housekeeper, who whispered to me that she had been caught there, was keeping house for him. Judge Marshall's residence also, is head-quarters for some high official of the Yankees. I went to see my cousins, C. H. & J., and was surprised at their air of cheerful composure. They had a Yankee officer lodging with them. Everybody is forced to do this for protection & maintainance, our funds being of no more value than so much waste paper, & few have any supplies in their house. I went of course to my other cousins' & saw my darling, who was delighted to see me, & I staid there until Mr. Taylor called for me, when we walked back home—(five miles) and arrived some time after dark. There had been no disturbances during my absence, but our only security was our trust in God. We heard of outrages being committed a round us, and for the next two days, every step & every sound filled us with terror. Our anxiety about Gusta was great—We feared she would be made sick with nervous terror. On Sunday morning we learned that George had come back the night before, and taken the cart and mule, and all the corn that was in the barn. Nothing to be done, but to submit. Sunday night we heard volleys of artillery all night. We afterwards learned it was in celebration of Genl. Lee's surrender to Grant. This was agony piled on agony—Rose sat on the floor before the fire, weeping bitterly. Gusta was dissolved in tears, and felt as if every ray of joy had departed from her young life. When Richmond fell I had given up all hope, so this was scarcely a new blow to me. I felt terrified as to what the consequences might be, and my fears absorbed my grief. I felt utterly miserable—That the earth might open & swallow us all up, was the only wish I could form. Gradually we felt that all was in the hands of God, and that He had willed this in His unerring wisdom, and that we must submit ourselves to Him—that in thus doing we were not humbled before our foes but before God. Other nations had been through similar and worse afflictions—we must bear our turn. The day was a dark, dreary, rainy day, in accordance with our feelings.

All this time rumours of desperate fights had reached us—we know nothing of the fate of those dear to us. We have to shut out all thoughts of them as much as possible, or we should be incapable of bearing our daily burden. On Sunday Rose was prostrated with despair about her sons. I reminded her that she had suffered similarly on other occasions, and yet they had escaped unhurt. But my words gave me little comfort—how could they her?—That afternoon a visit from Mr. Joe Linton cheered us up a little. He seemed to take a better view of things—Monday passed without other disturbance but alarm and dread. On Tuesday it was determined to send Gusta to town. She and I intended to walk in, but fortunately we had an opportunity of riding in with Mr. Taylor in Mr. Young's buggy. I started to walk the distance with a boy of the neighbourhood, but the roads were so miry that when Mr. Taylor overtook me, near Mr. Rose's, I got in and sent the boy back, and was glad to ride the rest of the way with Gusta in my lap. We heard that there was a chance of Rosina's silver being safe, as the vaults of the Bank were not destroyed by the fire. My object in going to town this day, was to procure a guard, which I succeeded in doing after much tedious delay, and escorted by a Lieut. and four soldiers, I reached home between eight & nine.

Mr. Taylor driving me in the old buggy until we got near his house, when our poor little blind, half fed, good little Berk, Mr. Young's faithful, willing little mare, gave out entirely, and could not pull another step. I had been so sorry for her all this way that it tired me to see her struggles to get along, and it was a relief to get out and walk the rest of the way. Rosina had had a quiet day and was so glad that she was really cheerful when I got home. The Lieut. (an Irishman) stationed a guard here and returned with Mr. Taylor to his house, where he staid all night. He was here, off and on all next day (Wednesday) & took dinner with us. We were much pleased with him, & he seemed disposed to do all in his power to keep order in the neighbourhod, & to make the negroes do their duty or quit us altogether. He left us before dark, promising to return in the evening, but as it is now noon of Thursday & he has not yet returned, and as he withdrew the guard last night, we conclude that his regiment has been ordered off.

Our conjectures concerning the Lieut. were correct. Mr. Linton who had kindly taken some butter and a few vegetables to Market for Rose, came Thursday afternoon to return her basket & bring her the money—(1.50 in Greenbacks). He told us that all the Yankee troops had been withdrawn from Richmond Wednesday night. That Genl. Lee's surrender was not credited—that he had heard Yankee Officers say they did not believe it, and we heard the same thing later in the afternoon from other sources. We do not know what to believe—we are <u>entirely</u> in the dark. The hogs, thirteen in all, were missing all day yesterday, and Fleming, the boy that minded them, went off and has not returned. This morning Cy. went and found all but four of them—no disturbance yesterday or last night.

Friday [April 14]

Some mounted Yanks came riding into the yard after breakfast this morning to buy eggs, but made no further disturbances. Rose

& I spent the rest of the day with the assistance of Georgiana and Caroline, cutting greens for Market, Mr. Linton having kindly offered to sell for us. While thus engaged, some Yanks came to the house, but finding we had a protection paper, they went away without disturbing anything. In the afternoon Cy took Caroline away and put her with a negro woman in the neighbourhood to whom he has hired her, without saying a word to Rosina upon the subject. We had no one left to take the two large bags of salad we had gathered in the morning, over to Mr. Linton's, so I walked over to Bridgewater's and got his son to come for them. Cy behaved abominably, and refuses either to leave the place or to do anything on it, unless sure of high wages & an increased allowance of meat. Sarah, his wife, does better, and Georgina does very well, but we do not know when it may suit her father to take her from us. He feels as if the whole place belongs to him.

April 15th Saturday

Felt stiff and sore with my unaccustomed labours of yesterday. Rosina too felt miserably. About 12 o'clock three armed Yankees came round the house in a boisterous manner, trying to catch our fowls—I went out, though frightened, taking the protection paper with me, and remonstrated with them. At first they professed to disregard the paper, but on my reading it to them, they thought it best to withdraw, but we did not contrive to save a hen which one of them, who had kept out of the way, had found in George's hen-house & took away. No other disturbance occurred, and our nights are always quiet, thank God, and though our thoughts about all that we are separated from are harrowing, I leave all in God's hands & endeavor to keep close under the shadow of His wings. Both Rose & I have lost flesh in the last two weeks—I keep strong & well, but she feels very feeble and sadly depressed.

April 16th

Mr. Linton called to leave the money 1.50 cts. in little Yankee notes, he got for the salad yesterday. He told us it was certain that Genl. Lee had surrendered—that he had seen several of the disbanded soldiers returning to their homes, and they told him of the safety of our boys. I don't know why, but we doubt the truth of this last piece of information. He thinks they will get home tomorrow. Genl. Lee arrived in Richmond yesterday he says. Rose feels wretchedly this morning—so weak and nervous. In the afternoon Mr. Young came to see us—he was terribly depressed and takes a sadly gloomy view of our future. Soon after he left us, we heard the foot-steps of men approaching the house—Of course we expected Yankees. It was John & George! Safe and well—Willie had got separated from them but was on his way with a mule he had been allowed to bring out with him. So they are all unhurt after such dangers, and exposure, privation & fatigue and hardships, as God's mercy and protection alone could have preserved them through. For 5 days and nights, they had marched and fought continuously, without one hour's sleep. They speak in grateful terms of the enemy's conduct to them after the surrender. Genl. Lee came along with them accompanied by his Staff, his wagons, ambulance &c. Genl. Grant refused to take his sword. Rose was overcome at seeing the boys. She had despaired of ever seeing them all three again, and here they are—not a hair of their heads injured. What a wonderful mercy! They had walked thirty miles yesterday. They are wonderfully cheerful, but like Genl. Lee they have the comfort of knowing they have done their whole duty as brave constant soldiers.

April 17th

Willie arrived soon after breakfast. He is well but looks worn & serious. We sat in the chamber talking all the morning. Much of the greatest interest, to hear & to tell on both sides. Mr. Young came over too, and told all his humiliating experience with the Yankee negro soldiers. We also had various visits from squads of white Yankees yesterday and today. No disturbances however. The afternoon was beautiful & I walked over to Mr. Martin Taylor's to make arrangements for going to town with him tomorrow. There heard the astounding intelligence of the assassination of Lincoln and Seward, but could not credit it.

April 18th

Walked to town with Deborah, the sempstress at Westbrook, and a white boy—William Gentry. Very windy and unpleasant. Attended to many matters. Saw Genls. Ord and Patrick about protection papers for ourselves and Mr. Young—permits for the boys—instruction as to many things we were in doubt respecting fire-arms, dealing with negroes &c all very satisfactory. Was treated with consideration and courtesy by the officers I had to see on these subjects. Went to my Broad St. Cousins', and finding them at dinner, dined with them. Their table is kept with the money they receive from a Yankee Officer who boards & lodges with them. He is gentlemanly and they have become quite reconciled to him. I was just too late to see Rosa Newton before leaving them to return to her home in Norfolk. Her father came up for her. Mr. Barsley too has gone via. Norfolk, Balt. & N. York to his home in northern Georgia. A sad, sad parting for them all.—Caroline is much depressed at not being able to hear from No. Carolina. No doubt is felt of Lincoln's death—and it is said that Seward too is in dangerous condition, from the injuries he has received. Saw many friends accidentally in the street. Walked home in the evening—footsore and much fatigued, but satisfied with my success. The boys were delighted with the privileges I had secured them—More of the pigs have been stolen—The few remaining have been sold to a butcher for 15 dollars.

April 19th

Willie & John walked to town to see about the mule, & to see Gusta. Minute-guns were firing all day. We hoped Seward was dead, but it was only in honour of Lincoln's funeral. The boys got home to dinner, unsuccessful. Report the City very quiet—all places of Public business closed. George at work in the garden all day. Work on the farm much retarded for want of a team. The mule Willie brought home needs recruiting before it can be worked. Willie had an interview with Cy. this morning, telling him he was willing for him to remain and keep his family here if they would work, as usual for their support, and behave themselves. He respectfully announced his intention to go away as soon as possible, which Willie assured him was the most satisfactory arrangement he could make. At night, Phil, Lizzie's husband, saw Willie about her, as he wishes her to remain here, but she desires to go with her parents, Cyrus & Sarah, so this remains undecided. We should greatly prefer Lizzie's remaining. She has been in her confinement ever since these troubles, so we have had no opportunity of knowing how she is disposed to conduct herself. Whenever we have been to see her, her manner has been as pleasing as usual, she is one of the nicest & best trained of servants. Her sister, Georgiana, for the last two days has been as sullen as a cow, and as perverse as a mule; & as slow as a snail. Willie threatened this morning to send her away if she did not behave herself, which produced a momentary change for the better. To have to submit to the Yankees is bad enough, but to submit to negro children is a little worse. They will, I hope, get ready to go soon. We have now had nearly three weeks of this state of things.

April 20th

Had a pleasant visit from Charles Small after breakfast this morning. He has his parole, and hopes to go to Baltimore soon. He told me of riots in N. York and Baltimore, in which, the mob incensed at the attacks on Lincoln & Seward, were killing our paroled prisoners. It is to be hoped the account is exaggerated. George walked to town in quest of the mule. Willie & John at work in the garden. Rosina very unwell today; did not get up. George, unsuccessful in the quest of the mule, and his feet pained him so much, that he staid at Westbrook all night. He has not recovered from the effects of his march and fight of five days and nights, without sleep, & almost without food, before the surrender at Appomattox Ct. House, & the march home afterwards.

April 21st

Walked to town with Willie to make another effort to regain the mule & horse. The weather was very warm but we had quite a pleasant walk. The road bordered with beautiful wild Honeysuckle, iris, violets &c &c. We found the mule to a cart just as we reached town! Willie claimed & identified it without difficulty, and brought it home in the evening. Walked with Willie to the quartermaster depot at Rocketts, where I sat in the Office & wrote a letter to send to sister Ellen by Mr. Patterson, while Willie examined the horses in search of Charles. I finished my letter by the time he got back. He did not find Charles. He got an order from some officer for transportation to Petersbg., to look among the captured horses there for him. Gusta walked home with Willie. I staid in town till Monday afternoon, when I came out on the cars which are again running. Richmond is a strange looking place—with its heap of ruins, its streets traversed by U.S. Army wagons—sidewalks thronged with Yankee soldiers, & saucy negro women. The Capitol Square over-run with the same, while troops of little negroes play at Soldier around the Monument. Everything looks unnatural & desecrated, and the eye is offended by all it sees, and the ear by all it hears—especially does the heart sicken at the music of their well-appointed bands. Still we have much to be thankful for so far, & I trust in God's mercy to preserve us from tyrannical oppression in the future—a thing much dreaded by many under the new administration. I found Willie & John at work in the field when I got back, George gone to Petersbg. to look for the horse. Rose and Gusta in the house—the former sewing, the latter practising. All had been quiet during my absence. The servants remain in the same unsatisfactory condition. Cy. spending his days away from here, somewhere, Georgiana acting like a mule—All doing as the please, and no one asserting any authority over them.

April 28th

Things remain as last recorded. No disturbances, though a large army corps is camped just within the fortifications. Fanny Young has been over twice to see us. We hear of our Southern towns & cities being in possession of the enemy, but we have no private accounts from Danville, where Edmund Myers & his family were living, from Raleigh or Mobile. George got home to dinner yesterday, but did not find the horse in Petersbg. The Fifth Mass. Negro Cavalry that stole him, is at Ft. Harrison. He staid with our friends the Simpsons in Petersbg.— Says they are all well and right cheerful. People there are better off than in Richmond, where so many have been completely ruined by the fire. Many who were in good circumstances hitherto, are drawing rations from the Yankees. Gusta is staying with the Stuarts since Tuesday morning.

April 30th

Papers of Friday contain accounts of the peaceable entrance into Raleigh of Sherman's forces—property respected and protected, which is a relief to our minds. Oppressive orders are being issued to our people in Virginia. No business can be carried on, no marriages contracted unless all the parties concerned take the oath of allegiance to the U.S. Government. Marylanders who left their home to join our struggle for independence, are now forbidden to return to them. This affects many in whom we are interested, and disturbs me particularly on account of my dear Edward Cohen. We must still wait on God in cheerful hope. George & Mr. Taylor made another effort yesterday to recover the horse, going down to Ft. Harrison, after that horrible Regiment, Col. Adams' 15th Massachusetts Negro Cavalry. Before reaching there, they heard of such abominable treatment, received the day before by some persons who had gone there for the same purpose, that Mr. Taylor, who was seeking a stolen horse of his own, declined going further. George, however, and another man went on, when lo: on their arrival they found that the demons had been removed to Petersbg. that morning early—so that was all—George describes the appearance of the country down there, so long the camping-ground of Grant's immense army, and of our smaller one, as desolate in the extreme. Whole farms without a sign of vegetation upon them—not a tree or a fence or a blade of grass—the ground as hard as a brick yard. Immensely strong & extensive fortifications on every side, and the numberless huts lately occupied by the Yankees, showing their vast superiority to ourselves in numbers as well as in comforts and resources of every kind. I forgot to record in the proper place, that on Friday, George got his mother's box of silver, which had been dug out of the vaults of the Farmer's Bank unhurt. The wooden box which contained it was not even scorched! Many were less fortunate, and the books & papers of the Bank were all destroyed. George saw a wheelbarrow load of silverplate, all melted up and blackened.

May 4th Thursday

Walked to town alone on Tuesday morning, anxious to hear something of Caroline and all my kin there, and to know if anything had been heard of Ed. Cohen, or from any of the family in Raleigh or elsewhere. The day was cool—no dust, no sun, no rain, & I walked in rapidly—passing through the enemy's camp on each side of the turnpike with the breastworks. They were very quiet & orderly. Met few persons on the road except negro men & women, and some very decent white women, bringing out baskets of cakes, apples &c. to sell to the soldiers, the only business at which any money can be got now.

I took in a gold thimble, and some gold trinkets to sell if possible, as I cannot bear to be without any money though I do not require much. I thought I would go into the cake business myself. I sold my gold for nine dollars—bought ½ Gal. molasses, and two lbs. flour, and some soda for sixty-two cts., & with this I have begun trade. I staid in town Tuesday night, having missed the cars, and being too tired after walking into & about town to walk back. I found Caroline well & in good spirits, as were all the rest, in spite of the want that was staring them in the face. Rebecca, Ella, & Caroline were busy making six shirts for the Yankee Officer who boards there—at one dollar and a quarter apiece. He had been with them nearly a week. Mr. Iglehart was reading aloud to them. He was waiting for a pass to visit Annapolis, but the late edict, forbidding all Marylanders engaged in "The Rebellion", to return to their homes, put an end to his hopes, & he returned to his Va. home at Mr. Brookes' the uncle of his wife. I went to see my cousins C. H. & J. They had got a letter from my brother Major Alfred Mordecai, making enquiries about all the family—it betrays dejection & solicitude tho' written very guardedly. The state of destitution of which the greater part of all classes in Richmond is reduced must be almost unprecedented. The utter and sudden worthlessness of our currency would alone produce poverty enough but the ruin to thousands, produced by the fire, in addition to this, has reduced almost everyone to the condition of pensioners on the Yankee Government. I must do these undesired authorities the justice to say that they are doing all they can to alleviate the universal distress, and that many of their regulations for the establishment and maintenance of order, are wise & efficient. The negro movement is still a most vexatious and mischievous one and its effects are painfully felt in every Southern household. This morning Cy. came to high words with George & John, insisting "he had a right to stay here—to bring here whom he pleased—to keep his family here—He was, he said, entitled to a part of the farm after all the work he had done on it. The kitchen belonged to him because he had helped cut the timber to build it." He also insists that all the land belongs to the U. States, and that it is to be divided among the negroes &c. Willie told him that he would give him three days to find a place to move to, a thing which he declared his intention of doing three weeks ago. Georgiana continues for the most part sullen & perverse. Lizzy, though she has resumed her duties in the house, is still in uncertain position, & devotes much time to her maternal cares, and though not impertinent, is rather too independent to be satisfactory. I made a good quantity of Confederate Cake this morning & gave it to William Gentry to sell for me at the Camp near his mother's—he thinks he can do a great business.

May 5th

This morning, without giving any warning of their intentions, all the servants were discovered to be packing up to go. Lizzy, whom we considered engaged for a month, was the first to get ready. Her husband told Rose he was mighty sorry to take her away from her, but that he liked to have his friends to visit him, & as this was not liked by the family, he had rented a room at Mr. Harwood's and was going to move there. Of course this was a false pretext, as this place has always been run over with negro visitors. Cyrus has rented a house on the turnpike, near the battery, and is moving there with the rest of his family. They all seem anything but joyous at the change, and Rosina is really and greatly distressed at parting with the foolish creatures. She thinks Cy. already repents of his late improper conduct which alone has brought about this change. Rose gave them all presents of old dresses &c. and also some meat, meal & potatoes, for all of which they seemed very grateful. We shall not be left entirely without a servant, as Willie told Cy. he wanted Georgiana to stay a few days, until we had found someone to take her place, and Elick to mind the cows, to which Cy. willingly consented; for which condescension on his part, Willie gave him leave to pick up fire-wood about here for his own use for a few days longer. His wife, Sarah, has behaved as well as possible the whole time, and we all respect her for it. She does not seem to approve of Cy's arrangements. They will now begin to find out how easy their life as slaves has been, & to feel the slavery of their freedom. Rose has walked over to Mr. Taylor's to make enquiries after other servants. The afternoon is lovely, I forgot to mention that when in town last, I met Mrs. John N. Gordon, a lady who has a very large family, and who was entirely burnt out in the conflagration of the fourth of April. She saved nothing but her beds. She told me all her servants have since left her, but she found it a great relief, as there were so many children among them to provide for. She now has a woman to cook for her, who was living at the place to which the family had gone, (a furnished house, from which the owners had fled on the approach of the enemy!) and she gets a woman to come & wash for them one day in the week, & they dispense with other service. I told her I had heard how wonderfully she bore her misfortunes. She replied, "I don't regard my private troubles as of the slightest importance—it is the public calamity, the loss of our cause and the misfortunes of the country that distress me—If that was all right, I should not care, & I do not care for my losses"!!

May 6th

The servants all went Friday evening—Georgiana & Martha returned at dusk & are still with us. They behave well so far, & are very useful. Willie milked the cows that evening & I strained the milk. Susan, one of the former Gardner servants, came up from the Mill & engaged to milk & to get breakfast every day until we get supplied with a cook. A niece of hers, a very nice girl who is out of a place, thinks of hiring herself here. She got dinner yesterday & cooked it very well. Poor Rose is miserably distressed. She scarcely slept at all Friday night. She is not only entirely upset in her domestic affairs, but she is grieved to part with Cy. & Sarah and Lizzy. She said, "If they felt as I do, they could not possibly leave me." Cy. came back yesterday after his fowls, & sought an opportunity to take leave of his "Mistress" (as he still calls her, in spite of his declaration to me, to the contrary,) and of the boys. He expressed to Rose his regret for his improper conduct the other morning, and was very much affected at parting with her. She could not take leave of him without emotion, & has felt miserable ever since. What an uprooting of social ties, and tearing asunder of almost kindred associations, and destruction of true loyalty, this strange, new, state of things produces!! The disturbance to the Whites & the privations it will at first entail upon the poor, improvident negroes, is incalculable. Augusta is still at the Stuarts. Her mother does not wish her to return until she is supplied with servants. She thinks she would be as much distressed as herself to see them all leave the place. I yesterday received a most unexpected visit. A gentleman in citizen's dress rode up to the gate accompanied by a Yankee Orderly, and alighting, came to the house & asked for me! He proved to be Mr. Marcus L. Ward of Newark, N. Jersey, whose acquaintance I had formed twenty years ago, when travelling at the North, in 1844! Our whole party had been much pleased with him, & as we travelled together for some days, we became well acquainted. A few years after that, seventeen years ago now, he visited the south for his health, being threatened with consumption. He found me out in Richmond, & I was delighted to see him and to extend to him whatever little attentions lay in my power. I felt deeply concerned about his condition, as his cough was very bad. I hoped to hear from him after he left Richmond but as I never did, had long ago concluded that he had died of his disease. My astonishment cannot be described, therefore at receiving a visit from him, in this secluded spot, under existing circumstances, after so long a period. He told me that he had written to me, and he expressed the greatest chagrin at my not having heard from him, saying that I must have thought him most ungrateful, &c.; that he had thought of me with the greatest solicitude through all our troubles, and longed to know how I was situated. He told me his wife knew me almost as well as he did, he had so often spoke to her of me. I had not recognized him, when I met him—He did not send up his name. He is much stouter, & of course looks older than when I last saw him. The sincerity of his expressions of regard, was sufficiently proved by his having ascertained in a three days' visit to Richmond, where I could be found, and securing means through friends of his in Gen. Meades' army, to come out and see me. Our interview was an exceedingly interesting one, only the time was too short to discuss or even to touch upon the many topics of interest which presented themselves. He asked me if there was nothing he could do for me—that he had so often when in N. York, longed to find something that would be suitable for him to send to me, and of use when received; that he never heard the so often repeated cry of "On to Richmond!" without remembering me with painful solicitude. Was there no book that I would like to have, and that could not be got in the South now, and was delighted, when swallowing my pride, I mentioned one, which I had long desired to possess. His visit was a most gratifying one to me, & so he said it was to himself—It was as long as he could make it, as he was to leave Richmond at 3 P.M. that day. His object in coming at this time, was to give his two sons the opportunity of seeing the grand Federal Army, then assembled here, before it was disbanded. I gave him a rose as he went away to keep in remembrance of Rosewood, at which he appeared much pleased, and asked me to add to it a piece of the Coral Honeysuckle, blooming on the little arbour. He had called at Westbrook on his way here to see Mr. Young who was of that same traveling party wh. he remembers with so much pleasure. He was from home, but Mrs. Young received the visit. He expressed to me the greatest desire to be able to do something to assist Mr. Young in his present difficulties, which Fanny had given him an idea of. I don't know when I have been as much interested, excited, touched & gratified as I was by this visit from one of our enemies. In the afternoon I went over to Westbrook. Several Corps of Grant's Army had been passing up the turnpike all day— returning to Washington, there to be disbanded. I went on top of the house to see the living stream, in one compact mass pouring up the road as far as the eye could reach in both directions. An admirably disciplined and well organized force—No straggling—no uproar—a quiet, steady stream—moving in an almost unbroken current. They have finished their work of destruction and subjugation, and are going in triumph to uninjured, undisturbed homes & customs, only ruining a few more farms in their progress, the owners of which have just returned from our army, destitute of everything, and having some hope of making something to live on, as the Surrender took place in time to plant. They camped all over the Farms above to Mr. Stuart's as far as the eye could reach—burning fences to make their Camp-fires, and treading down the wheat & oats. It is said Sherman's Army is also to pass this way. If so, all farming operations on their line of march had as well be suspended. Last night the coops with setting hens, and those with broods of young chickens were robbed of seven hens—Three large broods are thus left to shift for themselves, and four settings of eggs, two of the nests being duck eggs for which a high price was paid, all probably rendered useless. The eggs were left behind the pig-pen—This was doubtless done by Yankee soldiers who were prowling about the place yesterday.

May 7th P.M.

Martha (one of Cy's.) left us this morning, & Georgiana & Elick, this afternoon. Susan was sick and could not come up to milk—so Willie milked—I set up the supper-table, & Rose fed the fowls & attended to everything. Got a note from Caroline—giving the joyful news of the arrival in Richmond of Edmund (her brother) from Danville, and Edward Cohen from No. Carolina.

Tuesday A.M. [May 9]

Ned (*E. D. T. Myers*) came out in the cars last evening & staid all night, was very cheerful & agreeable & he and the boys being together again. He takes a less gloomy view of things than most people do, is determined not to be made unhappy by the state of the country. A white girl from the Orphan Asylum has come out on trial—is unhappy & lonesome, and doesn't intend to stay—She does not seem to be very competent. Georgiana who returned yesterday has gone for good, & we very badly off—have a temporary in the kitchen. I gathered strawberries yesterday & to-day for Rose to sell to soldiers—very fine ones. Rose is miserable at present trials & apprehensions of future ones—does not expect ever to have any servants on any terms again.

May 11th

A day of rare beauty, following a stormy night—The air so clear, & cool, the sky so blue, & the slopes of the leafy woods so green. The birds are numerous and the air is filled with their warbling. Thus it is in the outer world. Within, there is no beauty, no enjoyment, no harmony. Rose has had two days of nervous suffering & mental torture. She is still unsupplied with servants, & we have no definite prospect of getting any. I have been doing drudgery for the greater part of the week—assisted unwillingly & inefficiently by a little white girl from town, who is so miserable at being in the country, that she thinks of nothing, but how to get home again. My efforts do not meet with the only compensation I desire for them, the satisfaction of knowing that they afford one ray of comfort, or are in any way appreciated. The events of the last two days, have arisen from the moving of Sherman's army from Richmond to Washington. Last night a General (perhaps Sherman himself) and his staff were camped at Westbrook, & the troops are moving up the turnpike today—leaving behind then the ruin & desolation & misery they have spread through our land, to return to their own & find it untouched by these four years of cruel war—Sherman's army is perfectly ruthless, & now that the war is over, are as destructive as other armies are when engaged in hostilities. They are now giving us "the last Tag". They destroyed all the fencing & the large gate at Westbrook last night—Camped in the yard under the dining room windows, turned the horses out of the stables, to put theirs in, put their horses in the carriage house, & parked their wagons before the kitchen. I only hope they may continue such practices north of the Potomac.

May 13th

Willie & I gathered 12 qts. of fine strawberries Friday P.M., & John got four dollars for them in Market Saturday. Gusta returned from the Stuart's—Rose suffering all Saturday morning. A visit from her brother in the evening seemed of service to her. Annie the little white girl left us—Today Gusta & I have done all the house work except the boy's room wh. they did up themselves. Rose still in bed but seems more composed in mind. I must here record two anecdotes, told me by an eye & ear witness, illustrative of the new disorder of things. My informant was working in his garden which lies on the public road—he heard a negro man who was passing, thus soliloquizing. "Dis what you call freedom!—No work to do, & got to feed & clothe yourself". The same person was in town a few days ago, talking to an acquaintance on the street. A negro girl passed them, with her books on her way to school. They stopped her and asked what she was studying. She replied, "I studyin dis here book". "Let me look at it" said the gentlemen. It was a French Grammar. He returned it to her gravely remarking that it was a very suitable book for her to study.

The 15th Corps of Sherman's Army, (the last they say,) passed up the Brook turnpike yesterday exciting admiration, even among our own soldiers, by their numbers, equipment & discipline. How is it that we have sustained a four years war with an enemy who can present such armies at its close? The men boast of the destruction they have spread through So. Carolina & Georgia. They say they left nothing standing but houses, & destroyed many of them. They have in their train, cows that they have driven all the way from Georgia; mules, splendid horses & handsome equipages, all taken from once wealthy Southerners, whom they have left stript of even the necessaries of life. Doubtless the Officers' baggage wagons are loaded with stolen family-plate & other valuables. No news from Raleigh yet, but what we see in the Herald.

Wednesday [Monday May 15?]

As Monday was a fine day, & Augusta at home, I indulged myself in a visit to town, urged still further to do so by my desire to see Dr. Beale & get some spirits, for Rose if possible. I attended successfully to my business first, & then went down to my cousins'—On my way I met with Moses, my former slave, who was at work (he is a bricklayer) on Broad Strt. No servant could behave better than he has done. He showed great interest in me & all of us, and begged me to call upon him whenever he could do anything for me. His freedom will be little loss to me, nor gain to him, for as his wife who also belonged to me, is a very sickly woman & the children only an expense, it took nearly the whole of the wages he paid to me, to pay Dr's and druggists bills and to clothe them. I was truly glad to find my dear Edward Cohen at my cousin's. I spent several hours with them all, right happy in Ed. & C's. happiness & being allowed to share in it—I returned in the cars at 3:30, E. & C. walking to the depot with me. Heard of President Davis's capture, only hope it is not true that he was disguised in Mrs. Davis's clothes. I found R. sitting up—she looks very badly.

Tuesday [May 16]

Got up very soon—made fire & took up the ashes in R's room while Gusta swept, & then I dressed, strained the milk, swept back & front porch, fixed things on the table, got ice-water in the pitcher, by wh. time breakfast was ready. After breakfast we cleared away the table, washed up & I cleaned knives while she swept & dusted the dining-room—then she practiced while I gathered strawberries. Willie went to town servant hunting & returned with a woman & two little boys—the only one he could find, willing to come to the country. Rose says she is an untaught field-hand—She certainly cannot cook well, but is said to wash & iron well. At any rate her being here relieves Gusta & me from house-work, as Ellen the girl whom I omitted to record was cooking, can now come in the house. The new woman expresses willingness to learn what she does not know. Had a visit from Mrs. Oscar Taylor—all the talk, everywhere now is servants. Mr. Gardner came in the evening & staid all night—was very amusing—telling of Col. Fairchild's intoxicated visit to Westbrook. Went to town Friday & staid till Monday afternoon returning in the cars.

May 21st

There was a tremendous rain storm at night—doing much damage in town & country—collars overflowed &c. Out here the mill dam broke and the pond was emptied. Corn on hill sides washed up, Sunday—while I was in town. Before coming home on Monday I succeeded in getting some whisky for Rose at 1.15 a quart. I went to see Genl. Patrick, the Provost Marshal, who won my heart by his kindness, courtesy & attention. He gave me unsolicited an order to get a mule or horse, in place of Charlie the stolen horse, and an order on the Commissary to let me have two qts. whisky for R. Came home in triumph, but was caught in a hard rain on leaving the cars, & took refuge at Mrs. Johnson's until it was over—got very wet going there— Found R. better on my return, but unwilling to allow it—talked all the afternoon.

May 23rd Tuesday

I rose early—after our early breakfast did some mending—heard Gusta her French & I gathered about 10 qts. strawberries for market. R. helped me with them, (the heavy rains making this necessary) and this took till near dinner time—then changed my dress & lay down to rest until dinner was ready. Willie & George went to town after the promised mule, & returned while we were at dinner with the mule & a cow-boy, having also seen blk. George who told them where the stolen cart was—so we are making up for our losses. On

Wednesday Gusta went to Brook Hill with Willie to bid farewell to her good friends, the Stuart family, who leave for Europe Saturday.

May 24th

The fifth Army Corps, Genl. Wright, passed up the turnpike, occupying the whole day in the transit, consequently Gusta was detained at Brook Hill. We hear that many of the troops that have passed here to be disbanded, have been sent to Texas, Kirby Smith refusing to surrender & it is said being still in command of a large army. Some think the Trans-Miss. country will still achieve its independence. Willie went this A.M. after the stolen cart & succeeded in getting not only it, but the harness & cover—In our misfortunes we have been wonderfully fortunate—In the afternoon train, Edward Cohen came out. Willie went to Brook Hill for Gusta and I took a pleasant walk with Edward to Mrs. Johnson's to return a shawl & book. We sat under the pines on our return, & I read to him various letters & notes I wanted him to hear. We walked & talked till sunset. Gusta and Willie got back after supper. Gusta played for Edward, the "Blue Danube Waltzes", full of 6th Strt. associations, before the surrender, the boys smoked and talked with him, and we retired about ten.

May 26th

I intended going to town with Edward, but the rain fell in torrents nearly all night, and almost all day without ceasing. Many of the chickens got drowned in the yard. The rain is very destructive and injurious. The boys in the house all day. Ed. Cohen returned to town in spite of it. R. has been very much depressed all day—indeed is so all the time. How I wish she could be cheered! She is a victim to gloom & dependency. Today has been gloomy with us all. The cold pouring rain is depressing in itself—Gusta & Willie are very sad at parting with the Stuarts. Rose feels miserably about everything, which with her wretched health is not surprising, and I feel worried about the time on her account, and my own position and prospects are not cheering, and I can only seem to observe nothing, and to feel nothing. Gusta is plaiting a hat for John—

May 30th

Got a note from Caroline on Saturday telling me that brother Alfred was in town! Arrived Thursday afternoon. Felt very much agitated at learning this. Got Willie to walk in with me Sunday, (the cars not running)—to see him. On reaching my cousins' found that he had gone the day before, on his way to Raleigh. Instead of him found Edmund, Fanny, & Lill there. I felt at once disappointed & relieved—so much had I dreaded seeing him. They told me he was very sad, though he looked well. I staid in town till Monday afternoon when I returned in the cars. Got interesting letters from Raleigh while in town. They have suffered much more in the vicinity of Raleigh, than we have near Richmond. In the town, property was protected, but in the country, destroyed wantonly. Jacob Mordecai's place six or eight miles north of Raleigh—ruined. These letters contained the first direct information we have received of my dear, good brother Sam's death. He died on Sunday, April 9th, of Erysipelas, after a painful illness of a week's duration. His old friends in Richmond express the highest admiration of his character & intellect, and sincere regret at his loss. For himself he had little left to make life desirable. Although age had not rendered him incapable of enjoyment, circumstances deprived him of all its opportunities.

Aug. 1886

The tattered sheet containing this sad record is the last I can find of those containing my Diary—I will add a letter from Mrs. Ellen Mordecai, which I think worth preserving—Unfortunately it has no date—but the contents mark the period.

Raleigh. 1865.

To Miss Emma Mordecai. Richmond.
At last my dear E. I find myself actually seated to write to you—Where do I begin, and what to say, when so much will have to remain unsaid, for it would take a quire of paper to tell it all. What a summer this has been!—I feel, as does everybody, I reckon, that we are removed far, far away from everything that was Home—that we seem to be outcasts. No words can ever paint the bitterness, the hatred I feel to our despicable conquerors—ungenerous, low-minded, pitiful wretches. I will be just enough to say that at the hands of one or two I have had civility. I have had nothing to do socially with one. One or two favours, which I did not regard as favours so much as rights, I have asked, & fortunately applied, as I say, to the one in a thousand—a gentleman. For weeks before the Yankee came, I was living in a sort of whirl—wounded & sick Confederates in the house, and the daily administering to the wants of the passing soldiers. Then came Uncle's (*Mr. Sam Mordecai*) hurried and violent illness & death—then the horrid preparations for the enemy, & the heartbreaking emotions caused by the retreat of our Army. (*Genl. Johnson's.*) The very day before the Yankees came in, four or five Confederates breakfasted with us—all Charlestonians, and real gentlemen. I had never seen them before, but felt as if I knew them, while I was waiting on them, & putting up the last lunch I ever gave a soldier on duty. But there is no use in going back to those days—now gone forever—I feel as if there was nothing more to live for in this world. My very heart and soul were bound up in our cause, & while I can truly say I do not murmur at God's will, I feel utterly cast down, at our failure, and when I think of our President, the victim of their petty tyranny, my heart aches, & fervently my prayers ascend to Heaven, that he may be

sustained in these dark days, by a high, unfaltering trust in God! Well, you have heard of all our servant trouble—For weeks I got on marvellously well, without a cook—that is, a regular one—Jac's (*Capt Jacob Mordecai of Mobile—a first cousin*) servant did my cooking—and Sally (*a family servant*) was sick, and you know I had my two Confederate prisoners (*on parole*) and my dearest Jac with me. I would not have been without them for any thing. It was a balm to my heart to see Confederate grey constantly before me, & while so many had Yankee officers in their houses, I too feel I was protected by our own dear men. There could not be two more agreeable inmates than Col. Norris (*of Md.*) and Major Hennin (*of N. Orleans,*) and I was truly grieved when they were hurried off by that second cruel arrest. How my blood boiled to see Yankee muskets under every window of my house! I have been annoyed the whole summer by the constant presence of the Yankees. My back yard does not seem to me to belong to me. Till within the last ten days, it has been a perfect thoroughfare for soldiers, negroes and poor white folks. There was ever a group at the well, & soldiers hanging round my servants houses. The nuisance was intolerable. My gates were constantly open, & I dare not have them fastened—so cows were in the yard day and night. My poor little cedar hedge is a perfect wreck—my garden constantly pillaged—I was subjected to all sorts of petty annoyances & insults, and no representation of these facts to the officers produced anything but promises, until about ten days ago, when Jac went over and reported the insolence of a soldier at the well, & as, in his insolence he had cursed headquarters, the officer to whom Jac reported him, was very angry & sent over a subordinate officer at once, and put a sentinel at the well with strict orders, & as Jac is very prompt to report any negligence on the part of the sentinel, a different state of things prevails & the evils very much mitigated. Still home does not seem like home—nothing seems natural. I turn away from the contemplation of things as they are, and as they will be. Still you must not fancy me a picture of dejection. Until I became sick about five weeks ago I retained my energy, industry & spirit, but I have been suffering from quite a severe attack of jaundice, & I am the greatest sight you ever beheld, just as yellow and as withered as an old cucumber, put on the fence for seed. It is the effect of this disease to prostate the spirits & energies and I suffer in this way. I have fallen off considerably, & feel week and languid. Mag (*her little girl,*) is just recovering from a long attack of the same, which was preceded by a slight billious fever and followed by the severest eruption I ever saw—it was really alarming at first, it looked so much like smallpox. She suffered severely for two days & nights, and then began to grow better. Aunt Tempe has had a sick summer, but is now much improved in health. We attribute all this sickness to the offensive odours from the camps all around us—I rarely get a breath of real, pure, old timey air, & sometimes we are compelled to leave the front porch & shut the door to exclude the horrid stench. I have been interrupted by a visit from Sister Margaret & Nan—They have employed a very good man as table servant—he understands his business & they hope, with trembling, that he may prove a fixture. In other respects they get on pretty well. Brother Jac's Charlotte is cooking for the present, but they do not know how long she will remain—Edy (*another of the family servants*) is cooking for me, & is a very good servant, but will do nothing but cook. Sally and Alice wash & attend to the house, so I get on comfortably considering the times, but not as I once thought comfortably. Sam has not been going to school this summer, & what with the disorganized condition of household concerns, & sickness, I have not been able to carry out my plan of attending to his lessons and reading, so he has done little or nothing in the way of books, but he has been most useful to me. He is an excellent business man. He sells milk for me every morning, & while we had vegetables, sold them; but my garden, was so pillaged by the soldiers, that I stopped working it, so there is nothing in it but weeds, & a few tomatoes and some ochra. Aunt

Tempe staid a few days not long ago, with cousins Sally & Grizzy. Their servant had just left them, and they had not one—but a very good woman who was living on the lot, did their cooking—little enough it was. They are pretty well & quite cheerful, tho' feeling as we all do, the bitter change—and as cousin Sally said, it is the country, not the individual adversity that she mourns. Susan Raynor looks thin & badly—she has been sick—has had a summer of harassing care & pressing anxieties. Martha Mordecai is getting on tolerably—has had plenty of trouble—little Patty is very delicate. Poor Emily died a short time ago—a good, faithful creature. Most of the servants there have been horrid—Lucy good & faithful and one or two others right good. Write to me and tell me how you are all getting on. My very best love to Rose, Gusta, & the boys, and all the folks in town. Excuse this miserable affair of a letter, & write when you can & feel like it, to your aff. Ellen—

Copied—August 5th 1886. At 1219 Broad St. Richmond

Notes

1. Emma Mordecai Diary, 1864–1865 (hereafter EMD), Folder 103, Mordecai Family Papers, Collection 00847, Southern Historical Collection, University of North Carolina at Chapel Hill (hereafter MFP).
2. See, for example, J. David Hacker, "A Census-Based Count of the Civil War Dead," *Civil War History* 57 (December 2011): 307–348.
3. Gary W. Gallagher, *The Confederate War: How Popular Will, Nationalism, and Military Strategy Could Not Stave Off Defeat* (Cambridge, MA: Harvard University Press, 1997), 28–29.
4. Barbara Brooks Tomblin, *Bluejackets and Contrabands: African Americans and the Union Navy* (Lexington: University of Kentucky Press, 2009).
5. Paul Quigley, *Shifting Grounds: Nationalism and the American South, 1848–1865* (New York: Oxford University Press, 2011).
6. Early scholarship on Southern Jewish history emphasized distinctiveness, as seen in Leonard Dinnerstein and Mary Dale Palsson, eds., *Jews in the South* (Baton Rouge: Louisiana State University Press, 1973); Nathan M. Kaganoff and Melvin I. Urofsky, eds., *Turn to the South: Essays on Southern Jewry* (Charlottesville: University of Virginia Press, 1979); and Eli N. Evans, *The Provincials: A Personal History of Jews in the South* (New York: Atheneum, 1973), which was updated in both 1997 and 2005. More recent Southern Jewish history has downplayed Southern Jewish exceptionalism, as seen in Marcie Cohen Ferris and Mark I. Greenberg, eds., *Jewish Roots in Southern Soil: A New History* (Waltham, MA: Brandeis University Press, 2006), and especially in the collected works of Mark K. Bauman, *A New Vision of Southern Jewish History: Studies in Institution Building, Leadership, Interaction, and Mobility* (Tuscaloosa: University of Alabama Press, 2019).

7 For representative studies of the thorny issues of American Jews and whiteness, particularly in the context of slavery, in addition to sources cited elsewhere in this introduction, see Mark I. Greenberg, "Becoming Southern: The Jews of Savannah, 1830–1870," *American Jewish History* 86 (January 1998): 55–75; Laura Arnold Leibman, *Once We Were Slaves: The Extraordinary Journey of a Jewish Multiracial Family* (New York: Oxford University Press, 2021); Jacob Morrow-Spitzer, "The 'Theoretical Jew' versus the 'Southern Jew': Black Perceptions of Jewish Whiteness in the Nineteenth Century American South," *American Jewish History* 106 (January 2021): 31–54; Tudor Parfitt, *Hybrid Hate: Conflations of Antisemitism and Anti-Black Racism from the Renaissance to the Third Reich* (New York: Oxford University Press, 2020); and Jason H. Silverman, "'The Law of the Land Is the Law': Antebellum Jews, Slavery, and the Old South," in *Struggles in the Promised Land: Toward a History of Black-Jewish Relations*, ed. Jack Salzman and Cornel West (New York: Oxford University Press, 1997), 73–86.

8 Eric L. Goldstein, *The Price of Whiteness: Jews, Race, and American Identity* (Princeton, NJ: Princeton University Press, 2006). See also Eliza R. L. McGraw, *Two Covenants: Representation of Southern Jewishness* (Baton Rouge: Louisiana State University Press, 2005).

9 Major works on gender, slavery, Southern white women, and the Civil War, in addition to those cited elsewhere in the introduction, include Victoria Bynum, *Unruly Women: The Politics of Social and Sexual Control in the Old South* (Chapel Hill: University of North Carolina Press, 1992); Catherine Clinton, *The Plantation Mistress: Woman's World in the Old South* (New York: Pantheon, 1983); Catherine Clinton, *Stepdaughters of History: Southern Women and the American Civil War* (Baton Rouge: Louisiana State University Press, 2016); Laura F. Edwards, *Scarlett Doesn't Live Here Anymore: Southern Women in the Civil War Era* (Urbana: University of Illinois Press, 2000); Victoria E. Ott, *Confederate Daughters: Coming of Age in the Civil War* (Carbondale: Southern Illinois University Press, 2008); Giselle Roberts, *The Confederate Belle* (Columbia: University of Missouri Press, 2003); and Marli F. Weiner, *Mistresses and Slaves: Plantation Women in South Carolina, 1830–1870* (Urbana: University of Illinois Press, 1998).

10 For a classic summary of this interpretation, see Gallagher, *Confederate War*. For a classic summary of an alternate interpretation that emphasizes multiple forms of disaffection and resistance among both white and Black Southerners, see William W. Freehling, *The South vs. the South: How Anti-Confederate Southerners Shaped the Course of the Civil War* (New York: Oxford University Press, 2001).

11 A recent example of this type of synthesis in reference to women's history and the Civil War is Thavolia Glymph, *The Women's Fight: The Civil War's Battles*

for Home, Freedom, and Nation (Chapel Hill: University of North Carolina Press, 2020).
12 Emily Bingham, *Mordecai: An Early American Family* (New York: Hill and Wang, 2003), 12–13; and Myron Berman, *The Last of the Jews?* (Lanham, MD: University Press of America, 1998), 110.
13 Berman, *Last of the Jews?*, 9; and Jonathan D. Sarna, "The Democratization of American Judaism," in *New Essays in American Jewish History*, ed. Pamela S. Nadell, Jonathan D. Sarna, and Lance J. Sussman (Cincinnati: American Jewish Archives, 2010), 96.
14 Judith Myers Mordecai to Joyce Mears Myers and Myer Myers, December 5, 1792, Folder 1, MFP; Judith Myers Mordecai to Jacob Mordecai, February 11, 1793, Folder 1, MFP; Judith Mordecai to Joyce and Myer Myers, March 16, 1793, Folder 1, MFP; Bingham, *Mordecai*, 21; Berman, *Last of the Jews?*, 11.
15 Bingham, *Mordecai*, 22.
16 Berman, *Last of the Jews?*, 18.
17 Sheldon Hanft, "Mordecai's Female Academy," *American Jewish History* 79 (January 1989): 72–93.
18 Bingham, *Mordecai*, 84–86.
19 Bingham, 110.
20 See Rachel Mordecai Lazarus and Maria Edgeworth, *The Education of the Heart: The Correspondence of Rachel Mordecai Lazarus and Maria Edgeworth*, ed. Edgar E. MacDonald (Chapel Hill: University of North Carolina Press, 1977).
21 Bingham, *Mordecai*, 6–7; Samuel Mordecai to Solomon Mordecai, September 29, 1817, Box 1, Jacob Mordecai Papers, Archives and Manuscripts, Duke University (JMP hereafter); Rebecca Gratz to Maria Edgeworth, quoted in Edwin Wolf and Maxwell Whiteman, *The History of the Jews of Philadelphia from Colonial Times to the Age of Jackson* (Philadelphia: JPS, 1957), 47.
22 Berman, *Last of the Jews?*, 1–7.
23 Bingham, *Mordecai*, 100–101.
24 Quoted in Myron Berman, *Richmond's Jewry: Shabbat in Shockoe, 1769–1976* (Charlottesville: University of Virginia Press, 1979), 24–25.
25 Berman, 36–38.
26 Robert N. Rosen, *The Jewish Confederates* (Charleston: University of South Carolina Press, 2000), xii–xiii.
27 Bertram W. Korn, "Jews and Negro Slavery in the Old South, 1789–1856," *Publications of the American Jewish Historical Society* 50 (March 1961): 194. While this article is dated, it was the first professional historical assessment of the issue and remains worthwhile.
28 William A. Link, *Roots of Secession: Slavery and Politics in Antebellum Virginia* (Chapel Hill: University of North Carolina Press, 2003), 213; quoted in Jennifer

Stollman, *Daughters of Israel, Daughters of the South: Southern Jewish Women and Identity in the Antebellum and Civil War South* (Boston: Academic Studies Press, 2013), 190.

29 Link, *Roots of Secession*, 242.

30 Alfred Mordecai to Samuel Mordecai, March 17, 1861, Box 4, Alfred Mordecai Papers, MSS 33415, Library of Congress; Stanley F. Falk, "Divided Loyalties in 1861: The Decision of Major Alfred Mordecai," *Publications of the American Jewish Historical Society* 48 (March 1959): 147–169; Rosen, *Jewish Confederates*, xii–xiii.

31 Anne Murrell Taylor, *The Divided Family in Civil War America* (Chapel Hill: University of North Carolina Press, 2005), 1–3, 72–73.

32 Nelson Lankford, *Richmond Burning: The Last Days of the Confederate Capital* (New York: Penguin, 2002), 19.

33 Samuel Mordecai to George Mordecai, March 18, 1864, Box 43, George Mordecai Papers, Collection 00522, Southern Historical Collection, University of North Carolina at Chapel Hill (hereafter GMP); Bingham, *Mordecai*, 254–257.

34 Laura Arnold Leibman, *The Art of the Jewish Family: A History of Women in Early New York in Five Objects* (Chicago: Bard College and University of Chicago Press, 2020), 165.

35 Stollman, *Daughters of Israel*, 32–33; Anne C. Rose, *Beloved Strangers: Interfaith Families in Nineteenth-Century America* (Cambridge, MA: Harvard University Press, 2001), especially chapter 1, which profiles the Mordecai family.

36 Samuel Mordecai to George Mordecai, April 26, 1834, GMP; Ellen Mordecai to George Mordecai, September 7, 1834, Little-Mordecai Collection, PC 1480, North Carolina Division of Archives and History, Raleigh (hereafter LMFP); Emma to Ellen Mordecai, October 1, 1834, Patti Mordecai Collection, PC 185, North Carolina Division of Archives and History, Raleigh (hereafter PMC); Emma to Ellen Mordecai, August 19, 1836, Folder 68, MFP; Bingham, *Mordecai*, 118–121.

37 Marie S. Molloy, *Single, White, Slaveholding Women in the Nineteenth-Century American South* (Columbia: University of South Carolina Press, 2018); and Anne Firor Scott, *The Southern Lady: From Pedestal to Politics, 1830–1930* (Chicago: University of Chicago Press, 1970), 35–36.

38 Chandra Manning, *Troubled Refuge: Struggling for Freedom in the Civil War* (New York: Knopf, 2016); and David Silkenat, *Driven from Home: North Carolina's Civil War Refugee Crisis* (Athens: University of Georgia Press, 2016).

39 Julia Mordecai to Emma Mordecai, February 25, 1834, Folder 63, MFP; Bingham, *Mordecai*, 117.

40 Gallagher, *Confederate War*, 28.

41 John M. Sacher, *Confederate Conscription and the Struggle for Southern Soldiers* (Baton Rouge: Louisiana State University Press, 2021); Freehling, *South vs. the South*, 145.

42 Lankford, *Richmond Burning*, 21.
43 EMD, June 7, 1864. Note that diary citations are to the date of the entry, which is not always the same as the date of the events. Emma sometimes wrote about several days' events in one entry.
44 Link, *Roots of Secession*, 38.
45 Kimberly Harrison, *The Rhetoric of Rebel Women: Civil War Diaries and Confederate Persuasion* (Carbondale: Southern Illinois University Press, 2013), 12.
46 EMD, April 18, 1864.
47 Witold Rybczynski, *Home: A Short History of an Idea* (New York: Penguin, 1986), 50–79.
48 Elizabeth Fox-Genovese, *Within the Plantation Household: Black and White Women of the Old South* (Chapel Hill: University of North Carolina Press, 1988), 31–32, 39, 102; see also Thavolia Glymph, *Out of the House of Bondage: The Transformation of the Plantation Household* (New York: Cambridge University Press, 2008).
49 Lori Merish, *Sentimental Materialism: Gender, Commodity Culture, and Nineteenth-Century American Literature* (Durham, NC: Duke University Press, 2020).
50 EMD, April 18, 1864. The classic explication of nineteenth-century women's relationships is Carroll Smith-Rosenberg, "The Female World of Love and Ritual: Relations between Women in Nineteenth-Century America," *Signs* 1 (Autumn 1975): 1–29.
51 EMD, April 18, 1864.
52 On the antebellum reconstruction of work as something that took place outside the home, particularly in the industrializing North, see Jeanne Boydston, *Home & Work: Housework, Wages, and the Ideology of Labor in the Early Republic* (New York: Oxford University Press, 1990).
53 EMD, April 18, 1864.
54 EMD, September 8, 1864.
55 Anya Jabour, *Scarlett's Sisters: Young Women in the Old South* (Chapel Hill: University of North Carolina Press, 2007).
56 Elizabeth Fox-Genovese and Eugene D. Genovese, *The Mind of the Master Class: History and Faith in the Southern Slaveholder's Worldview* (New York: Cambridge University Press, 2005), 46; Bingham, *Mordecai*, 197.
57 Berman, *Last of the Jews?*, 67.
58 EMD, October 6, 1864.
59 For example, EMD, April 18, 1864; Link, *Roots of Secession*, 32–33.
60 Emma Mordecai Diary, 1838, Folder 100, MFP.
61 EMD, April 18, 1864.
62 E. Jennifer Monaghan, *Learning to Read and Write in Colonial America* (Amherst: University of Massachusetts Press, 2005).

63 Catherine A. Brekus, "Writing as a Protestant Practice: Devotional Diaries in Early New England," in *Practicing Protestants: Histories of Christian Life in America, 1630–1965*, ed. Laurie F. Maffly-Kipp, Leigh E. Schmidt, and Mark Valeri (Baltimore: Johns Hopkins University Press, 2006), 19–34.

64 Major studies of American women's diaries, in addition to titles cited elsewhere in this introduction, include Margo Culley, *A Day at a Time: The Diary Literature of American Women Writers from 1764 to the Present* (New York: Feminist Press, 1993); Gayle R. Davis, "Women's Frontier Diaries: Writing for Good Reason," *Women's Studies* 14 (1987): 5–14; and Penelope Franklin, *Private Pages: Diaries of American Women, 1830s–1970s* (New York: Ballantine, 1986).

65 Benedict Anderson, *Imagined Communities* (New York: Verso, 1983).

66 Stephanie McCurry, *Masters of Small Worlds: Yeoman Households, Gender Relations and the Political Culture of the Antebellum South Carolina Low Country* (New York: Oxford University Press, 1995).

67 Clara Solomon, *The Civil War Diary of Clara Solomon*, ed. Elliot Ashkenazi (Baton Rouge: Louisiana State University Press, 1995); Eleanor H. Cohen Diary, 1865–1866, reprinted in *Memoirs of American Jews, 1775–1865*, ed. Jacob Rader Marcus, vol. 3 (Philadelphia: JPS, 1956), 359; Phoebe Yates Pember, *A Southern Woman's Story* (New York: G. W. Carlton, 1879); Berman, *Richmond's Jewry*, 179. For more on Jewish women's Civil War writing, see Stollman, *Daughters of Israel*; and Dianne Ashton, "Shifting Veils: Religion, Politics, and Womanhood in the Civil War Writings of American Jewish Women," in *Women and American Judaism: Historical Perspectives*, ed. Pamela S. Nadell and Jonathan D. Sarna (Waltham, MA: Brandeis University Press, 2001), 81–106.

68 Dana McMichael, "Approaches to Life Writing: Confederate Women's Diaries and the Construction of Ethnic Identity," in *Teaching the Literatures of the American Civil War*, ed. Colleen Glenney Boggs (New York: MLA, 2016), 110.

69 Sandra M. Gilbert and Susan Gubar, *The Madwoman in the Attic: The Woman Writer and the Nineteenth-Century Literary Imagination* (New Haven, CT: Yale University Press, 1979), 3.

70 The next generation of feminist critical perspectives on women's diary practices can be found in Suzanne L. Bunkers and Cynthia A. Huff, *Inscribing the Daily: Critical Essays on Women's Diaries* (Amherst: University of Massachusetts Press, 1996).

71 Amy L. Wink, *She Left Nothing in Particular* (Knoxville: University of Tennessee Press, 2001), xii–xv, xvii, 131; Robert J. Yinger and Christopher M. Clark, "Reflective Journal Writing: Theory and Practice," Occasional Paper 50, Institute for Research on Teaching, Michigan State University, East Lansing, 1981.

72 Linda Kerber, "Separate Spheres, Female Worlds, Woman's Place: The Rhetoric of Women's History," *The Journal of American History* 75 (June 1988): 9–39.

Kerber problematizes the use of "separate spheres" as a hermeneutic but does not deny the deeply felt public/private dichotomy inherent in middle-class, white women's lives during the nineteenth century.

73 Catherine Clinton, *The Other Civil War: American Women in the Nineteenth Century*, rev. ed. (New York: Hill and Wang, 1999); Lindsay Morgan Cantwell, "'My Thoughts Must Find Vent': Disjuncture and Resolution in Slaveholding Civil War Women's Diaries" (PhD diss., University of Colorado at Boulder, 2017); Sarah E. Gardner, *Blood and Irony: Southern White Women's Narratives of the Civil War, 1861–1867* (Chapel Hill: University of North Carolina Press, 2004); Harrison, *Rhetoric of Rebel Women*.

74 Drew Gilpin Faust, *Mothers of Invention: Women of the Slaveholding South in the American Civil War* (Chapel Hill: University of North Carolina Press, 1996).

75 See especially Linda K. Kerber, *Women of the Republic: Intellect and Ideology in Revolutionary America* (Chapel Hill: University of North Carolina Press, 1980); Mary Beth Norton, *Liberty's Daughters: The Revolutionary Experience of American Women, 1750–1800* (Ithaca, NY: Cornell University Press, 1980); and Anne M. Boylan, *The Origins of Women's Activism: New York and Boston, 1797–1840* (Chapel Hill: University of North Carolina Press, 2002).

76 Fox-Genovese and Genovese, *Mind of the Master Class*.

77 The classic study is Barbara Welter, "The Cult of True Womanhood, 1820–1860," *American Quarterly* 18 (Summer 1966): 151–174.

78 Berman, *Richmond's Jewry*, 167

79 EMD, November 24, 1864.

80 Katherine K. Preston, *Opera on the Road: Traveling Opera Troupes in the United States* (Urbana: University of Illinois Press, 1993); Harlan F. Jennings, "Rossini Re-visited: Nineteenth Century Performances in the American Heartland," *Sonneck Society for American Music Bulletin* 19 (1993): 5–6. The most frequently performed opera was *The Barber of Seville*, sung in both Italian and English.

81 Heather Andrea Williams, *Self-Taught: African American Education in Slavery and Freedom* (Chapel Hill: University of North Carolina Press, 2005).

82 Stollman, *Daughters of Israel*, 120.

83 Judy Nolte Temple and Suzanne L. Bunkers, "Mothers, Daughters, Diaries: Literacy, Relationship, and Cultural Context," in *Nineteenth Century Women Learn to Write*, ed. Catherine Hobbs (Charlottesville: University of Virginia Press, 1995), 202.

84 Alan T. Nolan, "The Anatomy of the Myth," in *The Myth of the Lost Cause and Civil War History*, ed. Gary Gallagher and Alan T. Nolan (Bloomington: Indiana University Press, 2010), 15.

85 Edward Pollard, *The Lost Cause: A New Southern History of the War of the Confederates* (New York: E. B. Treat, 1866); *In Memoriam Sempiternam*,

commemorative book produced by the Confederate Memorial Literary Society (Richmond, VA: Confederate Museum, 1896), 39; David W. Blight, *Race and Reunion: The Civil War in American Memory* (Cambridge, MA: Harvard University Press, 2000), 255–256; Nina Silber, *The Romance of Reunion: Northerners and the South, 1865–1900* (Chapel Hill: University of North Carolina Press, 1993).

86 EMD, May 18, 1864.
87 George Fitzhugh, *Sociology for the South; or, The Failure of Free Society* (Richmond, VA: A. Morris, 1854), 17.
88 Jane E. Schultz, "Mute Fury: Southern Women's Diaries of Sherman's March to the Sea, 1864–1865," in *Arms and the Woman: War, Gender, and Literary Representation*, ed. Helen M. Cooper, Adrienne Auslander Munich, and Susan Merrill Squier (Chapel Hill: University of North Carolina Press, 1989), 74–75.
89 Emma Mordecai, Rosewood, to Edward Cohen, April 5, 1865, copied into EMD. Cohen was a relative from Baltimore who served in the Confederate army.
90 Freehling, *South vs. the South*, 153; Bruce Tap, *The Fort Pillow Massacre: North, South, and the Status of African Americans in the Civil War Era* (New York: Routledge, 2014).
91 James McPherson, *Battle Cry of Freedom: The Civil War Era* (New York: Oxford University Press, 2003), 724–726.
92 Gallagher, *Confederate War*, 8–11.
93 EMD, May 13, 1864.
94 EMD, May 13, 1864.
95 Stollman, *Daughters of Israel*, 73–75.
96 EMD, June 13, 1864.
97 Confederate States of America, "Tax and Assessment Acts, and Amendments: The Tax Act of 24th April 1863, as Amended," 16–17, Documenting the American South, UNC–Chapel Hill, accessed January 20, 2020, https://docsouth.unc.edu.
98 McPherson, *Battle Cry of Freedom*, 845.
99 EMD, May 12, 1864.
100 McPherson, *Battle Cry of Freedom*, 718–726.
101 EMD, May 7, 1864.
102 EMD, October 1–3, 1864.
103 Lankford, *Richmond Burning*, 19.
104 EMD, July 8, 1864.
105 Ernest B. Furgurson, *Ashes of Glory: Richmond at War* (New York: Knopf, 1996), 162; Berman, *Richmond's Jewry*, 178; Lankford, *Richmond Burning*, 103.
106 EMD, July 8, 1864.
107 EMD, August 24, 1864.
108 EMD, May 8, 1864.
109 Fox-Genovese, *Within the Plantation Household*, 86.

110 EMD, May 23, May 29, September 13, 1864.
111 Scott, *Southern Lady*, 43.
112 Damian Alan Pargas, *The Quarters and the Fields: Slave Families in the Non-Cotton South* (Gainesville: University Press of Florida, 2010); Brenda E. Stevenson, *Life in Black and White: Family and Community in the Slave South* (New York: Oxford University Press, 1996).
113 EMD, April 18, October 15, 1864.
114 EMD, October 24, 1864.
115 EMD, May 13, 1864.
116 Berman, *Richmond's Jewry*, 179.
117 EMD, May 18, May 23, 1864.
118 Ana Choperena, "Triumphal Narratives in the American Civil War: A New Nursing Professional Identity," *Journal of Advanced Nursing* 77 (2021): 1422–1431; Stephen B. Oates, *A Woman of Valor: Clara Barton and the Civil War* (New York: Free Press, 1994).
119 Rosalie E. A. Moses, Sumter, South Carolina, October 7, 1861, Rosalie Moses Collection, SC-8551, American Jewish Archives Center, Cincinnati (hereafter AJA).
120 Berman, *Richmond's Jewry*, 190; Francis B. Simkins and James W. Patton, "The Work of Southern Women among the Sick and Wounded of the Confederate Armies," *Journal of Southern History* 1 (November 1935): 478–490.
121 Rosen, *Jewish Confederates*, 226.
122 Pember, *Southern Woman's Story*.
123 EMD, June 7, 1864; Libra Rose Hilde, *Worth a Dozen Men: Women and Nursing in the Civil War South* (Charlottesville: University of Virginia Press, 2012); George Rable, *Civil Wars: Women and the Crisis of Southern Nationalism* (Urbana: University of Illinois Press, 1989), 121–122; Cheryl A. Wells, "Battle Time: Gender, Modernity, and Confederate Hospitals," *Journal of Social History* 35 (Winter 2001): 409–428.
124 EMD, May 18, 1864.
125 Louise L. Stevenson, *The Victorian Homefront: American Thought and Culture, 1860–1880* (Ithaca, NY: Cornell University Press, 2001), xxviii–xxix, 1–30.
126 EMD, May 14, 1864.
127 EMD, June 5, 1864.
128 EMD, May 10, 1864.
129 Simon J. Bronner, ed., *Jews at Home: The Domestication of Identity* (New York: Oxford, 2010).
130 Simon J. Bronner, "The Dualities of House and Home," in Bronner, *Jews at Home*, 7; Vanessa Ochs, "What Makes a Jewish Home Jewish?," *Crosscurrents* 49, no. 4 (1999): 491–510.
131 Émile Durkheim, *The Elementary Forms of Religious Life*, trans. Karen E. Fields (New York: Free Press, 1995); Arnold van Gennep, *The Rites of Passage*

(Chicago: University of Chicago, 1960); Jonathan Z. Smith, "The Bare Facts of Ritual," in *Readings in Ritual Studies*, ed. Ronald L. Grimes (Upper Saddle River, NJ: Prentice Hall, 1996), 473–483; Victor Turner, *The Forest of Symbols: Aspects of Ndembu Ritual* (Ithaca, NY: Cornell University Press, 1967); Jonathan Z. Smith, *To Take Place: Toward Theory in Ritual* (Chicago: University of Chicago Press, 1987).

132 Durkheim, *Elementary Forms of Religious Life*.
133 EMD, June 10, 1864.
134 Lance J. Sussman, "Another Look at Isaac Leeser and the First Jewish Translation of the Bible in the United States," *Modern Judaism* 5 (May 1985): 159–190.
135 There were very few ordained rabbis in the United States prior to the Civil War. Most synagogues were led by more or less knowledgeable religious functionaries, including Leeser. On the growth of numbers of ordained rabbis—all immigrants—and the resulting contestation over synagogue authority, see Zev Eleff, *Who Rules the Synagogue: Religious Authority and the Formation of American Judaism* (New York: Oxford University Press, 2016).
136 Lance J. Sussman, *Isaac Leeser and the Making of American Judaism* (Detroit: Wayne State University Press, 1995), 40–50.
137 David Weinfeld, "Isaac Leeser and Slavery: A Match Made in Richmond," *American Jewish History* 106 (July 2022): 231–254.
138 Scott, *Southern Lady*, 42–43.
139 James P. Byrd, *A Holy Baptism of Fire and Blood: The Bible and the American Civil War* (New York: Oxford University Press, 2021); Drew Gilpin Faust, *This Republic of Suffering: Death and the American Civil War* (New York: Random House, 2008); George A. Rable, *God's Almost Chosen Peoples: A Religious History of the American Civil War* (Chapel Hill: University of North Carolina Press, 2010).
140 Stollman, *Daughters of Israel*, 119–141; Diane Lichtenstein, *Writing Their Nations: The Tradition of Nineteenth-Century American Jewish Women Writers* (Bloomington: Indiana University Press, 1992); Michael Galchinsky, *The Origin of the Modern Jewish Woman Writer: Romance and Reform in Victorian England* (Detroit: Wayne State University Press, 2018).
141 Emma Mordecai to Ellen Mordecai, August 4, 1839, Box 5, JMP; Bingham, *Mordecai*, 194.
142 Laura Yares, *Jewish Sunday Schools: Teaching Religion in Nineteenth-Century America* (New York: New York University Press, 2023), 28; Berman, *Richmond's Jewry*, 56.
143 Dianne Ashton, *Rebecca Gratz: Women and Judaism in Antebellum America* (Detroit: Wayne State University Press, 1997), 121–140.
144 Bingham, *Mordecai*, 200–201.
145 Sussman, *Isaac Leeser*, 62–64; Ashton, *Rebecca Gratz*, 124.

146 Ellen Mordecai, Raleigh, to Emma Mordecai, Rosewood, ca. summer 1865, copied into EMD. Ellen was the daughter of Emma's brother Moses and the widow of her cousin Samuel Fox Mordecai.
147 Bingham, *Mordecai*, 46–48; Berman, *Last of the Jews?*, 29.
148 Bingham, *Mordecai*, 133.
149 Shari Rabin, "Jews in Church: Rethinking Jewish-Christian Relations in Nineteenth-Century America," *Religions* 9 (2018): 237–247; Bingham, *Mordecai*, 185–186.
150 EMD, August 30, 1864.
151 The term "antisemitism" was coined late in the nineteenth century and never appears in Emma's diary or any other Civil War–era document, but it is nonetheless used descriptively by scholars in reference to anti-Jewish phenomena of earlier time periods.
152 Rosen, *Jewish Confederates*, 31–32.
153 James William Hagy, *This Happy Land: The Jews of Colonial and Antebellum Charleston* (Tuscaloosa: University of Alabama Press, 1993).
154 Representative works on American antisemitism, in addition to the sources cited elsewhere in the introduction, include Leonard Dinnerstein, *Anti-Semitism in America* (New York: Oxford University Press, 1994); David A. Gerber, ed., *Anti-Semitism in American History* (Urbana: University of Illinois Press, 1986); Mark I. Greenberg, "Ambivalent Relations: Acceptance and Anti-Semitism in Confederate Thomasville," *American Jewish Archives* 45 (Spring–Summer 1993): 13–29; Frederick Cople Jaher, *A Scapegoat in the New Wilderness: The Origins and Rise of Anti-Semitism in America* (Cambridge, MA: Harvard University Press, 1994); Abraham J. Peck, "That Other 'Peculiar Institution': Jews and Judaism in the Nineteenth Century South," *Modern Judaism* 7 (February 1987): 99–114; and Howard N. Rabinowitz, "Nativism, Bigotry, and Anti-Semitism in the South," *American Jewish History* 77 (March 1998): 437–451.
155 Stollman, *Daughters of Israel*, 36–37.
156 See Randall M. Miller, Harry S. Stout, and Charles Reagan Wilson, eds., *Religion and the American Civil War* (New York: Oxford University Press, 1998); and Rable, *God's Almost Chosen Peoples*.
157 See, for example, Louis Ruchames, "The Abolitionists and the Jews," in *Jews and the Civil War: A Reader*, ed. Jonathan D. Sarna and Adam D. Mendelsohn (New York: New York University Press, 2011), 145–156.
158 David A. Gerber, "Cutting Out Shylock: Elite Anti-Semitism and the Quest for Moral Order in the Mid-Nineteenth-Century American Marketplace," *Journal of American History* 69 (December 1982): 615–637; Heather S. Nathans, *Hideous Characters and Beautiful Pagans: Performing Jewish Identity on the American Antebellum Stage* (Ann Arbor: University of Michigan Press, 2017).

159 Walter H. Sokol, "Dualistic Thinking and the Rise of Ontological Antisemitism in Nineteenth-Century Germany: From Schiller's Franz Moor to Wilhelm Raabe's Moses Freudenstein," in *Antisemitism in Times of Crisis*, ed. Sander L. Gilman and Steven T. Katz (New York: New York University Press, 1991), 154–211. See also the discussion of antisemitism in David Sorkin, *Jewish Emancipation: A History across Five Centuries* (Princeton, NJ: Princeton University Press, 2019).

160 W. W. Murphy, "Letter to the Editor," *Harper's Weekly*, April 30, 1863; Rev. Dr. McClintock, "Letter to the Editor," *New York Times*, August 3, 1863; Bertram W. Korn, *American Jewry and the Civil War* (New York: Atheneum, 1970), 160–161; Rudolf Glanz, "The Rothschild Legend in America," *Jewish Social Studies* 19 (January–April 1957): 3–28. Both letters to the editor, written in response to negative coverage in *Harper's Weekly* and the *New York Times*, exonerate the Rothschilds and blame Erlanger alone for the loan.

161 Eli Evans, "Overview: The War between Jewish Brothers in America," in Sarna and Mendelsohn, *Jews and the Civil War*, 27.

162 Alison Clark Efford, *German Immigrants, Race, and Citizenship in the Civil War Era* (New York: Cambridge University Press, 2013).

163 Quoted in Furgurson, *Ashes of Glory*, 191.

164 The most recent biography of Judah P. Benjamin is James Traub, *Judah P. Benjamin: Counselor to the Confederacy* (New Haven, CT: Yale University Press, 2021). An older take is Eli N. Evans, *Judah P. Benjamin: The Jewish Confederate* (New York: Free Press, 1988).

165 Korn, *American Jewry and the Civil War*, 177, 156.

166 Jonathan D. Sarna, "The 'Mythical Jew' and the 'Jew Next Door' in Nineteenth Century America," in Gerber, *Anti-Semitism in American History*, 57–78.

167 These numbers are constantly changing due to ongoing research, as best represented in Adam D. Mendelsohn, *Jewish Soldiers in the Civil War: The Union Army* (New York: New York University Press, 2022).

168 Robert N. Rosen, "Jewish Confederates," in Sarna and Mendelsohn, *Jews and the Civil War*, 233–234; Evans, "Overview," 29; Jacob Rader Marcus, "From Peddler to Regimental Commander in Two Years: The Civil War Career of Major Louis A. Gratz," in Sarna and Mendelsohn, *Jews and the Civil War*, 257; Furgurson, *Ashes of Glory*, 191.

169 Korn, *American Jewry and the Civil War*, 177.

170 *Sermon Delivered on the Day of Prayer, Recommended by the President of the C.S. of A., the 27th of March, 1863 at the German Hebrew Synagogue, "Bayth Ahabah," by the Rev. M. J. Michelbacher* (Richmond, VA: MacFarlane and Fergusson, 1863).

171 Quoted in Berman, *Richmond's Jewry*, 185.

172 Jonathan D. Sarna, *When General Grant Expelled the Jews* (New York: Nextbook, 2012); Gary L. Bunker and John J. Appel, "'Shoddy' Antisemitism and the Civil War," *American Jewish History* 82 (January 1994): 43–71.

173 Korn, *American Jewry and the Civil War*, 179, 182–183.
174 Berman, *Richmond's Jewry*, 130–131, 149–152.
175 Jonathan Frankel, *The Damascus Affair: "Ritual Murder," Politics and the Jews in 1840* (New York: Cambridge University Press, 1997); Bertram W. Korn, *The American Reaction to the Mortara Case, 1858–1859* (Cincinnati: American Jewish Archives, 1957); David I. Kertzer, *The Kidnapping of Edgardo Mortara* (New York: Knopf, 1997); Mark K. Bauman, "Variations on the Mortara Case in Mid-Nineteenth-Century New Orleans," *American Jewish Archives Journal* 55 (2003): 43–48.
176 Leonard Rogoff, "Is the Jew White? The Racial Place of the Southern Jew," *American Jewish History* 85 (September 1997): 195–230; Stollman, *Daughters of Israel*, 168. See also Goldstein, *Price of Whiteness*; and Karen Brodkin, *How Jews Became White Folk and What That Says about Race in America* (New Brunswick, NJ: Rutgers University Press, 1998).
177 A concise summary of this paternalistic attitude toward slavery, which also shored up gendered patriarchal authority, is Eugene Genovese and Elizabeth Fox-Genovese, *Fatal Self-Deception: Slaveholding Paternalism in the Old South* (New York: Cambridge University Press, 2011). This work offers a less romanticized view than Eugene Genovese's earlier *Roll, Jordan, Roll: The World the Slaves Made* (New York: Vintage, 1976). See also Korn, "Jews and Negro Slavery."
178 EMD, July 21, 1864.
179 Korn, "Jews and Negro Slavery," 159.
180 For stark descriptions of the all-encompassing horrors of slavery, see Edward E. Baptist, *The Half Has Never Been Told: Slavery and the Making of American Capitalism* (New York: Basic, 2015); and Walter Johnson, *Soul by Soul: Life inside the Antebellum Slave Market* (Cambridge, MA: Harvard University Press, 1999).
181 Bingham, *Mordecai*, 202–203.
182 Stollman, *Daughters of Israel*, 166–170; Stephanie E. Jones-Rogers, *They Were Her Property: White Women as Slaveowners in the American South* (New Haven, CT: Yale University Press, 2020).
183 On the "war within" slave-owning households, see Glymph, *Women's Fight*; and Stephanie McCurry, *Confederate Reckoning: Power and Politics in the Civil War South* (Cambridge, MA: Harvard University Press, 2010).
184 EMD, November 2, 1864.
185 EMD, November 2, 1864.
186 EMD, May 28, 1864.
187 EMD, June 11, 1864; Georgianna is most often spelled Georgiana in the diary.
188 Stollman, *Daughters of Israel*, 154–155.
189 On the last days of the war, see Elizabeth R. Varon, *Appomattox: Victory, Defeat, and Freedom at the End of the Civil War* (New York: Oxford University Press, 2015).

190 EMD, April 2, 1865.
191 Diane Miller Sommerville, *Rape and Race in the Nineteenth-Century South* (Chapel Hill: University of North Carolina Press, 2004).
192 Lankford, *Richmond Burning*, 83, 102–155.
193 Furgurson, *Ashes of Glory*, 338–339.
194 EMD, April 30, May 24, 1865.
195 Emma Mordecai, Rosewood, to Edward Cohen, April 5, 1865, copied into EMD.
196 Emma Mordecai to Edward Cohen, April 5, 1865.
197 Emma Mordecai to Edward Cohen, April 5, 1865 (emphasis in original). On elite Southern women's encounters with the Union army, see Lisa Tendrich Frank, *The Civilian War: Confederate Women and Union Officers during Sherman's March* (Baton Rouge: Louisiana State University Press, 2015).
198 Lankford, *Richmond Burning*, 3.
199 Caroline was the daughter of Emma's sister Eliza Mordecai Myers. She married Edward Cohen later that year. Emma Mordecai to Edward Cohen, April 5, 1865.
200 EMD, April 18, 1865.
201 EMD, April 13, 1865.
202 Glymph, *Out of the House of Bondage*, 99, 112.
203 EMD, April 13, 1865.
204 EMD, April 13, April 18, May 6, May 9, 1865.
205 EMD, May 8, April 15, 1865.
206 Fox-Genovese, *Within the Plantation Household*, 33.
207 Tera W. Hunter, *To 'Joy My Freedom: Southern Black Women's Lives and Labors after the Civil War* (Cambridge, MA: Harvard University Press, 1997).
208 Fox-Genovese, *Within the Plantation Household*, 63.
209 Anne C. Rose, *Victorian America and the Civil War* (New York: Cambridge University Press, 1992), 74.
210 Catherine A. Jones, "Reconstructing Social Obligation: White Orphan Asylums in Post-Emancipation Richmond," in *Children and Youth during the Civil War Era*, ed. James Marten (New York: New York University Press, 2012), 173–175.
211 EMD, May 11, May 8, 1865.
212 EMD, May 11, 1865.
213 EMD, May 4, 1865.
214 Berman, *Richmond's Jewry*, 64–88, 168–169.
215 Shari Rabin, *Jews on the Frontier: Religion and Mobility in Nineteenth-Century America* (New York: New York University Press, 2017), 14–15; Adam D. Mendelsohn, *The Rag Race: How Jews Sewed Their Way to Success in America and the British Empire* (New York: New York University Press, 2015); Berman, *Richmond's Jewry*, 64–95.

216 Lankford, *Richmond Burning*, 124–125.
217 EMD, April 15, 1865.
218 EMD, April 15, 1865.
219 EMD, April 13, 1865.
220 Quigley, *Shifting Grounds*.
221 Francis Charles Lawley, "The Last Six Days of the Grand Old Army of Northern Virginia: A Sketch by an Englishman," *Richmond Whig*, October 24, 1865.
222 Furgurson, *Ashes of Glory*, 176–177; Lankford, *Richmond Burning*, 108.
223 "To Our Patrons and Friends," *Richmond Whig*, October 24, 1865.
224 Harrison, *Rhetoric of Rebel Women*, 146–147.
225 "A Lady in Virginia" (Judith Brockenbrough McGuire), *Diary of a Southern Refugee during the War* (New York: E. J. Hale, 1867); "A Richmond Lady" (Sally Brock), *Richmond during the War: Four Years of Personal Observation* (New York: G. W. Carleton, 1867); Pember, *Southern Woman's Story*.
226 Representative recent work on Southern Jews during Reconstruction includes Michael R. Cohen, *Cotton Capitalists: American Jewish Entrepreneurship in the Reconstruction Era* (New York: New York University Press, 2017); Anton Hicke, *Jewish Identity in the Reconstruction South: Ambivalence and Adaptation* (Berlin: De Gruyter, 2013); and Stuart Rockoff, "Carpetbaggers, Jacklegs, and Bolting Republicans: Jews in Reconstruction Politics in Ascension Parish, Louisiana," *American Jewish History* 97 (January 2013): 39–65.
227 Blight, *Race and Reunion*; Charles Reagan Wilson, *Baptized in Blood: The Religion of the Lost Cause, 1865–1920*, 2nd ed. (Athens: University of Georgia Press, 2009).
228 Rebecca Kohut, *My Portion: An Autobiography* (New York: Thomas Seltzer, 1925), 16.
229 Matthew Dennis, *Red, White, and Blue Letter Days: An American Calendar* (Ithaca, NY: Cornell University Press, 2002), 221; Lloyd A. Hunter, "The Immortal Confederacy: Another Look at Lost Cause Religion," in Gallagher and Nolan, *Myth of the Lost Cause and Civil War History*, 190.
230 Quoted in Rosen, *Jewish Confederates*, 338–340.
231 Furgurson, *Ashes of Glory*, 364.
232 A useful scholarly summary of these debates is Karen L. Cox, *No Common Ground: Confederate Monuments and the Ongoing Fight for Racial Justice* (Chapel Hill: University of North Carolina Press, 2021).
233 Karen L. Cox, *Dixie's Daughters: The United Daughters of the Confederacy and the Preservation of Confederate Culture* (Gainesville: University Press of Florida, 2019); Caroline E. Janney, *Burying the Dead but Not the Past: Ladies' Memorial Associations and the Lost Cause* (Chapel Hill: University of North Carolina Press, 2008); Cynthia Mills and Pamela H. Simpson, eds.,

Monuments to the Lost Cause: Women, Art, and the Landscapes of Southern Memory (Knoxville: University of Tennessee Press, 2019); Silkenat, *Driven from Home*, 181; Blight, *Race and Reunion*, 272–273.

234 Faust, *Mothers of Invention*.

235 Teresa Roane, archivist, United Daughters of the Confederacy, personal correspondence with Dianne Ashton, May 19, 2020.

236 *Catalogue of the Confederate Museum of the Confederate Memorial Literary Society* (Richmond, VA: Ware and Duke, 1905), 89.

237 An edited version of Kate Stone's diary was later published as *Brokenburn: The Journal of Kate Stone, 1861–1868*, ed. John Q. Anderson (Baton Rouge: Louisiana State University Press, 1995); Sarah Morgan Dawson, *A Confederate Girl's Diary: The Civil War Diary of Sarah Morgan* (New York: Houghton Mifflin, 1913); Mary Boykin Chesnut, *A Diary from Dixie* (New York: Appleton, 1905). Published posthumously, Chesnut's "diary," in particular, is widely understood to be a rewritten, crafted narrative. See Julia Stern, *Mary Chesnut's Civil War Epic* (Chicago: University of Chicago Press, 2010).

238 Melvyn Stokes, *D. W. Griffith's "The Birth of a Nation": A History of the "Most Controversial Motion Picture of All Time"* (New York: Oxford University Press, 2007); Mark E. Benbow, "Birth of a Quotation: Woodrow Wilson and 'Like Writing History with Lightning,'" *Journal of the Gilded Age and Progressive Era* 9 (October 2010): 509–533.

239 Marie S. Molloy, "'A Noble Class of Old Maids': Surrogate Motherhood, Sibling Support, and Self-Sufficiency in the Nineteenth-Century, White Southern Family," *Journal of Family History* 41 (October 2016): 402–429; Finding Aid for GMP, https://finding-aids.lib.unc.edu.

240 "United States Census, 1900," database with images, FamilySearch, accessed July 2023, www.familysearch.org, Miss Emma Mordecai, in entry for Miss Va. F. Gay, 1900.

241 American Jewish Committee, *American Jewish Year Book*, vol. 8, *1906–1907* (Philadelphia: Jewish Publication Society, 1907), 225.

242 EMD digital version, https://finding-aids.lib.unc.edu.

Index

Page numbers in italics indicate photos

abolitionism, 48, 53, 59
The Absentee (Edgeworth), 9
African Americans: authority over, 64; 5th Mass. Coloured Cavalry, 189, 205–6; jobs for, 61; opportunities for, 3; speech of, 65; writing about, 62. *See also* slavery
Aguilar, Grace, 49
anti-immigration, 54
antisemitism: from accusation of poor-quality uniform production, 57; allegations of economic manipulation, 55–56; from alleged extortion, 56; anti-immigration and, 54; during Civil War, 54–57; coining of term, 233n151; guarding against, 56; ontological antisemitism, 54; restricted land ownership, 53; shadow of, 52–58; sources of, 53–54; worldwide, 57–58
Atlanta, Georgia, 146; fall of, 152, 157

Barton, Caroline Marx (Emma's cousin), 103, 132
Barton, Clara, 40

Barton, Willie (Emma's cousin), 103, 111, 116
battles: Battle of Chancellorsville, 33, 89, 90, 95; Battle of Spotsylvania Court House, 33, 110; Battle of the Wilderness, 31; Battle of Vicksburg, 81; battle sites, 160; defeats, 90; hearing, near Rosewood Farm, 31–34, 90, 93, 94, 99–100, 112, 123, 127–28, 146, 183; news of, 89, 98, 100, 142; observed at Rosewood Farm, 31–34; in Petersburg, 146–47, 149, 191; in Richmond, 150, 166; at Rosewood Farm, 96, 97; wounded in, 99–100
Bayth Ahabah (Richmond congregation), 56, 79
Beale, Dr., 135, 138, 140, 151, 215
Beauregard, Pierre Gustave Toutant, 90, 100, 122, 161
Belinda (Edgeworth), 173
Benjamin, Judah P., 54–55
Beth Shalome (Richmond congregation), 9, 13, 20; donations to soldiers, 41; Emma attending, 35, 86, 103, 159, 162, 164; Sunday school established, 49–50

239

240 • INDEX

Bettelheim, Rebecca, 79
the Bible: daily readings, 91; private reading of, 43; references in diaries, 22, 24; for trauma of Civil War, 48; versions of, 47
Birth of a Nation (film), 81, 83
Braxton, Armstead, 172
Braxton, Lucy, 125, 145, 147
Braxton, Mrs. (Mary Tomlin), 125, 147, 151, 152, 163, 165
Brock, Sally, 78
Brook Hill Farm (Virginia), 94, 97, 129, 135, 142, 145, 146; visits to, 149, 152, 156–57, 162, 217
Butler, Benjamin, 33, 111
buyers permit, 74, 75

Camp Lee, 65, 102, 186–89, 195
Camp Winder Hospital, 122
Caroline, 196, 200
Chamberlayne, Mrs. (Martha), 119–20, 126, 127
Chancellorsville, Virginia, 95
Charleston, South Carolina, 6, 24, 219
Chesnut, Mary Boykin, 81
Chiles, Mary, 117, 118
Chiles, Sally, 132, 133, 134
Chimborazo Military Hospital (Richmond), 24, 40
Civil War: antisemitism during, 54–57; Bible as comfort, 48; as bundle of crises, 3; commemorations, 79–80; Confederacy losing, 5; death toll in, 3; diaries as witness to, 22, 25, 81; of Emma, 30–42; end of, 64; last days, 1; as Lost Cause, 28–29, 79; refugees from, 15, 156. *See also* battles; Confederacy; Grant, Ulysses S.; Lee, Robert E.; Yankee forces
Clermont (Scribe), 148
Cohen, Edward (Emma's cousin), 65, 75, 97, 132, 205, 206; called out to meet enemy, 145; commission of, 172; on leave, 162–63; letters from, 121, 167; news from, 141; notes to, 91, 105; safe return of, 212, 215; visits from, 87, 107, 130, 141; walks with, 131, 172, 217
Cohen, Eleanor, 24
Cohen, Gratz, 126, 149, 151; news from, 157
Cohen, Jacob I. (Emma's step-grandfather), 6
Confederacy: allegiances to, 11; atrocities committed by, 30–31; Civil War loss, 5; claiming slavery as natural law, 61; Confederate Jews, 56–57; Confederate nationalism, 4–5, 10, 17, 62, 69, 79; conscription laws, 16; death toll in, 3; Emma on military, 29–31; food donations to, 39–40; free black men and slaves serving in, 16–17; gentility in, 69, 80; knitting, as work of Confederate women, 186; loss of ships, 133–34; military abilities, 29; nationalism of Emma, 17; news of battle defeats, 90; personal picture of fall, 76; prayers for, 21–22; Richmond Howitzers, 15, 90, 97, 99; seeking food and supplies, 123–24; social order of, 66; soldier casualties, 100; women supporting, in diaries, 26–27; worthless currency of, 207
conversion to Christianity: of Mordecai, R., 51; sister encouraging, 13–14
Couch, Deborah ("Miss Deborah"), 114–15, 121–22, 132, 167
Cyrus ("Cy"), 62, 87, 93, 118, 185; apology from, 111, 209–10; demands of, 207–8; emancipation of, 68, 186, 195, 200; putting out fire, 111

Dallam, Mr. (Henry), 147
Dallam, Mrs. (Elizabeth Braxton), 145, 149, 156, 158, 163
Damascus Affair, 57–58

Davis, Jefferson, 55–56, 81, 194, 219–20; capture of, 215
Deborah (seamstress), 88, 132, 146, 202
Devereux, Annie ("Nan," Emma's great niece), 87, 113, 139, 143, 146, 149
Devereux, Tom (Emma's great-nephew), 107, 157
diaries, 77; Biblical references in, 22, 24; Confederacy supported in, 26–27; for documenting Jewish identity, 43–46; editing of, 34; Emma copying, 78, 85; for identity, 22; inner self in, 25–26; for memorializing and vindicating Old South, 78–79; of nineteenth century women, 21–30; as scrapbook, 74–75; as secure location, 19–21, 24–25, 30; survival of, 4; training children to write, 28; transgressing gender norms, 25; as witness to Civil War, 22, 25, 81; women's sphere and, 26
Diary of a Southern Refugee during the War (McGuire), 78
Draper, Alonzo, 188–89, 191
Durkheim, Émile, 45–46

Early, Jubal, 39, 76, 133, 136, 139; defeat of, 157, 164; drives of, 101
Edgeworth, Maria, 9, 173
emancipation: of Cyrus, 68, 186, 195, 200, 207; of Fleming, 199; of George, 195; of Georgianna, 68, 212; of Lizzy, 208–9; of Mary, 67–68, 197; at Rosewood Farm, 63–72; self, 3
Ewell, Richard, 63, 108, 110, 114, 119, 128
Ezekiel, Moses, 8

The Farmer's Register, 10
Faust, Drew Gilpin, 80
5th Mass. Coloured Cavalry, 189, 205–6
Fitzhugh, George, 29
Fleming, 61, 154, 168, 169; emancipation of, 199

food: clauber, 37, 107, 108; coffee, 88; Confederate soldiers seeking, 123–24; desserts, 37, 108, 113, 119, 137, 141, 152, 156; donations to Confederacy, 39–40; Emma on, 36–37; Emma selling, in Richmond, 71; evening meals, 107–8, 112, 119, 128, 132, 134, 138, 141–43, 147, 156, 170; food shortages, 36–37; to hospitals, 122; peach preserves, 155; search for, 72, 123–24; selling in Richmond, 71; sorghum, 37, 154, 160, 163; tea shortage, 155; trading of, 67; for visitors, 91
Foote, Henry, 54
Forrest, Nathan Bedford, 30
Fort Gilmer (Virginia), 160
Fort Harrison (Virginia), 160
Fort Pillow (Tennessee), 30
Fox-Genovese, Elizabeth, 18

Gardner, Mr., 88–91, 94, 102, 136, 144, 155, 175; news from, 90, 100; staying at Rosewood, 88, 92, 124, 126, 154, 175, 216
Gennep, Arnold van, 45
gentility, 69, 80
Gentry, William, 202, 208
George, 93, 94, 184–85, 203; emancipation of, 195; finding in Richmond, 190, 192–93; garden work, 139; harvesting wheat, 133; looting by, 197–98; selling butter, 118
Georgianna, 62, 65–66, 93, 118, 187, 200; emancipation of, 68, 212; peach gathering, 141; scolding of, 203
Glymph, Thavolia, 67
Goldstein, Eric, 4
Grant, Ulysses S., 30, 33, 57, 88, 101, 128; campground of, 64, 206; disbanding army, 211–12; Overland Campaigns by, 31; rumors of death, 136; at surrender, 198, 201; withdrawing from Petersburg, 145
Gratz, Rebecca, 9, 50

Halyburton, Fanny, 104, 164, 191
Hannewinkel, Mrs. (Roberta Campbell), 103, 106–7, 122, 137, 149, 164
Harrington (Edgeworth), 9
Hebrew Ladies Memorial Association, 79
home as social ideal, 17–19
Horton, Mr. (hospital patient), 108, 114–16, 121
hospitals, 29; Camp Winder Hospital, 122; Chimborazo Military Hospital (Richmond), 24, 40; Emma visiting, 96, 111, 121; Emma working in, 41–42, 101–3, 105–6, 115–17; food to, 122; fundraising for, 40–41; hospital ships, 40; Howard Grove Hospital, 150; overfilled with wounded soldiers, 132–33; Rosina visiting, 101, 111, 126; Rosina working in, 107; Seabrook Hospital, 41, 100–101, 111, 121; St. Francis de Sales hospital, 41, 115, 121; visits to, 39–40; women working in, 39–41, 104, 109
Howard Grove Hospital, 150

Iglehart, Mr., 191, 207

Jackson, Thomas Jonathan ("Stonewall"), 80
Johnston, Joseph E., 56, 128, 154
Jones-Rogers, Stephanie E., 60
Judaism: collective Jewish consciousness, 46; Confederate Jews, 56–57; diary for documenting Jewish identity, 43–46; Emma as Jewish elder, 4; Jewish migration, 47, 54; Mordecai, Jacob, knowledge of, 9–10; Mordecai family history and, 5–21; mythical Jew, 55; observance of rites and services, 117, 129, 159–60, 162–64; Philadelphia Hebrew Sunday School, 50; Philadelphia Jewish community, 6, 9, 47; rabbis, 79, 232n135; in Richmond, 9; veiling of, 43; women replacing life-cycle events from Christianity, 49. *See also* antisemitism; Bayth Ahabah (Richmond congregation); Beth Shalome (Richmond congregation); Mikveh Israel (Philadelphia)

Ku Klux Klan, 81

Lady Audley's Secret (Braddon), 125–26
Lawley, Francis Charles, 75–76
Lazarus, Aaron (Emma's brother-in-law), 51
Lazarus, Rachel Mordecai (Emma's sister), 8, 13; church attendance, 51; correspondence with Maria Edgeworth, 9; deathbed conversion to Christianity, 51; death of, 21
Lee, Lizzie, 112, 156
Lee, Robert E., 11, 30, 43, 76, 101, 128, 194; defeats of, 104, 136, 160; illness of, 110; monuments to, 79–80; observed as secular saint, 31; in Petersburg, 125; surrender of, 64, 66, 198, 201; victories of, 94, 98; withdrawing from Petersburg, 136
Leeser, Isaac, 47–48, 50
letters: from Cohen, Edward, 121, 167; to Cohen, Edward, 181–94; from Mordecai, Ellen (niece), 218–22; from Mordecai, Ellen (sister), 139, 144, 155; from Mordecai, George, 116, 148, 157; from Mordecai, George Washington, 158, 166; from Mordecai, John Brooke, 147, 153, 163, 166; from Mordecai, Samuel, 146, 149, 155, 175; from Mordecai, William Young, 171, 174; to Mordecai, Ellen (sister), 49, 126, 133, 140, 144, 170, 204; to Mordecai, George, 91, 152; to Mordecai, Samuel, 154, 165; to Mordecai, William Young, 153, 169; from Myers, Caroline, 112, 145, 153, 218; to Petersburg, Virginia, 107; from Ra-

leigh, North Carolina, 107, 139, 173–74, 218, 219–22; to Raleigh, North Carolina, 99, 108, 110, 133; to Richmond, 177–81; from Rosewood Farm, 181–94
Levy, Ezekiel, 148
Levy, Isaac, 51–52, 148, 150–51
Lewery, Anna, 69–70, 212–13
Lincoln, Abraham, 11, 57, 192, 193; assassination, 202; funeral of, 33, 203
Linton, Joe, 95, 100, 198; news from, 114; selling produce, 199–201
Lizzy, 93, 99, 203; emancipation of, 208–9; rug making by, 167
Lost Cause: Civil War as, 28–29, 79; commemorations, 79–80
The Lost Cause (Pollard), 29
Luck family, 184, 185, 190, 192

Manning, Gen., 190–91
Le Marriage au Tambour, 28, 171
Martha, 196, 211
Marx, Joseph (Emma's uncle), 7
Marx, Richea Myers (Emma's aunt), 7–8
Mary, 65–66, 93, 187, 190; berry picking with, 147; emancipation of, 67–68, 197; peach gathering, 142
Massie, 186, 190
Mayo, Willie (Emma's cousin), 102
McGuire, Judith Brockenbrough, 78
McKee, Capt., 188–89, 193
Michelbacher, Maximilian Joseph, 56–57
Mikveh Israel (Philadelphia congregation), 47, 50
Mobile, Alabama, 120, 142, 143, 146, 148, 205
Moise, Penina, 49
Morais, Sabato, 50
Mordecai, Alfred (Emma's brother), 12, 13, 14, 207, 218; as anti-secession, 10–11
Mordecai, Alfred, Jr. (Emma's nephew, son of Alfred and Sara Hayes Mordecai), 11, 13

Mordecai, Augusta ("Gusta," Emma's niece, daughter of Augustus and Rosina Young), 15, 86, 107, 125; anxious about home, 94; anxious about Lee, R. E., surrender, 196; anxious for aunt, 193; attending music lessons, 127, 134, 141, 144, 145, 147, 155; attending school, 30–31, 87, 91–92, 97, 100, 109, 115, 168, 169, 173; attending Sunday school, 91, 118, 154, 156; attending wedding, 139, 176; church attendance, 143, 149, 152, 167, 169, 175; dread of Yankees, 182; dresses for, 88; French lessons of, 215, 216; horseback riding, 131, 135; news of battles from, 89, 98; plaiting straw, 130, 135–37, 139, 141, 147, 218; straw hat of, 147; visiting Brook Hill, 149, 152, 156, 162; visiting brothers, 117, 119; visiting with cousins, 88; weaving straw hats, 35
Mordecai, Augustus (Emma's brother), 8, 13, 15, 120
Mordecai, Ellen (Emma's sister), 8, 11, 85; Confederate nationalism of, 17; embracing Christianity, 13; letters from, 139, 144, 155, 218–22; letters to, 49, 126, 133, 140, 144, 170, 204; move to Raleigh, 13; receiving refugees, 146; selling slaves, 59
Mordecai, Ellen Mordecai (Emma's niece, daughter of Moses and Margaret Lane Mordecai), 50, 64, 75; Yankee soldiers invading, 220–21
Mordecai, Emma, 2; attending Congregation Beth Shalome, 35, 86, 103, 159, 162, 164; on battles observed at Rosewood Farm, 31–34; belief in white supremacy, 81; on benefits of slavery, 58–59; Civil War of, 30–42; on Confederate military, 29–30; Confederate nationalism of, 17; copying diary, 78, 85; death of, 83; diary as secure location, 19–21, 30; displacement and fear, 1, 3, 19;

Mordecai, Emma (*cont.*)
engagement ending, 14; on food, 36–37; on food shortages, 36; hiring orphans for household work, 69–70, 212; hospital visits, 111, 121; hospital work of, 41–42, 101–3, 105–6, 115–17; on independent position, 153; Judaism and family history of, 5–21; legacy of, 74–83; literary life of, 28; observing Jewish rites and services, 117, 129, 159–60, 162–64; patriotism of, 5; paying freed slaves as cooks, 69; privacy of, 1; quarrels with sister-in-law, 98–99; racism exhibited by, 60–62, 168, 192–93, 197, 207; religious discourse of, 51; religious world of, 42–52; room of, at Rosewood Farm, 45–46, 48, 86, 142, 146–47, 152, 154, 168, 175; selling gold trinkets, 207; selling goods and food in Richmond, 71; selling slaves, 59–60; settled in Richmond, 5; sewing and knitting by, 35; as slave owner, 10, 59–60; as Southern, white, Jewish elder, 4; Sunday school established by, 49–50; support of secession, 10; tombstone, 82; translating by, 28, 159, 165, 167, 169, 171; as tutor, 20; on visiting, 38–39. *See also specific topics*

Mordecai, Esther (neé Elizabeth) Whitlock (Emma's grandmother): first marriage of, 5–6; second marriage of, 6

Mordecai, George (Emma's brother), 10, 14, 85; bringing news of war, 35; buying slaves, 60; letters from, 116, 148, 157; letters to, 91, 152; punishing slaves, 62, 118; safe return of, 201; visits with, 86–87, 144

Mordecai, George Washington (Emma's nephew, son of Augustus and Rosina Young Mordecai), 13, 31, 39, 85–86; anxiety for safety of, 165–66; at Brook Hill, 162; church attendance, 138; family silver retrieved by, 206; fleeing to mountains, 164; horseback riding, 131, 139, 141; illness of, 174; letters from, 147, 158, 166; recovering from wounds, 102, 105, 127, 131, 134; rejoining command, 162; as Richmond Howitzer, 97; running errands, 130; seeking mule, 204, 216; seeking stolen horse, 205–6; tithing business, 129, 131; visits from, 118–19; war news from, 112, 133, 136; wounded in battle, 99–100

Mordecai, Henry (Emma's nephew, son of Moses and Margaret Lane Mordecai), 81

Mordecai, Jac (Emma's nephew, son of Moses and Margaret Lane Mordecai), 220

Mordecai, Jacob (Emma's father), 6, 7, 47; Christian church attendance, 51; death of, 4; knowledge of Judaism, 9–10; as patriarch, 4; school established by, 8

Mordecai, John Brooke (Emma's nephew, son of Augustus and Rosina Young Mordecai), 31, 39; garden work by, 204; home visit, 118–19, 134, 141; letters from, 153, 163, 166; reporting for duty, 143; as Richmond Howitzer, 97; safe return of, 201; safety, in camp, 164

Mordecai, Judith Myers (Emma's father's first wife), 6–7

Mordecai, Margaret Cameron (Emma's sister-in-law), 13, 170

Mordecai, Martha ("Patty," Emma's great niece), 81, 83, 222

Mordecai, Moses (Emma's brother), 6–7, 81

Mordecai, Moses (Emma's grandfather), 5–6, 9

Mordecai, Peggy (Emma's great niece), 108, 163

Mordecai, Rebecca Myers (Emma's mother), 7–8, 11

Mordecai, Rosina Young ("Rose," Emma's sister-in-law), 8, 13–15, 28, 31; anxious for soldier sons, 90, 165–66;

anxious over Lee, R. E., surrender, 198; attending to wounded cousin, 104; buyers permit, 74, 75; chronic headaches of, 17, 87, 118, 124, 130, 133, 153, 182; confined to bed, 139, 141, 143, 145, 149, 168, 170; entertaining by, 37; as feeble and depressed, 201, 217–18; greeting Emma, 86; grieving loss of slaves, 209, 213; hiring servants, 69–70; horse stolen from, 64–65; hospital visits, 101, 111, 126; hospital work, 107; operations performed on, 140, 151; preserving peaches, 155; protecting livestock and valuables from pillagers, 36, 87, 92–93; quarrels with Emma, 98–99; as rich poor person, 91; rug making by, 167; as slave owner, 59–60; at smoke house, 159; walks with, 165, 167; whisk for, 216

Mordecai, Samuel (Emma's brother), 10, 11; death of, 218, 219; letters from, 146, 149, 155, 175; letters to, 154, 165

Mordecai, Solomon (Emma's brother), 8, 13, 148; fire losses, 171

Mordecai, William (Emma's nephew, son of Solomon and Caroline Waller Mordecai), 135

Mordecai, William Young ("Willie," Emma's nephew, son of Augustus and Rosina Young Mordecai), 32, 39, 109–10; at Brook Hill, 146, 152, 162; church attendance, 138, 143, 149, 154, 156, 167; foraging by, 140; garden work by, 204; home visits by, 112–13, 117, 124; horseback riding, 135; illness of, 157–59; letters from, 171, 174; letters to, 153, 169; medications for, 144; milking cows, 209; mule retrieved by, 204, 216; as Richmond Howitzer, 97; safe return of, 201; scolding freed slaves, 203; servants sought by, 215; tithing business, 129–31, 134–35, 155; unfit for duty, 143;

visiting Brook Hill, 149, 157; war news from, 142; at Westbrook, 163

Morgan, Sarah, 81

Moses, Octavia Harby, 49

Moses, R. J., 181, 191

Moses, Rosalie E., 40–41

Myers, Caroline (Emma's niece, daughter of Samuel and Eliza Mordecai Myers), 87–88, 97, 125, 130, 148; attending wedding, 139; during evacuation, 181–82, 191; in good spirits, 207; horseback riding, 139, 141; ill, with diphtheria, 111, 115; letters from, 112, 145, 153, 218; shopping with, 163; talks with, 173; visits with, 137–38, 144

Myers, Edmund ("Ned," Emma's nephew, son of Samuel and Eliza Mordecai Myers), 144, 176, 205, 212, 218; asthma attack, 157; observing battle sites, 160; safe return of, 212

Myers, Eliza Mordecai (Emma's sister), 144

Myers, Ella (Emma's cousin), 103, 144, 148, 207

Myers, Gustavus (Emma's cousin), 115

Myers, Moses (Emma's cousin), 103

Myers, Rebecca (Emma's cousin), 103, 144, 207

Myers, Samuel (Emma's uncle), 8, 38

mythical Jew, 55

nature: comfort in, 91, 114, 119, 213; delight in, 102, 151; drought conditions, 125, 126, 130–33, 143, 146, 148, 179; frost, 163, 170; refuge in, 70, 88; snow, 171; Southern ideas of, 14; tranquility in, 108; walks in, 164, 166, 170, 172

news: of battle defeats, 90; of battles, 89, 98, 100, 142; from Cohen, E., 141; from Cohen, G., 157; from Gardner, Mr., 100; from Linton, 114; from Raleigh, 132; of war, 35, 112, 133, 136, 142; from Westbrook Farm, 169;

news (*cont.*)
    of Yankee forces approach, 88–89, 91–92, 95, 139; of Yankee forces atrocities, 104; of Yankee forces battles, 98, 100, 142; of Yankee forces defeat, 90, 91
Newton, Rosa ("Rose"), 103, 115, 121, 176, 202
Nightingale, Florence, 40
Norrill, Moses, 16–17, 60, 115; repairs by, 167–68

The Occident, 48
orphans, as household workers, 69–70, 212

Patrick, Marsena Rudolph, 202, 216
Pegram's Battery, 140–41
Pember, Phoebe Yates Levy, 24, 40, 78
Petersburg, Virginia, 6, 8, 13, 51, 204–5; battles in, 146–47, 149, 191; casualties in, 148, 150–51, 161, 175; devastation in, 206; evacuation from, 154; Grant withdrawing from, 145; Lee, R. E., in, 125; Lee, R. E., withdrawing from, 136; letters from, 107; refugees from, 131–32, 148–49; under siege, 34; Yankee attacks, 122–23, 130, 140
Phil, 68, 203
Philadelphia, Pennsylvania, 11; Hebrew Sunday School, 50; Jewish community in, 6, 9, 47, 50
Pickett, George, 80, 90, 100
Pollard, Edward, 29
protection pass, 72, 73, 199–200, 202

Rabin, Shari, 51
race: assumption and attitudes toward, 4–5; in Southern society, 58
racism: absorption of, 4; Emma exhibiting, 60–62, 168, 192–93, 197, 207; social order of Southern society and, 58–63
Raleigh, North Carolina: alarm bells ringing in, 35; family in, 141; letters from, 107, 139, 173–74, 218, 219–22; letters to, 99, 108, 110, 133; news from, 132; refugees in, 146; requests from, 112, 163; Sherman in, 205; sister moving to, 13; slaves in, 60; Yankee forces in, 205
Reconstruction, 79
refugees: Civil War, 15, 156; Mordecai, Ellen, receiving, 146; from Petersburg, 131–32, 148–49; in Raleigh, 146
Rehine, Zalma, 47
religion: church attendance, 51, 138, 143, 149, 152, 154, 156, 167, 169, 175; Emma and, 42–52; for entertainment and social life, 48; objects as religious, 45; Puritan dogma, 178; revivals, 48; Sunday school attendance, 91, 118, 154, 156. *See also* Bible; conversion to Christianity; Judaism
Richmond, Virginia, 1; battles in, 150, 166; beleaguered city, 97; burning of, 63–64, 66, 185–86; capture of, 184, 189; departure from, 11, 13–15, 85–86; Emma selling goods and food in, 71; evacuation of, 181–83, 191; family network in, 8; hospitals in, 24, 40; Judaism in, 9; letters to, 177–81; Mordecai family settled in, 5; refuges in, 131–32; ruins in, 204; stirring times in, 155; visits to, 38, 40, 164; Yankee forces in, 158, 160, 162
Richmond during the War (Brock), 78
Richmond Examiner, 100
Richmond Howitzers, 15, 90, 97, 99
Richmond Whig, 75–76
Rogoff, Leonard, 58
Rosewood Farm (Virginia), 8, 13, 14–15; battles fought near, 96, 97; battles heard near, 31–34, 90, 93, 94, 99–100, 112, 123, 127–28, 146, 183; emancipation at, 63–72; Emma as useful addition to, 17–19; Emma's room at, 45–46, 48, 86, 124, 142, 146–47, 152, 154, 168, 175; evacuation from, 63; gardening at,

138–39; Gardner staying at, 92, 124, 126; hiding and removing valuables from, 183–85; horse stolen from, 187–90, 197, 205–6, 216; housing volunteer troops, 95–96; letters from, 181–94; making up for losses, 216–17; protection for, 72, 73, 199–200, 202; seeking guard for, 195–96, 198–99; smoke house, 159; stealing from, 124, 196, 202; tithing oat crop, 129–31, 134–35; tithing wheat crop, 155; trading fresh food from, 67; visiting at, 38, 149, 153, 163–64; wheat harvest at, 123–24, 133; Yankee forces at, 202

Sally, 17, 59, 115, 116; illness of, 137, 220
Sarah, 62, 68, 118, 200
Scott, Anne Firor, 48
Scribe, Eugène, 148
Seabrook Hospital, 41, 100–101, 111, 121
secession, 10
Seward, William H., 202–3
Sheridan Philip, 101, 105, 120, 125, 129, 161; Sheridan's Cavalry, 37, 104–5, 125, 129, 161
Sherman, William Tecumseh, 24, 31, 128; army of, 213–14; in Raleigh, 205
Sinclair, Mrs. Dr. (Lucy Jones), 134, 160, 167
Sinclair, Willie, 160–61
slavery: barbarous treatment in, 27; capture of escaped slaves, 120; Confederacy claiming as natural law, 61; destruction of Southern slave society, 81; Emma as slave owner, 10, 59–60; Emma on benefits of, 58–59; Emma selling slaves, 59–60; free black men and slaves serving Confederacy, 16–17; freed slaves, 16–17, 69, 196, 203; literacy among slaves, 28; Mordecai, G., buying slaves, 60; Mordecai, G., punishing slaves, 62; paternalistic attitude, 58, 235n177; permeating Southern society, 18; in Raleigh, 60; religious support for, 24; Rosina as slave owner, 59–60; runaway slaves, 142; slaves joining Union forces, 3; Southern population displacement and, 3; young slaves serving masters, 150

Smith, Jonathan Z., 45
Smith, Kirby, 217
Sociology for the South (Fitzhugh), 29
Sokol, Walter, 54
Solomon, Clara, 24
A Southern Woman's Story (Pember), 78
Southern society: diaries for memorializing and vindicating, 78–79; displacement of population, 3; food shortages, 36–37; home as social ideal, 17–19; literacy in, 28; public performances in, 28; race as factor in, 58; racism and, 58–63; religion for entertainment and social life, 48; slavery permeating, 18; straw hats in, 133, 147; structural violence in, 62; visiting in, 38–40; women working in, 20. *See also* visiting
Spring Farm (Virginia), 8, 87, 147
St. Francis de Sales hospital, 41, 115, 121
Stockdell, Mrs., 39, 102, 151, 154, 165; church attendance, 152, 169; rug making by, 167
Stollman, Jennifer, 58
Stone, Kate, 81
Storrs, Patsey, 39, 124, 165
St. Paul's Church, 13, 176
Stuart, Bell, 98
Stuart, James Ewell Brown ("Jeb"), 33, 95, 98
Stuart family (Brook Hill Farm), 94, 97–98, 108, 114, 129, 140, 145, 147, 149, 156, 168, 186, 205, 210, 212, 214, 217

Taylor, Martin, 197–99, 202, 206, 209
Taylor, Mrs., 95, 136, 147, 156

tithing business, 129–31, 134–35
Tolcott, Mrs., 175
Tomelin, Mrs. Harrison, 151
translating, 28, 159, 165, 167, 169, 171
Turner, Nat, 27

United Daughters of the Confederacy, 80–81

visiting: Brook Hill Farm, 149, 152, 156–57, 217; by Cohen, E., 87, 107, 130, 141; Emma on, 38–39; family visits, 149, 153, 158, 165; by Gusta, 88, 117, 119; home visits of Mordecai, George Washington, 118–19; home visits of Mordecai, John Brooke, 118–19, 134, 141; home visits of Willie, 112–13, 117, 124; hospitals, 96; with Mordecai, George, 86–87, 144; to Mrs. Young, 151, 173; neighborhood visits, 128–29; with nieces, 137–38, 144; in Richmond, 38, 40, 164; at Rosewood Farm, 38, 149, 153, 163–64, 168; in Southern society, 38–40; Westbrook Farm, 88, 90, 116–17, 119, 138, 145, 147, 151, 156, 163, 174, 196, 211

Waldrop, George John, 135, 136
Walker, Mr. (minister), 91, 99, 110, 133, 152
Ward, Marcus L., 210–11
Warrenton, North Carolina, 6, 8, 51, 124, 165
weddings, 139, 175–76
Weinfeld, David, 48
Weitzel, Godfrey, 72, 75, 197
Westbrook Farm (Virginia), 125, 127, 128; intoxicated colonel at, 216; messages from, 93; news from, 169; visits to, 88, 90, 116–17, 119, 138, 145, 147, 151, 156, 163, 174, 196, 211
white supremacy, 4, 79; belief in, 81
Wilmington, North Carolina, 51, 83, 155
Wilson, Woodrow, 83
women: Confederacy supported by, 26–27; diaries of nineteenth century, 21–30; Jewish ideals for, 49; knitting as work of Confederate, 186; model of true womanhood, 27; Republican Motherhood, 27; separate spheres and, 229n72; women's sphere, 26; working, in hospitals, 39–41, 104, 109; working, in Southern society, 20

Yankee forces: attacks in Petersburg, 122–23, 130; blockades by, 32, 36, 133; communications cut off by, 97; confronting, 30; death toll in, 3, 130; disbanding of, 211–12; dread of, 182; as educated and accomplished, 180; Emma on African American, 65–66; 5th Mass. Coloured Cavalry, 189, 205–6; gun boats, 131, 160; hatred for, 123; news of approach, 88–89, 91–92, 95, 139; news of atrocities by, 104; news of battles with, 98, 100, 142; news of defeat of, 90, 91; prisoners of, 161; raids of, 177–79; in Raleigh, 205; in Richmond, 158, 160, 162; at Rosewood Farm, 202; Sheridan's Cavalry, 37, 104–5, 125, 129, 161; Sherman's army, 213–14; slaves joining, 3; Southern mobilization to defeat, 16
Young, Frances Churchill Braxton ("Fanny," "Mrs. Young," Rosina's sister-in-law), 87–89, 108, 120, 170, 175, 196; Beavercloth cloak from, 174; dinner invitation from, 125–26; news from, 205; trouble with hogs, 152; visits from, 149, 153, 158, 165, 168; visits to, 151, 173
Young, John Brooke ("Mr. Young," Rosina's brother), 89, 92, 104, 155, 171; freed slaves of, 196; losses of, 194, 201–2; on runaway slaves, 142; traveling with, 120–21; troubles of, 211; visits of, 135
Young, Lawrence (Rosina's cousin), 41, 100–104; recovering from wounds, 108–9, 111, 121, 126
Young, Rosa (Rosina's cousin), 106, 109, 121

About the Authors

DIANNE ASHTON was Professor Emeritus of Philosophy and World Religions at Rowan University. She was a pioneering scholar of feminist religious studies and American Jewish women's history, and she served as editor of *American Jewish History*. Her major works include *Four Centuries of Jewish Women's Spirituality*, coedited with Ellen Umansky (1992); *Rebecca Gratz: Women and Judaism in Antebellum America* (1997); and *Hanukkah in America: A History* (2013).

MELISSA R. KLAPPER is Professor of History and Director of Women's and Gender Studies at Rowan University. She is the author of *Jewish Girls Coming of Age in America, 1860–1920* (2005); *Small Strangers: The Experiences of Immigrant Children in the United States, 1880–1925* (2007); and *Ballots, Babies, and Ballots of Peace: American Jewish Women's Activism, 1890–1940* (2013), which won the National Jewish Book Award in Women's Studies. Her most recent book is *Ballet Class: An American History* (2020).

THE GOLDSTEIN-GOREN SERIES IN AMERICAN JEWISH HISTORY

General editor: Hasia R. Diner

Is Diss a System? A Milt Gross Comic Reader
Edited by Ari Y. Kelman

We Remember with Reverence and Love: American Jews and the Myth of Silence after the Holocaust, 1945–1962
Hasia R. Diner

Jewish Radicals: A Documentary Reader
Edited by Tony Michels

An Unusual Relationship: Evangelical Christians and Jews
Yaakov Ariel

All Together Different: Yiddish Socialists, Garment Workers, and the Labor Roots of Multiculturalism
Daniel Katz

1929: Mapping the Jewish World
Edited by Hasia R. Diner and Gennady Estraikh

Hanukkah in America: A History
Dianne Ashton

Unclean Lips: Obscenity, Jews, and American Culture
Josh Lambert

Jews and Booze: Becoming American in the Age of Prohibition
Marni Davis

The Rag Race: How Jews Sewed Their Way to Success in America and the British Empire
Adam D. Mendelsohn

Hollywood's Spies: The Undercover Surveillance of Nazis in Los Angeles
Laura B. Rosenzweig

Cotton Capitalists: American Jewish Entrepreneurship in the Reconstruction Era
Michael R. Cohen

Making Judaism Safe for America: World War I and the Origins of Religious Pluralism
Jessica Cooperman

A Rosenberg by Any Other Name: A History of Jewish Name Changing in America
Kirsten Fermaglich

A Mortuary of Books: The Rescue of Jewish Culture after the Holocaust
Elisabeth Gallas

Dust to Dust: A History of Jewish Death and Burial in New York
Allan Amanik

Jewish Radical Feminism: Voices from the Women's Liberation Movement
Joyce Antler

Jews Across the Americas: 1492–Present
Edited by Adriana M. Brodsky and Laura Arnold Leibman

Forged in America: How Irish-Jewish Encounters Shaped a Nation
Edited by Hasia R. Diner and Miriam Nyhan Grey

Black Power, Jewish Politics: Reinventing the Alliance in the 1960s, Revised Edition
Marc Dollinger

The Threshold of Dissent: A History of American Jewish Critics of Zionism
Marjorie N. Feld

The Civil War Diary of Emma Mordecai
Edited and with an Introduction by Dianne Ashton with Melissa R. Klapper

www.ingramcontent.com/pod-product-compliance
Lightning Source LLC
Chambersburg PA
CBHW030635150426

42811CB00077B/2153/J